Memories and Melancholy: Reflections on the Mahoning Valley and Youngstown, Ohio

Memories and Melancholy: Reflections on the Mahoning Valley and Youngstown, Ohio

Richard S. Scarsella

iUniverse, Inc.
New York Lincoln Shanghai

Memories and Melancholy: Reflections on the Mahoning Valley and Youngstown, Ohio

Copyright © 2005 by RICHARD S. SCARSELLA

All rights reserved. No part of this book may be used or reproduced by any means, graphic, electronic, or mechanical, including photocopying, recording, taping or by any information storage retrieval system without the written permission of the publisher except in the case of brief quotations embodied in critical articles and reviews.

iUniverse books may be ordered through booksellers or by contacting:

iUniverse
2021 Pine Lake Road, Suite 100
Lincoln, NE 68512
www.iuniverse.com
1-800-Authors (1-800-288-4677)

ISBN-13: 978-0-595-37269-0 (pbk)
ISBN-13: 978-0-595-81664-4 (ebk)
ISBN-10: 0-595-37269-4 (pbk)
ISBN-10: 0-595-81664-9 (ebk)

Printed in the United States of America

For those whom believe, *"Strands of memories are woven together and neither time nor the world can break them apart."* (Unknown)

Contents

Introduction xvii
Acquaintances 1
Affairs of the Heart 3
Afterthoughts 5
"All for Love" 7
American Hercules 12
Angels Amidst Us 14
Around the Corner 16
Autumn Leaves 18
Back to Idora Day at Yankee Lake 20
Bridal Traditions 22
Calvacade of Stars 24
Canfield Fair 26
Christmas Recollections 28
Christmas Yore 30
Cityscape 32
Clouded Mirror 35
Declination 37
Déjà Vu 39

Memories and Melancholy: Reflections on the Mahoning Valley and Youngstown, Ohio

Downtown Youngstown Department Stores 41

Drive-in Theaters: Summer Ritual. 43

East End 45

Easter Parade 48

Eastertide Reflections. 50

Ebb Tide 52

Eclipse 54

End of Summer 57

Environs 59

Epitaph 61

Faces of Poverty. 62

Fading Idora 64

Family Helpers 67

Family Matters 69

Fifty Some Years Ago. 71

Fine Dining from the Past 73

Flashbacks 75

Good-bye Five and Dimes. 77

Gothica 80

Grandmother's China 82

Hardware Memories 84

Harvey Firestone: Neglected Native Son 86

Historic McGuffey Letters Donated to Butler Institute 88

Historic Restaurants Still Linger on Our Minds. 90

Historical Perspectives on Mahoning Valley Labor 92

Holiday Thoughts	98
Hollywood Eulogy	100
I Sometimes Recall	102
Ice Kingdom	104
Idora Ballroom	106
The Idora Century: 1899-1999	108
The Idora Century Mark	112
Idora Facts	114
Idora Park Memories Still Bright After Twenty Years	117
Idora Wars	119
In the Day	121
In the Land of McGuffey: Hope from the Heartland	123
Interdependence of Local Communities Based in History	129
Intermigration of Mahoning Valley Has Long History	131
Isaly's and Me	134
Isaly's Neighborhood Memories	136
John Kennedy, Jr.: A Profile in History	138
Labor Day Facts	140
Lake Erie Recollections	142
Lamentations	144
Land of Promise	146
Legacy	148
Legends	150
Life at the Movies	152
Life Without Lucy	154

Life Without Perry Como	156
Local McGuffey Society Sole Survivor	158
Mahoning Valley: Home of Historical Giants	160
March Memoirs	162
Memories of Memorial Day	164
Messages	166
Milestones	168
Mill Creek Metroparks' Historical Points of Interest	170
Minutia	172
Mirage	174
Modern Martyr	176
Mortality	178
Musings	180
Neighborhood Theaters	183
New Years Observances	185
Oblivion	187
Ode to Bozo	189
Of Aunts, Uncles, & Others	191
Old Friends	193
Omnibus Nostalgia	195
On the Riverfront	198
Only Yesterday	201
Parochial School Days	203
Patron of the Arts	205
Personages	207

Contents   xi

Pianoforte 209

Planting Time 211

Plaza Appeal 213

Post-Holiday Melancholy 215

The Power of Fashion 217

Preachers, Sisters, and Brothers 219

Random Thoughts 221

Remembrances 223

Renaissance 225

Riparian Rites 227

Roller-Skating Days 229

Ruminations About Life 231

Sanctuary 233

School Haze 235

Seems Like Old Times 237

Shades of the Seventies 239

Shadows of Time 241

Somewhere in Time 243

Summer Icons 245

Summer Solstice 247

Summertide Holiday 249

Summertime Hospitality 251

Sunday Drives 253

Thanksgiving Traditions 255

The 1940's 257

The 1950's	260
The 1960's	262
The Forgotten Giant	265
The Long Goodbye	268
The World I Once Knew	270
The Y and I	272
Theaters of the Past	274
Things I Miss	276
Things I'll Never Do Again	278
Things My Child Will Never Know	280
Things You Don't See Anymore	282
Thinking Back	284
This and That	286
Trading Stamp Days	288
Transfiguration	291
Traveling Son	293
Tribulations	295
Twilight of a Dynasty	297
Unforgotten	299
Uptown: Crossroads to Suburbia	301
Urban Legend	303
Vanished Tableaus Live on in Memories	305
Vanishing Youngstown	307
Victuals	309
Virtual Family	311

War Fervor 314
Water Delights 316
Whatever Happened to. 318
When I Go Shopping 320
When Youngstown Turned Irish. 322
Whispers of Time 325
Wonderland Lost 327

Acknowledgements

Writing *Memories and Melancholy: Reflections on the Mahoning Valley and Youngstown, Ohio* has been a work in progress for over a decade. I have had numerous requests over the years to compile my articles in an anthology. All of the selections have previously appeared in one or all of the following: *Austintown Town Crier, Boardman News, Boardman Town Crier, Canfield Town Crier, Mahoning Valley Update,* and *Poland Town Crier.*

My beloved eloquent late father, Alfred M. Scarsella, Sr., known as Al, and my indomitable unforgettable mother, Marie Antoinette Modarelli Scarsella, provided continued support and encouragement for this undertaking. To them, I will be forever grateful.

My wife, Debra Ann Mettee, provided necessary proofreading and expert guidance in the use of computer technology. My daughter, Natalie Marie Scarsella, provided untold energy and hours during the editing process. My daughter's cat, Tinkerbell, provided steady company over the composition process. A kindred spirit, Gene Gonda, provided perspective and a sounding board.

Readers and fans were a constant prod and inspiration to begin, finish, and submit my work for publishing. Although many scoff at those that hold memories close to the heart, those that believe the past is important in more ways than one are legion.

Some few have remarked that the melancholy that permeates my manuscript is ever present. I prefer to think of this characterization as a compliment. Why? The past is bittersweet. To portray it otherwise would be deceitful.

Introduction

The Mahoning Valley and the metropolitan Youngstown, Ohio area are rich in oral and written history. Many forget how diverse, successful, and memorable the people are in a land of a half-million inhabitants known as the Connecticut Western Reserve Territory. Others do not cherish the colorful customs and priceless institutions that made this environs an archetypal symbol of the American dream and a democracy of the common man.

Memories and Melancholy: Reflections on the Mahoning Valley and Youngstown, Ohio is an attempt to document and preserve the life force that sustained generations in our midst. Topics such as Idora Amusement Park, Mill Creek Park, the Canfield Fair, the steel industry, traditional holidays, the vanishing agrarian society, and extended family are timeless and still influence our lives. Legendary native sons with names like William Holmes McGuffey, President William McKinley, Harvey Firestone, the Warner Brothers, Joseph Butler, and Edward J. DeBartolo changed both the local landscape and the nation.

The eclipse of downtown Youngstown, movie palaces, anchor department stores, urban neighborhoods, and family farms are all mourned to this day by those old enough to remember another world quite unlike the one we now inhabit. Callous disregard for a way of life that has all but disappeared is unsettling for those of a certain sensitivity. In days of yore, we can find wisdom, sustenance, and courage to face our cloudy futures.

If anything, the selections I have offered will hopefully help the reader to recreate their own personal coherent narrative. The unsettled past will not quiet peacefully. It demands to be reckoned with, at some point. So, a trip down memory lane can be entertaining, nostalgic, and therapeutic.

Historical giants, gypsies, freak shows, and Native American folklore all are subjects in my anthology. Hopefully, reminiscences of all but forgotten times, places, events, and figures in our lives will be cathartic and worthwhile.

Acquaintances

by Richard S. Scarsella

In the 1950's, Americans fell in love with television. The kinescope, as television was once called, brought the world to our homes. No longer did one have to attend downtown Youngstown movie palaces for the latest newsreels played between features. Television both entertained and informed us in the comfort of our own homes.

As film icons such as Jimmy Stewart, William Holden, Gary Cooper, Spencer Tracy, Joan Crawford, Bette Davis, Gloria Swanson, and Marlene Dietrich dimmed in popularity, television "personalities" gripped our attention and commanded our affection. We were soon hooked.

Milton Berle, Ernie Kovacs, Red Skelton, David Jansen, Lucille Ball, Donna Reed, Mary Tyler Moore, and Carol Burnett all became household names. All of them appeared weekly for years on network broadcasts nationwide. They became familiar faces and friends. Literally, these celluloid figures became very much a part of our everyday lives, since the personas they evoked were of the common man in common circumstances.

It was reassuring to know that our television heroes were also confused by an increasingly modern, complex, and turbulent world. Ernie Kovacs' comedic madness reflected our own exasperation. Milton Berle's burlesque spoofs on culture, complete with men in drag, assured us we were not alone in our doubts about the status quo. Red Skelton's gentle vaudeville-like images of tragic clowns, noble tramps, and other marginal members of society mirrored our concern about the dispossessed in an impersonal age. David Jansen's gritty "The Fugitive" foreshadowed our morbid curiosity with a nation descending into violence and litigation. Unlike motion pictures, television was very grounded in real-life issues, not escapism.

Female characters during television's "golden age" were predecessors of a cultural shift that redefined traditional male and female roles in the home and in the workplace. Women were given a voice and were shown to no longer be at the mercy of men or other forces beyond their control.

Lucille Ball evolved from a dutiful strong-willed ditzy wife into a divorced working mother over a period of years, right in front of our eyes. As she grew up, we grew up. Donna Reed became the symbol of suburban, refined, and "sanitized" domestic partnership. Unbeknownst to her professional husband, she "knew" better and ran the household, not vice-a-versa. Mary Tyler Moore pioneered new territory by personifying a single career woman in a big city. She broke the mold of women as only wives and mothers. Truly, she was a liberated contemporary woman ahead of her time.

Carol Burnett was a forerunner of Saturday Night Live and other irreverent comedy genres. She satirized Hollywood, Washington, D. C., royalty, television, family, and stereotypes with sassy bravado. She made it clear women knew the score and would not be held captive by artificial limits such as middle-class conventions and sexual stereotypes. Her boldness and outspokenness helped level the playing field for women performers too long overlooked and given second billing.

Sadly, television friends have passed on, just like real-life acquaintances. Fred McMurray, Raymond Burr, Jackie Gleason, Gail Storm, Dinah Shore, Loretta Young, Ozzie and Harriet Nelson, and scores of others all are part of television heritage and national lore. They were all part of our collective consciousness and made social and cultural history as well. The extended family television provided us changed our lives.

It is comforting to know that when we need to reconnect with an "anchor" in our lives, that television legends can still be visited, courtesy of perpetual reruns. Their times are still very much a part of our times now.

Affairs of the Heart

by Richard S. Scarsella

Until the 1970's, dating rituals were fairly formal and standardized. Eligible young men were introduced to available maidens at church events, school functions, or society occasions. If all went well, the potential suitor would phone his new acquaintance and follow up with a personal visit. Once the family gave him the once over and a seal of approval, he would be allowed to call upon the young lady if his intentions were beyond reproach. Obviously, both his and her credentials were checked by both families so as to avoid scandal or a mismatch. By today's standards, this all seems impossibly quaint. Some few courtship practices prevail. Despite the casual dating scene, the dating game still points towards engagement and eventual marriage.

At Christmastime, it was once fairly common for those going steady to announce their engagement and wedding dates. A diamond engagement band was considered to be the ultimate romantic holiday gift. Valentine's Day, spring, or fall matrimony dates followed the engagement parties. A whirlwind of planning ensued.

Of all the surviving pre-nuptial customs, attending bridal shows is still in vogue. In January, exhibitions are still held displaying everything a bride-to-be could possibly need or want. These galas literally merchandise love and wedding bliss.

Those old enough to remember can easily recall when style-leading Strouss-Hirschberg's and McKelvey's downtown department stores hosted bridal extravaganzas in their music halls. They also booked Idora Ballroom, the Elms Ballroom, Stambaugh Auditorium, and the Rayen-Wood Auditorium for their bridal fashion shows.

Audiences were dazzled by haute couture gowns, rhinestone headpieces, exotic fur wraps, and sophisticated tuxedoes. Mothers-of-the-brides, bridesmaids, and brides-to-be all took copious notes on what was seen. When these shows reigned supreme, divorce was uncommon and couples married for life. Therefore, few had thoughts of second or third marriages. The first time down the aisle was to be the last time and had to be perfect in every detail.

Unlike today's department stores, venerable Strouss-Hirschberg's and McKelvey's were one-stop emporiums for those to be married. Engagement and wedding bands were purchased in the better jewelry departments. Furniture, draperies, appliances, and carpeting were put in lay-a-way in the home furnishings departments. China, tableware, flatware, and kitchen utensils were listed on the gift registry. The trousseau, honeymoon wardrobe, and travel arrangements all were handled by specialized department store staff. These stores catered to generations of the same area families and sought to make dreams come true. Wedding consultants became like one of the family.

Youngstown's "ladies department store" was named Livingston's. This New York inspired downtown firm catered to an upscale clientele. Its bridal boutique was unrivaled in the valley. Within it velvet draped walls one could find exquisite garments tailored from French chiffon, Italian satin, Flemish lace, and Asian rainbow sequins. Fifth Avenue creations by Milady, Bianchi, Dior, Givenchy, and Chanel all were stocked for viewing by appointment only. These exclusive dresses were all featured in national publications and supplies were limited. Until it closed, Livingston's was considered a trendsetter.

Though these legendary stores have long ago passed from the scene bridal pageants continue to be held and attract huge throngs. They now charge admission, feature vendors of all kinds, and award door prizes. Grand prizes usually include free honeymoon trips, airline tickets, or wedding gowns. Today's merchants of love continue an old tradition that Strouss-Hirschberg's, McKelvey's, and Livingston's pioneered.

Oddly enough, even in this jaded contemporary unglamorous society we now inhabit, women and girls of all ages still have their hearts quicken when they attend a bridal show.

Afterthoughts

by Richard S. Scarsella

It never fails. Once July 4th has been celebrated, back to school sales begin in earnest. School age children know their days of summertime bliss are numbered. Once August arrives, one can even catch a whiff of fall in the early morning breezes.

I remember when Buster Brown, Red Goose, and U.S. Keds footwear were favorites amongst students. Our parents would drag us into Lustig's, Strouss', and McKelvey's to be fitted for "sensible shoes". Strict dress codes forbade faddish or stylish footgear. Penny loafers were considered chic. Saddle shoes were seen as fashionable. Occasionally, younger children were allowed to wear Buffalo Bill or Sky King cowboy boots to school. Gym shoes were called sneakers or tennis shoes.

I remember shopping at Murphy's, McCrory's, Woolworth's, Kressege's, or Grant's for book bags, binders, pencil sharpeners, rulers, and other supplies. A quarter could purchase five hundred sheets of first-rate "bonded" lined writing paper, complete with red margin lines. Composition books, now known as notebooks, were priced below fifty cents. Erasers were a penny. Many times, a free bookmark or miniature calendar was given to each child who made a school purchase at one of these variety stores.

I remember my grandparents expressing disdain for the newfangled ballpoint pens. They steadfastly clung to their fountain pens and little bottles of ink. Generally, children were dissuaded from buying red pens. These penmanship tools were considered the province of teachers and parents.

I remember being measured and tailored at A & A Department Store in Struthers for school uniforms. We also shopped downtown Penney's youth departments, Strouss' mezzanine girls' and boys' shops, and McKelvey's young women and men boutiques for school apparel. Boys had to have a collar on their shirts. Girls had to wear blouses to match. Pants, skirts, and blazers were made of all wool cloth. When it rained, drenched students smelled like a herd of sheep.

When this happened, the obvious distress of the teachers was worth the discomfort.

I remember the cafeteria ladies as being stern, matronly, and frenzied in pace. All wore hairnets. They served up beets, lima beans, and rice pudding with aplomb. Pupils were coerced into taking a helping of everything served. All were expected to eat a "complete meal". Lunch mothers, who took their duties seriously, would not allow a child to leave their table without cleaning their plates. Food allergies and delicate stomachs were no excuse for not eating a well-balanced meal.

I remember small cartons of Isaly's, Lawson's, and Sealtest's milk and juice being served for lunch and snack time. We would pick the wax off the containers with our fingernails. Being chosen a milk/juice deliverer was a much-envied badge of honor and privilege. The payoff? An extra carton of milk or juice at no charge. Of course, getting out of class to clean the milk cooler was an added bonus.

I remember watching the early NASA rocket launches in science class. Local merchants would loan schools black and white television sets for a day or two. Adjusting the antennae was an art unto itself. The Mercury, Gemini, and Mariner televised space programs seemed Flash Gordon-like in reality and fueled dreams of budding astronauts. During these years, space seemed miraculously attainable.

I remember viewing during class-time memorable news broadcasts and documentaries concerning the life, times, and death of iconic President John F. Kennedy. We literally watched history in the making on television, with narration by Walter Cronkite and Huntley and Brinkley. Here was a slice of life not normally found in the curriculum. Suddenly, history came alive, as we grimly watched the transfer of power to Vice President Lyndon B. Johnson. From our wooden desks, in our austere classrooms, we somehow knew our nation would never be the same again.

I remember a wise teacher saying, "Bad things happen to good people." Our class agreed. We all grew up a little the day J.F.K. was buried. From that day on, I saw life as one big lesson after another.

"All for Love"

by Richard S. Scarsella

Historical Background of Valentine's Day:

February 14 was declared Valentine's Day in about 498 A.D. by Pope Gelasius. The holiday has both Roman pagan and early Christian roots. The truth behind the holiday is murky. Yet, it lives on in the United States, Canada, Mexico, the United Kingdom, France and Australia.

Legend describes Valentine or Valentinus, and there are three saints by this name, as a priest in the third century. He supposedly incurred the wrath of Emperor Cladius II for marrying soldiers and young men. Why? Those betrothed were not as fearless in battle as single men. Valentine was subsequently jailed and put to death, all for love.

Chronicles speak of Valentine helping Christians escape brutal Roman prisons, as well. Regardless, there is general agreement that Valentine either sent a note or letter to a young woman, perhaps his jailer's daughter, expressing some soft sentiment. Romantics believe he signed the correspondence 'From your Valentine', an expression still used today. This and other touching tales dwell on Valentine's appeal as a heroic, compassionate and tragic figure.

The February date of the memorial to Valentine coincides with the pagan Lupercalia festivals, which celebrate the beginning of spring. This fertility and purification celebration also paralleled the Middle Ages' belief that birds mated at this time. A 1415 greeting by Charles, Duke of Orleans, written to is wife, while he was imprisoned in the Tower of London, still exists today in the British Museum. King Henry V later instructed the writer John Lydgate to send a similar greeting to Catherine of Valois. Others in the king's court followed suit.

By the seventeenth century, the British widely exchanged tokens of affection or elegantly written notes. By the end of the eighteenth century, improvements in typesetting made printed cards affordable and convenient. Lower postage rates fueled the popularity of valentines. Esther A. Howland is credited with selling the first American mass-produced cards. Only Christmas rivals Valentine's Day as the largest card-sending holiday.

Local Practices:

In the Mahoning Valley, St. Valentine's Day was greatly celebrated by all classes of people, both Christian and non-Christian alike. No longer considered a saint's holy day, it had gradually been secularized, like Christmas. Merchants gradually viewed Valentine's Day as an opportunity to herald in spring merchandise and begin the Easter selling season early. All the hype that accompanied Valentine's Day made it a consumer's delight.

A cavalcade of goods competed for disposable incomes, especially in the post World War II years. The top items on everybody's lists were cards and candy. Old-timers doggedly made cards out of hand-woven or store bought doilies. They also laboriously melted down baker's chocolate and poured the same into heart or truffle molds. However, savvy merchandising soon pushed such quaint practices aside by making mass produced greetings and confections more affordable and convenient.

Hallmark, Gibson and American greeting card companies targeted consumers with eye-popping displays and sentimental poetry and prose, which few could resist. Color, style, texture, balance and scale were all expertly translated into materials as diverse as velvet, foil, satin and cardboard. For under a dollar, one could send a first-class card and gift of Shakespearean quality. Sonnets were literally sold for pennies a line. Memories could be purchased retail. Generations were hooked on valentines as a result.

Candy became synonymous with Valentine's Day. Children delighted in giving out little Necco brand multi-colored, sugared hearts with pithy phrases printed on both sides. "Be My Valentine", "I Love You" and "Forever Yours" were favorite messages. The blushes of children receiving their first valentines is testimony to the power of words expressing emotions not easily spoken.

Adults reveled in the giving and getting of red papered, heart shaped, ribbon and bow covered boxes of chocolates, diets not withstanding. Both maids and matrons could look forward to a symbol of affection or appreciation on this day. Husbands, lovers, children, and relatives all ritually gave candy to important women or girls in their lives. Not to receive candy and a greeting card on Valentine's Day was a traumatic event, not soon forgotten or forgiven.

The once prevalent Fanny Farmer Confection Shoppes, corner pharmacies and variety stores all catered to teenage Romeos and Juliets during this season of love. Fanny Farmer once offered exotic pink chocolate and heart-shaped suckers alongside its famous cherry cordials. Gray Drug Stores once featured an endless array of Russell Stover milk, dark and ivory chocolates, wrapped in red coverings, suitable for any budget. Woolworth's, Murphy's, Grant's and Kressege's all competed vigorously for these holiday sales. Shirts, hats, socks, hairclips, bows and scarves all were emblazoned with valentine motifs, like modern day coats of arms. Red-hot cinnamon hearts were especially cherished by youngsters and bought by the scoop.

Flowers also made this holiday memorable for recipients and profitable for florists. Young lovers and mature couples alike favored red, long stemmed roses. Matrons preferred orchids, to be worn either on the wrist or as a corsage. In the 1940's, camellias enjoyed brisk sales, courtesy of Bette Davis' dreamy blockbuster film "Now Voyager". With Paul Henried as a co-star, Bette Davis epitomized the bitter sweetness of a love affair too short-lived and much remembered.

Poignantly, area cemeteries came alive mid-February, with valentine shaped carnation wreaths standing sentinel over loved one's graves. The long processions of widows and widowers in and out of graveyards were dire warnings of the fragility of life and love and the preciousness of time.

Well into the early 1960's, young men and women of school age, society figures, and business types all earnestly purchased or cleaned outfits in anticipation of gala Valentine's Day dances and balls. Livingston's specialized in Sandra Dee and Lana Turner inspired creations. Toile, full skirts with matching crinolines, lame sheaths, fox fur trims, sequin encrusted poodle skirts, soft-hued fuzzy cashmere sweaters, and dyed shoes to match made Livingston's ensembles ooze style, attitude, and cachet.

Strouss' and McKelvey's offered women complimentary makeovers. Revlon, Max Factor, Maybelline and Cover Girl products all guaranteed that "Hollywood glamour" at affordable prices. New shades of red lipstick, rouge, and blush were heavily promoted. The in-store beauty salons recommended seaweed facials, color, cuts and tints, pedicures and manicures in their package deals. Undergarment specialists, along with seamstresses and tailors, made off-the-rack dresses and gowns fit like couture clothing. These stores were truly makers of illusion.

Men would frequent tuxedo and tailor shops so as to complement their dates fashionably, if unobtrusively. Hartzell's, Rose and Sons, Shy Lockson, and Bond's all catered to men of distinction wanting to look their best. Evening garb, from white tails to blue serge suits, all were nattily fitted, sewn and pressed for men emulating Fred Astaire, Cary Grant, and Troy Donahue.

Stout yellow cabs and sleek, dark funeral limousines all escorted couples to high school and college gyms, the Elms and Idora ballrooms, and private clubs, such as the Youngstown Club. American Bandstand Top 40 records, Big Band music standards, and classical quartets all created magic on the darkened dance floors. Green sherbet punch, champagne fountains, and very dry martinis helped create a New Year's Eve type of ambiance. This evening for lovers was meant to be special, regardless of cost.

Finger sandwiches, angel food cake, and stern chaperones all made school-age partygoers remember that they did not discover romance. It had been ritualized and immortalized by others long ago as a precursor to marriage and settled life. Somber admonishments were liberally given prior and during the schools sponsored Valentine's Day events. Young people were told to keep a firm grip on their emotions and not get carried away, lest they be "lost".

Young adults had more freedom to indulge in this commemoration of affairs of the heart. Beaus and sweethearts all congregated, like bees to honey, at the Elms and Idora ballrooms. The intimate Elms was a veritable sea of hormones. Phosphates were tenderly shared, with two straws per soda glass. However, once on the dance floor, the Lotharios went into their acts. Cupid's presence could be heavily felt amongst the warm embraces.

At the Idora Grand Ballroom, a mirrored, revolving globe reflected rainbow hues of color across Youngstown's largest dance hall. Guy Lombardo and Lawrence Welk once recreated a touch of Camelot here, with string music guaranteed to melt any hardened heart. With the mighty Wild Cat and curvaceous Jack Rabbit coasters and Dutch Impressionistic Tunnel of Love windmill rapids ride as a backdrop, Idora was the quintessential Valentine's Day idyllic setting for young love that dwelt in fantasy.

For those not inclined to don mink wraps, pearls, patent leather shoes or black tie apparel, simple Valentine's Day customs took many forms. Testimonies of affection would be printed in local newspapers, for a small fee, replete with original poems and cryptic initials. Western Union telegrams also were tasteful expressions of endearment. Candy grams, oftentimes accompanied with a love song, were used by the more daring Don Juan suitors. Dedicated tunes on the radio also conveyed heartfelt emotions. Naturally, television variety shows such as Ed Sullivan and Carol Burnett would use Valentine's Day as a theme. No one could escape the national obsession with this ancient inspired holiday.

Valentine's Day became a right of passage. Charles Schultz's Peanuts cartoon immortalized how all the Charlie Browns of the world feel when gone unnoticed in a world awash in longing. From simple paper cutout heart chains to classical cherubs targeting our hearts, Valentine's Day is a memorial to the sublime importance and tenaciousness of love in our lives and in history. After all, the ardor for Cleopatra by Augustus Caesar and Marc Anthony changed the course of Western civilization. Love knows no bounds.

In Tennessee Williams' play Streetcar Named Desire, his lovesick character, Blanche DuBois, succinctly summed up the power of love and fatal attraction. Her lament? "The opposite of death is desire."

American Hercules

by Richard S. Scarsella

History is made of larger than life figures. Zeus, Apollo, Poseidon, Athena, Cyclops, David and Goliath, to name a few, all belong to a pantheon of legends still known to us today.

In America, new traditions were built upon the basis of old ones. Likewise, attributes of mythical deities and actual historical characters were transferred to contemporary celebrities.

Paul Bunyan, Johnny Appleseed, and Daniel Boone were embodiments of distinctive Yankee characteristics including rugged individuality, determined independence, and the ethos of a "new man." An Italian immigrant named Angelo Siciliano came to the United State via Ellis Island in 1903 and blended Old World civilization with the emerging American culture. His name was Charles Atlas.

Dubbed the American Hercules by the popular press, Atlas symbolized the Greco Roman ideal of the faultless sculpted male. The fact that he pioneered an isometric program guaranteed to turn any hollow-chested pint into a "man" made him a founder of the current fitness craze.

Atlas' use of Madison Avenue advertising techniques made him widely known and very wealthy. His rippling muscled leading man image immortalized him in ubiquitous colorful adventure comic books and pulp fiction magazines. Atlas became one of the nation's first popular culture symbols.

In 1922, Charles Atlas was labeled the "World's Most Perfectly Developed Man" in a contest at New York's old Madison Square Garden. His rags to riches story, an evocative tale of the harsh immigrant experiences, was heartwarming to a country that believed anyone could pull themselves up by their bootstraps and improve himself or herself. His true-to-life tale of having sand kicked into his face by a beach bully and his resolve to never be taken advantage of again struck a chord with Americans looking for heroes. Atlas literally typified the American belief in self-reliance, hard work, luck, and pluck.

Ahead of his time, Atlas harnessed direct mail to spread his formula for success. The result was a mail order empire. Young men from across the continent eagerly sent in money and anxiously awaited their muscle building kits. Gyms, weight rooms, boxing clubs, and YMCA's all over the heartland subscribed to Atlas' exercise regime. Atlas' personal appearances were his best advertisements and gave him legitimacy detractors could not counter.

Atlas trained beloved athletes such as fighter Jack Dempsey and baseball player Joe DiMaggio. In the 1950's, his methods of conditioning were endorsed by the American Medical Association. In the 1960's, President John F. Kennedy's physical education challenges for school age children were in part inspired by Atlas' legacy of wellness and health maintenance.

Well into old age, Atlas continued to tour, demonstrating unbelievable feats of strength for a man of his years. Atlas passed away in 1972. His name still conjures images of an idealized man reminiscent of the neo-classical age. This modern titan has not been forgotten in his adopted country. Like the mythical gods Atlas and Hercules, he has been immortalized by a people hungry for Olympian superheroes.

Atlas' brawn was only matched by his ambition, business acumen, and foresight. His persona has become in effect public property. Atlas' transformation and shifting identity from a foreigner into the epitome of American masculinity mirrored a world transfixed with the future but still rooted in the past.

Angels Amidst Us

by Richard S. Scarsella

History is replete with accounts of supernatural beings intervening in earthly affairs. Christian, Judaic, and Islamic traditions all mention angels in our midst. The archangels Gabriel and Michael are just two of many such famous celestial beings referred to in ancient sacred texts and discussed by theologians, scholars, and believers of agents of the divine.

In the Mahoning Valley, guardian angels of a human kind were once found in abundance. Elderly woman, closer to the afterlife than to life itself, were oftentimes conduits of comfort and goodness. Most children in the Youngstown area could depend on the help of strangers in time of trouble. I recall well the years when neighborhood crones, although unsightly to behold, would readily pick up fallen children and salve their knees with peroxide and bandages.

Hoboes were once colorful familiar urban figures around these parts. These intrepid followers of the rails moved with the change of seasons, like shabby migratory birds. Creatures of habit, they regularly stopped for handouts at the doorsteps of merciful folks known to share leftovers and seasonal bounty. Although persecuted by many, hoboes were oftentimes a gentle lot and had just experienced "hard times" through no fault of their own. They relied on angels of mercy for food, shelter, and clothing as they endlessly traipsed across the country.

Infamous gypsies were both dreaded and tolerated during their annual sojourns into town. Forced to the edges of "respectable society", due to their birthright, culture, and customs, these so-called "heathen Christians" were consorted with for pleasure, entertainment, and commerce. Their gift for song and dance, magical cures, potions, and creams, and genuine European, Oriental, and Middle Eastern silks, tapestries, and notions made them purveyors of exotica. However, these cursed nomads were made scapegoats for all petty crimes, drunkenness, and immoral pursuits. Efforts to imprison adult gypsies, decency league court proceedings demanding that gypsy youth be institutionalized and taken away from their parents, and sheriff actions to deny gypsies a livelihood elicited many extended hands bearing refuge and aid. Helping a gypsy, under the veil of darkness, out of town to avoid the long arm of the law earned the benefactor untoward gypsy loyalty, blessings, and gratitude for one's lifetime. It was said gypsies never forgot anyone whom assisted them.

Religious orders of the Roman Catholic, Byzantine Catholic, Anglican, and Orthodox faiths all were caretakers of the downtrodden and unfortunates. The saintly priests, sisters, monks, and brothers routinely aided those in need, with no expectations of reward or acknowledgement. In fact, truth be told, those of the cloth ministering to the gypsies were many times the recipients of harsh criticism for their good deeds. Like the legendary heavenly hosts, the avowed cared for the needy long before social welfare agencies and professionals came upon the scene.

The steel valley once hummed with hard labor, prosperity, and hardships. Health breaking work, gambling, fraud, and industrial accidents all took their unrelenting toll amongst families. Escape was welcomed. Touring circuses and festivals were warmly embraced. Carnivals, though sometimes vaguely sinister, were popular as well. Adult entertainment, games of chance, and sideshows were a radical change of pace for those mired in the workday grinds.

Turtle boy, the bearded lady, the snake woman, and Siamese twins were sights to behold. Carnival managers gave a wide assortment of freaks protection and employment in a world hostile to the handicapped or infirmed. The carnie encampments had strict social codes that were readily enforced for the safety of the patrons and carnival workers alike. Owners of the carnivals literally rescued, for a profit, the abnormals of society from certain hunger, persecution, and premature death. In effect, they were trustees of those most vulnerable, like ministering spirits of lore.

Our world has become wildly chaotic and dangerous despite all of our prosperity and modernity. Simple folk tales about fireflies being angels in search of wings are rarely heard now. Some believe we are alone in the universe.

I do find some measure of comfort though when I see lightening bugs on humid summer nights. These twilight sentinels exist despite all odds and are our constant companions, just within hands' reach. If I choose, I can still believe in kindred spirits looking out for us all. And, with this in mind, I invariably have a good night's sleep.

Around the Corner

by Richard S. Scarsella

Life is the ultimate journey. Words cannot do justice when describing the rich, colorful, and complex days of our lives. In a real sense, memories have a padlock on time. They preserve the essences of previous experiences. Try as I might not to, I still invariably revisit the past daily. Like old grizzled friends, dim reflections from days gone by are familiar much missed landmarks in an increasingly unrecognizable world.

When I travel down car-choked Route 224 between Poland, Boardman, and Canfield, I still habitually scan the horizon for once plentiful signs of my youth. Where have all the Amoco, Pure, Sinclair, Atlantic, Fleet Wing, Texaco, and Cities Service fuel station signboards gone? I still mistrust buying generic gasoline from self-service pumps. In the not-so-distant past, uniformed attendants filled your tank, knew your name, and washed your windshield with radiant smiles on their faces. Today's pit stops are jarringly impersonal uncomfortable experiences in comparison.

Now, it is rare to go shopping anywhere other than sterile malls and gray slab-like plazas. Until the 1960's, families routinely made purchases at corner establishments located on Market and Oak Streets and Mahoning, Belmont, and South Avenues. Buying Kosher meat at Lazar Brothers Groceries, selecting fresh produce at Pyatt Street Market farm stands, and paying for egg white-based frozen custard at Parker's or Fron's ice cream parlors were once weekly chores for area households. These corner merchants made doing business a pleasure, since they were all personable family-owned enterprises. A cheery hello and heartfelt goodbye were hallmarks of these latter day entrepreneurs.

The blue-collar intensive Mahoning Valley was once a beehive of corner bars and sanctuaries. Rough and tumble working-class saloons—as my grandmother derisively labeled them—reeked for blocks around of rancid cigar smoke, steamed hot dogs, and draft beer. These watering holes anchored ethnic enclaves. They were havens for those seeking contact with the Old World countries left behind.

Many taverns had theme-inspired décor. Bavaria, Napoli, and the Emerald Isle were favorite motifs.

Stern Gothic inspired hand-carved churches dotted the smoky Youngstown skyline and its varied subdivisions. Catholic, Orthodox, and Protestant places of worship seemed to be in view around most every corner. Sacred chants, solemn hymns, and heavenly chimes filled our ears with the voices of angels and the word of God. Neighborhoods could not escape the sanctified intonations emanating from holy places. Those up to no-good could not go far unchecked, because the haunting refrains of the blessed seemed to reach out to them throughout the environs.

A metropolitan area that still boasts of a half-million inhabitants is no stranger to death. Industrial accidents, childhood mortalities, and father time all made funerals commonplace. Lavish purple-draped funeral processions could easily be witnessed every day throughout the valley. Stately Cadillac and Lincoln hearses and limousines filled with black-attired relatives, elaborate carnation floral arrangements, and ebony caskets oftentimes met our unwary eyes at the intersections of well-traveled street corners on their way to area funeral homes and cemeteries. To bless yourself in the wake of grief was not uncommon. Long before inner belts rerouted heavy traffic away from our abodes, funeral entourages snaked lugubriously through our community and reminded us that the hand of death was amongst us.

No longer do I expect to see uniformed Girl Scout troops hawking cookies door to door. I have not seen a gypsy peddle wares or occult services for years around these parts. Sadly, Amish buggies will not hazard the risk of suburban traffic jams in order to sell organic duck eggs at our doorsteps. Time marches on and takes no prisoners.

Yet, for some unknown reasons, I still sense fleeting ghostly images around some corners. Perhaps, they are metaphors for life. Or, errant signals from the twilight zone.

Autumn Leaves

by Richard S. Scarsella

When the first chills of fall blanket the Mahoning Valley, I oftentimes think back to days long gone. For years, the area had its own unique rituals, when dealing with the change of the seasons.

Area homesteaders once laid in a truckload of coal or a tank of heating oil in anticipation of "firing up" long dormant furnaces. Chimney sweeps could easily be viewed high above rooftops as they performed their Dicksonian-era tasks.

Awning service companies were booked solid with appointments from residences taking down canvas window coverings. Storm windows were thoroughly scrubbed with hot vinegar water concoctions and mounted with great care.

By October, gardeners were losing the battle with Jack Frost. Tomato vines were wrenched from the soil by their roots and hung upside down in fruit cellars to dry in an effort to ripen green tomatoes.

Orchard growers started up apple stills and distilled both apple juice and apple cider. City folk cruised the countryside and bought bushels of apples for pies, crisps, and applesauce. Old-timers would mash apples into apple butter throughout the winter solstice.

The turning of the leaves signaled that the raking season was upon us. Children once went door-to-door soliciting neighbors for jobs. At one time, leaves were regularly deposited into street gutters, awaiting the street cleaners. For a time, residents burned leaves on the curb, in metal trashcans, or in incinerators. The result? A haze of smoke over a neighborhood was to be expected during the peak of leaf removal.

Those well traveled looked for revised train and bus schedules come October. Railroad depots usually added runs to New York City and Chicago, in order to accommodate increased freight and passenger demands. Greyhound and Trailways bus lines offered additional "express service" to locales such as Philadelphia, Washington, D.C., Baltimore, Detroit, and St. Louis. The familiar hoboes from the railroad yards began to head south and west just as the flocks of Canadian geese and mallard ducks began the trek to warmer nesting grounds.

In the months leading to Christmas, catalogues began to appear in mailboxes. Sears, Montgomery Wards, and Spiegel all sent glittering publications brimming with the latest styles, "affordable luxuries", and value pricing. As the fall quarter gave way to the winter quarter of the year, the Parcel Post and UPS trucks were seen more often making deliveries of brown wrapped packages.

Lake Erie denizens began the watch for "lake reports" threatening choppy water, whitecap waves, and gale winds. Marinas would begin to dry-dock speed boats, yachts, and canoes as the days grew increasingly short.

Like clockwork, Mill Creek Park patrons found roads temporarily blocked, in anticipation of the snow. These scenic closed drives were ideal paths for leaf watchers and doubled as sled routes during wintertime.

The brilliant hue of turning leaves made Mill Creek Park picture postcard perfect. Its neighbor, historic Idora Park, strangely was becalmed amid all the beauty. It was mothballed with great care and expertise, for a long winter's nap. When the carrousel was uncharacteristically stilled and the midways were hauntingly empty, one knew a change of season was underway.

An endless cycle of birth, life, and rebirth was repeated perpetually in our midst. Traditions endured and customs were honored without fail. Like autumn, life in our community once had a distinctive rhythm that changed little from year to year or season to season.

Today, I sometimes reflect that the way of life I once intimately knew has vanished. Nothing of comparable meaning has replaced it. I feel as naked and vulnerable as a tree shorn of its protective foliage. Only a suitcase of dried memories remain.

Back to Idora Day
At Yankee Lake

by Richard S. Scarsella

On August 29, 1999 Mahoning Valley residents were able to revisit a part of a social and cultural landmark, Idora Park. Area merchants held an event, called "Back To Idora", at the Yankee Lake grounds, which was once a site of a small amusement park. The event services an ever-growing cottage industry of Idora memories and memorabilia.

Idora Park, which is listed on the National Registry of Historic Places, closed in 1984. It has been much celebrated locally, in the 100th year of its opening, by this and similar commemorative gatherings of Idora vendors. Why? The historic amusement park continues to exert a mesmerizing influence on the imagination and collective sense of loss in a community unwilling to let go its rich magical-like presence.

This late summer happening offered a brief tantalizing glimpse of a gone, but not forgotten, grande dame amusement park. Food stands, offering distinctive Idora French fries, satiated a modest crowd, which was hungry for a taste of what once was the Idora experience. Big-band music in the quaint Yankee Lake Ballroom somewhat recreated the ambiance of the Idora Grand Ballroom. Small displays of vintage postcards, artwork, shirts, and a few artifacts of Youngstown's "Million Dollar Playground" were a feast for eyes longing to revisit the valley's now defunct entertainment complex. Here, seeing an authentic Idora coaster car or arcade sign was as close as one could hope to get to the rapidly fading icon.

A highlight of this nostalgic centered enterprise was the book-signing by Professor Rick Shale and Charles Jacquist of their new book titled "Idora Park: The Last Ride of Summer". This near definitive tome focuses on Idora's beginning, heyday, fires, and auction with rare photographs, detailed narratives, and eclectic statistics. Although previously available in area bookstores, the Idora biography, with its haunting visages of an Idora we all knew and still love, continues to radiate the true spirit and legacy of a time and place our eyes will never witness again locally.

The recent unveiling of a commemorative sign at Idora Park, by the Idora Park Institute, the Idora book, an Idora United States Postal Service stamp cancellation, and other Idora themed promotions all are graphic testimonials for a landmark that now stands forlorn, derelict, and close to oblivion.

"Back To Idora" was promoted by Creative Corners and Bob Barko Graphic Arts and was not associated with the recently proposed Idora Museum at Conneaut Lake Park, the Idora Park Institute, or the Mahoning Valley Historical Society.

It is ironic and telling that Idora Park is still widely popular a century after its founding. It can easily be argued that Idora be called the amusement park that refuses to die. Apparently, local merchants still see profit in a tradition that valley leaders are doing little to preserve.

Bridal Traditions

by Richard S. Scarsella

The Mahoning Valley is a rich tapestry of varied, colorful ethnic customs. Of them all, the solemn ritual of weddings has steadfastly grown and endured through the generations. In good times, like the rich post-World Ware II 1950's, and in the bad times, like the 1970's steel collapse, hopeful couples splurged on the weddings of their dreams. Families of Greek, Italian, and Hispanic origins especially celebrated the unions of their children, with lavish displays of hospitality for their guests.

Unbeknownst to many, the love-based bridal industry is a huge economic engine for the metropolitan area. Virtually recession-proof, purchases of gowns, rings, food, cookies, cakes, invitations, photography, limousines, tuxedoes, and entertainment are part of a steady, growing, vibrant right of passage for most adult men and women.

Of all the trappings associated with marital union, the bridal attire conjures up the most vivid images. Long, jewel encrusted cathedral trains, empire waistlines, yards of taffeta, imported lace, and fingertip length veils make weddings truly out of the ordinary. A dedicated, patient cadre of specialists known as bridal consultants once expertly delivered the magic. New York and continental fashions, primarily from Italy and France, were glamorized and advertised to a local market, hungry for haute couture at affordable prices.

Livingston's, with an anchor store on West Federal Street, in downtown Youngstown, was the fashion leader for brides-to-be. An elegant bridal saloon, ensconced in this mini-department store, complete with crystal chandeliers, velvet wallpaper, and antique furnishings, catered to every whim and desire of the newly engaged. This exquisite store, with suburban branches, offered complete makeovers, bridal trousseaus, honeymoon wardrobes, and an in-house furrier. The local Alfred family, owners of this legendary women's chain, provided a touch of New York's 7th. Avenue, for discriminating brides. Customers from the tri-state area frequented this mercantile landmark.

The Bride and Formal Shoppe, on Market Street, in Youngstown's once trendy Uptown district, offered a wide selection of leading designer gowns, at moderate to high price points. Here, a bride-to-be could browse through styles ranging from the romantic to the contemporary. Regardless of size, age, taste, or budget, the racks of garments in this store literally made dreams come true. With a sister store, named Marlane Bridals, the Rose family made "high style" affordable to the emerging middle-class of the greater Youngstown area. The Youngstown Vindicator society pages were filled daily with new brides pictured in the best finery the wedding industry manufactured.

Marie Antoinette Bridal House, on the West Side's Mahoning Avenue, near Mahoning Plaza, was Youngstown's first bridal boutique open by appointment only. A New York Greenwich Village type of informal ambiance awaited prospective brides at this unique establishment, which was located in a house turned into a storefront. Here, Marie Antoinette Modarelli Scarsella personally selected and fitted one-of-a-kind garments for trusting clients. Dresses were also handmade for more discerning tastes, courtesy of seamstresses that learned their trade on the European continent. Surgical-like alterations and custom fittings were the "secret" trick of making every bride "beautiful" for her special day.

Sadly, all these fine establishments have passed from the local scene, due to the retirements of the owners. Their legacies live on in priceless images, frozen in time in the thousands of wedding albums that families cherish. Most would agree that the money spent on these occasions was well worth the memories.

Calvacade of Stars

by Richard S. Scarsella

At one time, radio entertained a nation hungry for amusement. Venerable vaudeville acts, slightly risqué burlesque routines, and folksy amateur contests all enthralled us for hours on end. Soap operas first found their national audiences on the AM dial and radio made baseball a national pastime.

When kinescope, popularly known as television, debuted in the late 1940's, many said it would not amount to anything. The critics were wrong. By the early 1950's, this new medium had gutted radio's dominance and threatened Hollywood's mighty film studio empires. The end result? A steady stream of "stars" became available at no cost to viewers in the comfort of their own homes.

At first, leading men and women of the silver screen shunned the small screen. As Hollywood lost its mortal grip on Americans' leisure time and dollars, Hollywood royalty began to appear nightly on ABC, NBC, CBS, and independent television networks. This drain of talent sealed Hollywood's fate and cemented television's longevity. Television's voracious appetite for talent welcomed Hollywood's elites and has-beens.

Loretta Young's anthology series showcased her formidable creative talent, both as a producer and as a performer. Her style, elegance, and versatility thrilled viewer for many years. Ironically, she is now best remembered for her grand entrances, through double doors, at the beginning of her shows, coifed perfectly in flowing exotic gowns, made of exotic silks, flowing chiffons, imported laces, and shimmering jewels.

Ronald Reagan, our ex-president, hosted a popular General Electric series in the 1950's as well. This former film union president and B movie contract player honed his easygoing all-American personae week after week on this pioneer display of drama. He later became the ultimate made-for-television personage and used the camera expertly for political gain and influence. Had it not been for television, the history books would read very differently now.

Red Skelton blended circus, vaudeville, burlesque, Broadway, radio, and motion picture traditions seamlessly into a television art form. His classic gags, full of pathos and mischief, kept alive venerable practices of stage, screen, and performance artists. Skelton's clown character endeared him to generations and makes him unforgettable still. In the best spirit of television, his craft bridged the void between all classes and spoke to all.

Of all the famous, glamorous, and notorious legends television featured, Judy Garland was the most loved and pitied. When she took her idolized voice and tortured psyche to televisionland, she had embarked on yet another "comeback". Due to a dependency on pills, mismanaged affairs, and lack of confidence, Garland's life had spun out of control when she was but a starlet on the MGM movie sets. Her failed marriages, bouts of depression, attempted suicides, and estrangement form her mother all haunted this larger than life performer. On television, we saw Garland simultaneously glitter and fade away in front of our disbelieving eyes. When the variety hour was cancelled, it was almost a relief. The rawness of television translated her disintegrating personality on many levels. Garland's nervous mannerisms, pleading eyes, and piercing vocals are still vivid in my memories of the early television years.

Lucille Ball, Jackie Gleason, Donna Reed, and Jack Benny, to name a few, all belonged to an era of television giants the likes of which will never be witnessed again. I still miss them all. When I tune in my "tube", I still half expect to see old familiar faces light up my screen. Alas, the golden age of television is long gone and only glimpsed in occasional reruns.

Canfield Fair

by Richard S. Scarsella

In the Mahoning Valley, Labor Day weekend always meant more than going back to school or the final weekend of Idora Park's season. It screamed "Canfield Fair!"

For farmers, suburbanites, and city dwellers, the Mahoning County Fair in Canfield was the official end of summer and the beginning of fall activities. Local media saturated the region with previews of the fair and related human-interest stories. Going to the fair was as much a tradition with area families as was getting a picture with Santa Claus, having a picnic at Mill Creek Park, or attending a reunion at Idora Park.

Generations of valley residents have fond memories of the fair. It was and is a smorgasbord of sights, sounds, smells, and tastes. Children loved the sight of baby animals. The petting zoo's fuzzy ducklings, silky rabbits, and smooth calves are annual favorites. The over-sized antique smoke belching farm machinery also captured impressionable imaginations.

The sounds of snorting horses, scolding pigs and shrill chickens were mesmerizing, in their own way, for people used to seeing such animals only on television. The Canfield Fair was a potpourri of smells. Fresh cut hay, chilidogs, fresh roasted peanuts, manure, and fertilizer all intermingled freely. The earthy smells seemed to be subtle reminders that this celebration of harvest was not just a festival, but also a celebration of the land and its fruits.

Food was always a fair trademark. Here, one could find fresh off the farm corn-on-the-cob, sweet strawberries, juicy watermelon, and onion flavored steak sandwiches. Lemon shakes, real buttered popcorn, hot dogs on a stick, pecan filled fudge, elephant ears, and sausage sandwiches all put one into the fair mood, regardless of age, income or gender.

The fair's midway was a carnival unto itself. Double Ferris-wheels, freak shows and games of skill all competed for one's attention. It was hard to believe, that just a couple feet away, wholesome 4H students were sleeping with and guarding their prized entries.

Canfield Fair was and is larger than most state fairs. It was and is second in size in Ohio only to the Ohio State Fair. It has been a source of local pride and a dependable tourist attraction. For over a century and a half, it has been a meeting place for a diverse valley population, while in turn being a generator of commerce. Unlike many area institutions, it has endured and prospered, among the ruins of the so-called "rust belt".

The giant pumpkin patch, riding shows, bandstand revues, blue-ribbons, arts and craft displays, quaint home-making entries of preserves, marching bands, talent shows, tractor pulls, and the Western Reserve Village Museum, all make this event a genuine expression of Americana, with a distinctive local touch.

Canfield Fair is a living montage of rich cultures, colorful traditions, and the living past. Here, one can find a Strouss malt, Parker's custard, and Idora French fries. Hopefully, the day will never come when Labor Day weekend does not mean a trip down memory lane at the Canfield Fair.

Christmas Recollections

by Richard S. Scarsella

The Mahoning Valley's many ethnic cultures gave birth to varied, colorful, richly textured expressions of holiday cheer. Steel magnates, mercantile titans, white-collar professionals, tradesmen, and factory workers all united in good will for a day of thanks, remembrance, and celebration.

Naturally, the hub of excitement was in downtown Youngstown, well into the 1960's. Bargain hunters scoured East Federal Street for good deals. The Central Store and Klein's Department Store, Youngstown's first discount chain outlet, specialized in stocking uptown fashions at off prices. The Brass Rail catered to hungry, hassled shoppers by serving up coffee house entrees such as grilled cheese and tomato sandwiches, club sandwiches, with colorful toothpicks, pepper steak and onion rings, and lemon meringue pies.

The Christmas tree unveiling and lighting ceremony on Central Square attracted thousands of shoppers from the tri-county area. Santa's parade was a spectacle of rainbow hued tinfoil, perky high school bands, and amateur floats, pulled by steel hauling diesels. The fact that there was a Santa Christmasland high atop both McKelvey's and Strouss' Department Stores did not appear incongruous to gullible children. It seemed very in keeping with the holiday magic.

Majestic theaters, with two and three lobbies, lush marble in-laid floors, heavy velvet draperies, and cut glass chandeliers glittered. The Palace, Warner, State, and Paramount all advertised extra showings of their holiday blockbuster movies. Film offerings always included wholesome family fare, such as Disney's Swiss Family Robinson, lush romantic stories, such as Romeo and Juliet, tearjerkers, such as Love Story, and escapism action tales, such as James Bond's Gold Finger. Dressing up to go shopping, taking in a movie and having lunch downtown at Raver's, The Italian Restaurant, Strouss' Grille, and McKelvey's Dining Room was a hallowed practice for most residents, regardless of age or income, during this festive season.

Livingston's display windows were truly breathtaking. This touch of New York's 7th Avenue in our midst mesmerized us with blue dyed mink stoles, crystal encrusted pill boxes, genuine hand-tailored, imported couture Dior fashions and alligator leather shoes and handbags.

Located on West Federal Street, McKelvey's and Strouss' were veritable fortresses of gold gilded wreaths and pinecones, aluminum Christmas trees, and white cotton-covered decorations. Organs bellowed out venerable tunes, such as It Came Upon A Midnight Clear, while perfume clerks spritzed customers with the fragrances of Chanel No. 5 and Old Spice Cologne.

Before heading home, almost everyone stopped at Fanny Farmer Candies. This Chicago chocolate confectioner dazzled our senses with ultra-pure milk chocolate Santas, pink chocolate angels on a stick, and white chocolate snowmen. Genuine peppermint sticks and oversized candy canes were the perfect treat after a big day of pounding the pavement downtown. For good measure, most shoppers dropped a few coins into the ubiquitous red Salvation Army kettles, located at almost every street corner.

On the way home, most households would stop at a nearby Isaly's and purchase a long narrow block of ice cream. Inside this frozen dessert, which was to be sliced, one would find a green Christmas tree, topped by a red star. To accompany this sublime pleasure, most residents would buy a Paradise Fruit Cake, baked by the now closed Ward Bakery. This holiday staple was full of mixed nuts, jellied fruits, rum, and sugar and lingered on the palette. The tin container, festooned with white, neo-classical angel-like pixies, was considered a collectable. For many, these tins are all they have left to remind them of this bygone era.

Time has moved on. And so have we. The downtown is silent now, victimized by the strip plazas and cavernous malls. Movie palaces are all shuttered. Their screens are permanently dark. Most movies are viewed at home on television.

Few travel downtown anymore. We can now shop by e-mail. Our memories, however, are frozen in time, when the silhouette of downtown Youngstown's skyline, once in view, was a passport to urban raptures now unimaginable.

Christmas Yore

by Richard S. Scarsella

Holidays rekindle fond memories of times past. Regardless of what has or has not happened in our lives, we inevitably revisit yesterdays for comfort and reflection during the holidays.

In the once bustling Mahoning Valley, tri-county area residents doggedly headed to Youngstown's crowded central business district in search of memorable gifts. Glittering specialty boutiques, trendy shoe stores, fashionable diamond jewelers, fussy gentlemen tailors, style salons, and landmark department stores welcomed intrepid shoppers with great hospitality.

Well into the 1960's, Federal Street was a thriving avenue of trade. Fleets of yellow and checkered cabs delivered patrons to storefronts. Elephantine-like buses stopped at each downtown corner block, much to the exasperation of motorists. Throngs of pedestrians choked walkways and intersections, with jaywalkers receiving tickets from ever-vigilant traffic officers. Festive decorations hung elegantly by the Downtown Board of Trade adorned store facades, although they were scarcely noticed by time-pressed consumers.

The traditional Central Square Christmas tree and crèche were breathtaking in their symbolism and size. Despite automobile fumes, industrial smog, flocks of pigeons, and steam escaping from street manholes, we enjoyed our days of "going to town". Eating lunch at a chrome counter in an art deco five-and-dime store was a novelty. Buying a Strouss' malt in the bargain basement department was a special treat. "Taking in a movie" at a grand movie palace was a side trip into another dimension. A journey into the city was full of welcomed diversions.

Area churches, usually somber and drab, suddenly came to life, once they were festooned with boughs of evergreens, colorful ribbons, and fresh garland. European clarions chimed robustly with religious favorites, such as "Silent Night" and "Come All Ye Faithful." Of course, the ubiquitous Salvation Army red kettles and bell ringers encouraged us to share with those less fortunate. Our strident Mid-western ethic constantly reminded us to guard against frivolity.

The observation of the birth of Christ and of New Years necessitated obligatory visits to ancestral cemeteries. Hand-carved headstones, both new and weathered, were lovingly decorated with votive candles, religious emblems, artificial poinsettias, and black wreaths. Local graveyards became hosts to carloads of kin paying earnest respects. Oddly, the departed seemed particularly close to us as we rejoiced without their earthly presence. Widows, widowers, and orphans were known to be stricken with a touch of melancholy as the merriment commenced.

I can still clearly recall inviting the mailman and milkman in on Christmas Eve for fresh eggnog and fruitcake. It seems like yesterday when we would peruse corner Christmas tree lots, debating the pros and cons of long and short needle freshly cut trees. Purchasing extra greenery for the mantle, staircase, and dining room table was a task entrusted to the youngest children.

When all the gifts had been wrapped, after the Christmas tree was lit, and when company had gone home, the evenings were oftentimes ended with families singing carols around an old upright piano. Special radio and television programs also fueled our holiday cheer.

To this day, when I hear Bing Crosby, Frank Sinatra, Perry Como, Judy Garland, Kate Smith, or Brenda Lee sing Christmas standards, such as "White Christmas", I am transported back to earlier simpler times. We did not know it then, but we do now. Those were the good old days. And I expect them to be time immemorial.

Cityscape

by Richard S. Scarsella

Youngstown once was a montage of colorful, vibrant, multi-ethnic neighborhoods. Before suburbia zapped their energies, urban avenues, streets and boulevards were alive with the rich heritages of English, Irish, Italian, German, Jewish, African—Americans, and other cultures.

The 1940's and 1950's were golden years for the Mahoning Valley. The war effort and the subsequent peacetime economic expansion solidified once transient enclaves situated on the hills of the murky Mahoning River. Wick Park, Fosterville, Lansingville, Brier Hill, Cherry Hill, and Brownlee Woods were all environs one knew and visited without hesitation.

In our midst, a steady stream of sojourners also frequented these city districts. Traveling salespeople routinely pitched their products to prosperous homeowners. Many sold products to several generations and became trusted consultants to area families. It was not unusual to invite these vendors up onto our porches and drink lemonade and gossip. They were a welcomed relief to our routines and broke the everyday monotony.

Many of us still fondly remember the Fuller Brush man. He would regally unveil, from his velvet lined valises, genuine whalebone combs and authentic horsehair brushes. He would also give "expert" advice on balding, thinning hair, and split ends. The Fuller Brush products were considered top-of-the-line, expensive, and good investments, since they were made of long-lasting materials not readily available in local variety stores. These toiletries were considered a status symbol and were not available in any stores.

Knife-sharpeners often frequented local homesteads. The grinders were usually gruff, bearded, spoke with foreign accents, and reeked of perspiration. They not only sharpened cutlery and scissors, but also sold new and used blades. Neighbor children would stare in amazement, as sparks would fly off dull daggers being burnished on flint. These craftsmen from another era were all important to busy housewives who trusted them with their prized house wares.

At a time when most homes had chimneys attached to working fireplaces or incinerators, the chimney sweeps customarily appeared in the autumn before the first frost. Tall, slender, lightly muscled, these men of soot usually were sparse of words and as agile as cats. Their dirty, dangerous, and mysterious profession seemed perversely alluring to youngsters in search of danger.

Farmers also hawked goods within the city boundaries. Vine-ripened strawberries, sweet corn, apple cider, hen and duck eggs, fresh cream, and country-cured meats all could be sampled and purchased in the comfort of one's own front yard. Home bakers had the bounty of the valley brought right to their pantries and fruit cellars. Supermarkets had their profit cut by this direct buying. Family picnics and reunions always boasted the best from these rural peddlers. Sunday dinners were planned around the harvest of our country cousins.

In the 1940's and 1950's, kitchen freezers were not yet perfected. Ice buildup and uneven temperatures took their toll on the flavor and storage of ice cream and sherbet. The nomadic ice cream man, ringing a bell or playing a tune over a loudspeaker, was an irresistible sound on hot, humid, languid summer days. Nickels and dimes could buy Eskimo Pies, Isaly's Klondikes, Dilly Bars, and Good Humour frozen confections. These tastes became firmly entrenched in our childhood recollections.

Other visitors were tinged with a less savory hue. We were very cautious of the intermittent hoboes and tramps that drifted into town. From the rail yards, tattered hoboes came uptown in search of odd jobs, food, and shelter. They told epic stories of the West and South, where they sought out warm climate during our winters, and seemed pathetically noble and tragic in their cross-country treks. Tramps, dressed in patched rags, sometimes lingered for days. They were eager to take on handyman chores for low fees or in exchange for food. Many were well educated, clinically depressed, or alcoholics. They regularly dropped by our parts and seemed like luckless, broken-hearted, distant kin in search of safe harbor from their troubles. Both tramps and hoboes were familiar figures in our metropolitan lives. They taught us much about "hard times" and the greater world outside city boundaries.

Gypsies were the most memorable characters to briefly touch our lives. Lurid tales of baby snatching, curses, and the evil eye made these migrants extra-special guests in close-knit communities. These much persecuted and stereotyped descendants of Central and Eastern Europe offered imported silks, tapestries and brocades, medicinal herbs, pungent, rare spices, magical potions and powders, and bargain-priced gold and silver jewel-encrusted jewelry to curious spectators.

The more daring of us had our fortunes told. We much enjoyed their calling on us. However, we breathed easier when they left town.

Bee Line representatives, Tupperware agents, sweeper salesmen, evangelical preachers, missionaries, and faith healers, Native-American medicine men, and dairy and bread trucks all once unvarying appeared in the course of a year in any given neighborhood. They were part of the very essence of the city. We felt very cosmopolitan for having met and dealt with them all.

Modern day life has all but squeezed these once prevalent characters off the contemporary scene. They live on in stories, teleplays, and movies. Our lives are much poorer for their untimely exit into local history and lore. Why? They made remembrances out of everyday life that now are priceless to behold.

Clouded Mirror

by Richard S. Scarsella

When I think of the past, I have to catch myself. Why? I try to guard against remembering things that did not happen as I recall. It is easy to embellish days gone by through the dim portal of time.

Holidays oftentimes are prone to be exaggerated in our subconscious mind. The uncertain present is no match for the familiar gauzy yesteryears. Try as we might, it is impossible not to use the olden days as a quick reference for the contemporary era we sometimes uneasily inhabit.

I remember well the post-holiday rush crowds in downtown Youngstown hell-bent on scooping up bargains at a myriad of merchants. Strouss' and McKelvey's ran pages of enticing advertisements in local newspapers and flooded the radio and television airways with urgent announcements of "once in a lifetime savings." City traffic officers dreaded the end-of-the-year clearances, which attracted thousands of pedestrians and led to intransigent traffic jams.

Smart consumers took lumbering public transit buses into the heart of town. Buying a transfer for another bus route was only a nickel at one time. Many area residents had year-round and seasonal passes. It was not unusual for many riders to know the bus drivers on first name basis. Sometimes, gracious transit employees dropped off older or younger passengers at unscheduled stops. Hitching a ride into Central Square on a long curvaceous bus was half the fun of our once routine trips into the city.

These erstwhile days reeked of cigar smoke, Chanel No. 5 perfume, Old Spice aftershave, and diesel smoke. Strolling upon the wide sidewalks of Federal Street was like a taste of a big city. Window-shopping was an honored pastime. Newspaper boys yelling "Extra, extra, read all about it!" and bedraggled bag people asking people humbly for change were all familiar sights in our lives. The dramatic fashionable show windows, displaying European elegance and New York chic, were sharply contrasted by the Dicksonian environs of rancid dirt, pungent fumes, and rag covered beggars which surrounded them. We embraced all of this.

We knew no other world. The antiseptic malls and faceless strip plazas we now frequent were not even part of our imagination.

Colorful ethnic shopkeepers, hourly sales clerks, and professional salaried salespeople more than "earned their keep" during the post-holiday sales season. They could size up a client and pull from overflowing markdown racks suitable garments and accessories with flare and aplomb. We trusted their taste, integrity, and sincerity. To this day, these vanquished loyal legions of retailers are without equal. They are still fondly held in high esteem and much missed by those they so well served.

Maybe my memory is tricking me, as I reminisce. Were Jay's hot dogs the best I ever tasted? Could Woolworth's lunch counter make the most delicious grilled cheese sandwich in town? Did the Strouss' and McKelvey's toy lands stack goods to the cathedral ceilings? Did gritty downtown Youngstown assume a mantle of grace, hospitality, and magic during the yuletime season?

My mind questions what my heart feels. Due to the clouded mirror of times past, I may never know for sure. I know one thing for certain. Even now, the call of the past is as strong and as real as anything I have ever known.

Declination

by Richard S. Scarsella

In an annual rite of autumn, the daylight hours shorten the darkness increases, and the countdown for the New Year begins. Once Halloween passes, thoughts turn to Thanksgiving and Christmas. With little effort, I can summon up vivid memories of days gone by.

I clearly recollect the Youngstown Transit Company increasing their bus runs to and from the city in the fall. Valley residents all traveled to the downtown to window shop, browse, put items in lay-a-way, and to purchase holiday supplies and gifts. Parallel parking on side streets was perilous at best. Finding an indoor parking garage with open spaces was also exasperating.

Although the Christmas season officially began the day after Thanksgiving, merchants began to stock, price, and display holiday goods in late October. Variety stores, such as Murphy's McCrory's, Woolworth's, Kressege's, and Grant's usually were the first retailers to debut festive merchandise.

These emporiums popularized cardboard images of Santa Claus, Rudolph, and Frosty the Snowman. Silver artificial trees, Lionel trains, manger scenes (crèches), and copies of "The Night Before Christmas" adorned five and dime store shelves long before snow ever fell to the ground. Ribbon candy, pudding candles, and "fancy cocktail nuts" all were prominently showcased for eager shoppers.

Swanky women's stores, such as Livingston's and Betty Goodman's, once held trunk sales for select clientele. These private showings of New York, Parisian, and Italian haute couture fashions were once common events in our metropolitan area. Garments were carefully selected for major festivities, which marked the holiday calendar. The famous Esther Hamilton Christmas Show and the New Year's Eve parties at the Youngstown Club were two events where founding family society matrons glittered to their fullest. The Vindicator society column dutifully documented the social gatherings of our local "jet set".

In Mill Creek Park, drives were closed for sledding, leaves were turned into mulch, and the boats at Glacier and Newport lakes were dry-docked, all in anticipation of father winter. Hayrides, bonfires, and apple cider festivals all drew city dwellers into the nearby countryside for pastoral past-times. Awaiting their return was a city full of belching smoky chimneys.

As the valley cooled, the languid Mahoning River would become steamy and foggy. The steel mills' insatiable thirst for water literally turned this once scenic waterway into a hissing sewer of fumes and smog. Oddly, we took some measure of comfort in this unnatural sight, since old-timers assured us that dirty air and fouled water were small prices to pay for continued prosperity. The soot and haze that engulfed downtown Youngstown became part of the shopping experience and was taken into stride by locals. As temperatures dropped in the later part of the year, the stark beauty of denuded Mill Creek Park, rusty iron railways, gray cavernous steel factories, and towering central city office buildings became more readily apparent to even a casual observer. The longer fall evenings were perfect venues for fire spewing open-hearth furnaces, spectacular Strouss' and McKelvey's department store window displays, and well-lit steeples of St. Columba Cathedral and First Presbyterian Church.

As people dutifully installed storm windows and doors, cleaned gutters, and stored porch furniture, other landmarks in the valley made adjustments for the encroaching inclement weather. Rayen and South Side stadiums would paint their bleachers. Calvary and Tod cemeteries would clear graves of warm-weather decorations. Putt Putt golf courses would mothball their diminutive fairways and shutter their doors. Geneva-On-The-Lake boardwalk would literally become a ghost town until spring.

One by one, carnivals, festivals, and circuses left town for the year, heading south to warmer climates. Only fabled Idora Park remained in our midst, as the "mistress of amusements". Although the Grand Ballroom remained open year-round, booking shows such as Lawrence Welk and Guy Lombardo, the midways fell silent as we entered the dark months. Wintertime was a type of limbo for Idora Park.

For almost one hundred years, the Tunnel of Love/Rapids water ride was drained, the Idora Limited train was put into its roundhouse, and the carrousel was draped in sturdy canvass for a long winter's nap. Then, as now, only the reptilian skeletons of the Wild Cat, Baby Wild Cat, and Jack Rabbit marked the Idora grounds as a haven for sun and fun. These haunting silhouettes still endure. And with the end of each year, Idora's hold on existence slips with the passage of time. Sadly, time waits for nothing.

Déjà Vu

by Richard S. Scarsella

The years come and go unrelentlessly. Our hurried lives take on the quality of old snapshots, with only highlights of existence documented for posterity. Holidays in particular make us take a breathless pause from our routines. When we do so, we take stock of our presence in a valley both transfixed and mired in the past.

Not so long ago, holidays were prepared for by patronizing long established locally owned and operated merchants. Families would head downtown to purchase a new pair of shoes at Lustig's, a new outfit at Strouss' or McKelvey's, or a pound of hand-dipped chocolates at Fanny Farmer. The central city was once the hub of holiday shopping for the entire valley. Smoky streets were filled with window-shoppers and consumers ready to buy some holiday cheer.

Downtown retailers were staffed by generations of family employees. Once you entered the thresholds of legendary stores with names such as Livingston's, Hartzell's, Bond's, Glasgow's, Brenner's, Simco Shoes, and Betty Goodman's, you knew you would be treated with a level of professionalism rarely found in today's stores. Career sales "clerks", usually uniformed in dark colors, knew your tastes and preferences. They acted as knowledgeable consultants. We trusted them. Commissions were not the top priority with these salespeople. They knew if you were satisfied you would remain a loyal customer and make referrals to them. They were right.

Buying a new holiday wardrobe was a must. Girls were partial to velvet dresses, trimmed in lace and satin bows. Black patent leather "Shirley Temple" slippers, with a white rabbit fur muff, completed the ensemble. Boys were attired in "Buster Brown" suits, caps, bow ties, and suspenders. Babies were dressed as elves, angels, or fairytale characters. Of course, having a picture taken at an area portrait studio, such as Schween-Wagner or Blackford, was a must to commemorate the festive season. In fact, family portraits were taken at this time and sent throughout the country to extended family. Ironically for many, only these posed photographs remain as testaments to days gone by.

Well into the 1960's, ladies and gentlemen "dressed" for a formal series of society events. Women would carefully select hostess, church, club, golf, cruise, and New Year's garments. Stores would record your purchases, so no one would appear at a function wearing "your" clothing. Hats, gloves, and matching handbags were all coordinated with stylish costume and fine jewelry pieces. It's a cliché, but true nonetheless, women made every effort to glow for the glittering parties, dinners, and performances held during this time of year.

Men also put on their best threads to complement their wives and significant others. Gentlemen purchasing classic suits, hats, shoes, ties, French cuff shirts, and accessories kept local tailors and haberdasheries busy. Tuxedoes were cleaned, pressed, and altered for more formal affairs, such as the symphony, ballet, opera, and Monday Musical Club attractions. Country clubs, the Youngstown Club, and fraternal lodges all required "formal dress" for their annual soirees. Many refer to these days as a golden age of manners, civility, decorum, and aspirations.

I vividly recall many things about the past Christmas seasons. Boy Scout, Girl Scout, and Camp Fire troops could be seen visiting nursing homes and hospitals, with tins of homemade cookies and handmade crafts in their hands. Salvation Army kettles could be found at every downtown street corner, with solemn volunteers ringing bells as advertisements. Brightly lit theater marquees grandly announced blockbuster films "suitable for family viewing". Panhandlers meekly asked for change so they could buy a cup of coffee at nearby grilles. The hissing steam from the street manholes gave the downtown environs an old London, England aura.

The focal point for shoppers was the Central Square Christmas tree, which towered over storefronts and acted as a backdrop for high school choirs, parades, and crèche displays. Santa Claus signs heralded his arrival at Strouss', McKelvey's, and all five and dime stores. The strings of colored light, which hung over East and West Federal Streets, gave the downtown a magical feeling.

Although the downtown presently sits in silent slumber, the memories it once made for us all are endearing and enduring. I oftentimes travel the innerbelt highway around the central city. The skyline still stirs me. Sights of the stately Home Savings signature clock, the art deco Metropolitan Tower, and the orange roofed B&O passenger terminal whisper to me that these places, and all they represent, still survive.

As a famous sportsman once exclaimed, "It's déjà vu all over again."

Downtown Youngstown Department Stores

by Richard S. Scarsella

At the height of its popularity, downtown Youngstown was the retail, professional, and cultural hub of the Mahoning Valley. Federal Street was lined with nationally and locally owned stores, bustling skyscraper office buildings, and first-run movie houses. A network of trains, trolleys, and buses connected Central Square with towns and villages in the tri-county area. Going downtown was a big event. And, with good reason.

Why the attraction? Youngstown once boasted six large department stores. McKelvey's—"Youngstown's Greatest Store"—was the fashion leader in town. Its designer collections, fur salon, bridal boutique, china department and furniture selections were all from McKelvey's New York City buying offices. One had to go to Cleveland or Pittsburgh to find items of similar style, taste, and quality.

Strouss-Hirschberg was also a retail leader. It was known for elegant casual wear, fur-trimmed coats, after-five suits, Hollywood cosmetics, Parisian perfumes, Italian leather goods, boys' and girls' departments, and its famous chocolate "malts". Both McKelvey's Restaurant and Strouss' Grille lured shoppers into their stores' wide aisles, escalators, and elevators. Both stores became integral parts of our lives. In-house bakeries, "bargain basements", and "halls of music" captivated area families. Strolling through Christmas displays and meeting Santa Claus were traditions with several generations. Sadly, both flagship stores closed—victims of mall shopping trends.

Bargain-hunters browsed East Federal Street. The Central Store catered to thrifty buyers. Reasonably priced boots and britches, broadfronts (underwear), and work clothes were the drawing cards for this establishment. Before jeans became fashionable, the Central Store had the biggest selection around. This austere firm proudly displayed good, sturdy, Yankee-made, no-nonsense items at fair prices. Grandmothers, preachers, and teachers frequented this store.

Down the avenue, Klein's Department Store pre-dated locally founded Hill's Department Stores, by using the same merchandising philosophy of plain displays, big selections, and everyday discount prices. Uptown couture styles were imitated here at affordable prices and dubbed as "fashion" items for the average women. Like so many landmarks, both the Central Store and Klein's were leveled for urban renewal.

Sears, Roebuck and Company was a magnet for male consumers. Its selections of tools, power equipment, garden, and auto supplies could not be equaled anywhere. Located on Central Square, men spent whole afternoons examining, pricing, and ordering items, either from the world famous Sears catalogue or at one of the huge oak counters. Children and teens would spend hours in the toy and radio/stereo aisles. Homemakers stocked up on house wares, at this family friendly merchant.

Penney's—located between McKelvey's and Strouss'—catered to solid, conservative middle class tastes and values. Coffee-coats, lingerie, "women's foundations", school uniforms, and an extensive infants department outfitted most young homemakers' homes. In a quest to move towards suburbia, both Penney's and Sears shuttered their downtown anchor stores. Both were torn down for development projects.

Old-timers will tell you, that the age of the grand downtown department stores cannot be beat by sterile, box-like suburban stores. The downtown shopping experience was truly unique. Why? One's senses were engaged by: steam coming out of the manholes, flocks of pigeons overhead, bumper to bumper traffic, smoke emitting buses, garishly lit theater marquees, life-like window displays, pungent smelling food stands, barking newspaper boys, and Dickinsonian bag-people. Following the lead of the steel mills, this era has regrettably passed into local urban lore and history. The likes, of which, will never be seen again.

Drive-in Theaters: Summer Ritual

by Richard S. Scarsella

Baby-boomers still fondly remember a time honored summer ritual that has all but vanished from the Youngstown area. Its name? Drive-in theaters.

In their heyday, drive-ins were a mainstay in the 1950's and 1960's family life and youth culture. Their appeal? Wide screens, great seats (your own car!), good food, playgrounds, and a double feature for one low price.

Drive-ins used to open for their seasonal business shortly after Easter and close for the year in late September. They heralded the summer's debut and finale. Drive-ins gave everyone a chance to see films again that had long ago played the first-run movie palaces of downtown Youngstown. If one missed a movie at the State, Warner, Paramount, or Palace Theaters, one could probably catch it the following summer at the West Side, North Side, South Side, or Sky-Hi drive-in theaters.

These venerable roadside landmarks were all located on the outskirts of town, in former pastures. Just driving to them was an adventure. As the city slipped behind, one approached these Hollywood outposts with the cool, country breeze wafting into the car. The enticing smells of buttered popcorn, hot dogs, hamburgers, and cotton candy reached the car, long before one gained entrance into the admittance arch. The excitement was in the anticipation of joining others on acres of land devoted to the movies.

In farm country, it was odd to see city folks, in bumper-to-bumper cars, creeping along, in not quite single-file, at dusk, on Mahoning Avenue, Belmont Avenue, Market Street and McCartney Road. Even more unusual were the car occupants themselves. Children in pajamas, complete with slippers, were major fans of this pop culture. Dutiful parents packed pillows, blankets, toys, coolers, and more for this night out with the kids. Hordes of teen-agers, full of hormonal angst and gang psychology, also fueled the prosperity of the drive-ins. These rustic cinemas were a bargain, especially when the ticket price was per car, and not per head. Even retirees joined the crush of youth to see the "big screen".

Drive-in theaters were a quintessentially American invention. America's wide-open spaces gave birth to this unique silver-screen culture. The blend of giant screen spectacle, fast food, and somnolent attitude made the drive-in very chic. No one had to dress up to go to this theater. All one had to do was roll down one's window and attach the speaker. How democratic!

Drive-ins usually catered to young families and older folks with the early-evening fare that featured Walt Disney films and middlebrow comedies. The Parent Trap, Swiss Family Robinson and 20,000 Leagues Under the Sea all had great crossover appeal for parent and child alike. One could truly appreciate the Disney magic when it was projected on a screen four stories high.

Mid-evening double features targeted the teens and young adults. Horror flicks, action films, and beach party movies predominated this time slot. Christopher Lee, Steve McQueen, and Frankie Avalon all could be seen in their full glory in this wide-screen presentation. Dracula, Angie Dickinson, and Annette Funicello all looked mesmerizing on the bright, Technicolor lit behemoth of a screen that was outlined by a sepia-hued summer evening sunset.

Midnight features offered films with an edge. One might see Psycho, Who's Afraid of Virginia Woolf, or House on Haunted Hill. Blood, cleavage, "adult themes", and "adult language" reigned here. The sounds of riotous crickets and tossed beer cans were standard happenings at this showing, as were steamed windows. The bugs, flies, and manure smells of nearby fields affected all the crowds. This was part of the experience.

The 1970's and 1980's have been unkind to the drive-ins. Rising land prices, new housing developments, strip plazas, malls, chain restaurants, vcr's, cable, central air conditioning, and increasingly sophisticated audiences have doomed area drive-ins. All the Youngstown drive-ins have been demolished. Even the Mid-Way Drive-in, between Boardman and the Pittsburgh Airport, has closed. Now, one has to travel to the Warren area to attend a drive-in.

In some towns, drive-ins double as flea markets or as outdoor churches. It's hard to believe that all the drive-in screens of suburban Youngstown and all of the movie palace screens of downtown Youngstown are now darkened. These unique pieces of Americana no longer exist in our midst. Like the flickering screen images in the moonlight, we now just have fleeting, fading memories of another era that has passed all too soon into the basement of history.

East End

by Richard S. Scarsella

Youngstown is a collage of various ethnic groups and races. Founded by New Englander John Young, it later attracted hordes of European immigrants in search of work and the American dream. Although the Mahoning Valley was a verdant farm area, it slowly evolved into a thriving urban center. Steel was its soul.

When one thinks of "Y-town", images of the murky fetid Mahoning River lined with gray belching mills comes to mind. However, this scene is only one of many creating the Youngstown imagery. The elegant North Side, home to civic leaders, industrial barons, university professors, and the artistic elite, gave the city a cosmopolitan veneer. Magnificent Stambaugh Auditorium, the nationally known Butler Gallery of Art, and the tree-lined boulevard of period mansions called Fifth Avenue all exuded area style, culture, and tradition.

The trendy South Side, home to the Uptown retail district of boutiques, fine eateries, and sophisticated nightclubs, attracted emerging society figures. Having dinner at the Colonial House, the Mansion, or the original Antone's was once the "in" thing to do if one wanted to see and be seen. Cocktails at the Cave Lounge, catching an art film at the Uptown or Foster theaters, or dining late at The Oven Restaurant all were South Side rituals enjoyed by all. Of course, living near historic Idora Park attracted many homeowners wanting to be near entertainment.

Youngstown's West Side was stolidly middle-class. Home to a wide array of churches and bars, it was clean, safe, and conservative in values. Anchored by the Isaly's art deco dairy complex at the Mahoning Avenue Bridge on one end and the Mahoning Plaza on the western boundary, this district was a living testimony that hard work, thrift, and right living paid much-deserved dividends. West Siders considered Mill Creek Park to be their own personal backyard.

Of all the parts of town, the oldest was the most colorful. The East Side oozed rags to riches toil, brick streets, depression-era architecture, Gothic churches, neighborhood gangs, hard-drinking taverns, and brutally competitive sports. All typified the East End reality. Wedged between downtown Youngstown, Campbell, Hubbard, and the Pennsylvania line, this earthy environs was home to Italians, Irish, Germans, Englishmen, Greeks, and African-Americans. Family meant everything. For many, it was all they had.

Oak Street, commonly known as Route 422, was the main road on the East Side. It stretched between downtown Youngstown and New Castle, Pennsylvania. It once ranked with Belmont and Mahoning Avenues as a main thoroughfare, until the advent of the freeways. Youngstown's first supermarket, named Century Foods, was located on the old Oak Street School property. The legendary Royal Oaks Tavern, owned by the DeMain family, was an institution located at the corner of Lansing Avenue. Boilermakers, pink ladies, steamed hot dogs, and uniquely chilled draft beer all made this business thrive. On payday, one had to wait in line to get a booth, since the DeMain's cashed paychecks so as to enable their clientele to pay their weekly tabs.

Montella's Isaly's, in the shadow of austere Immaculate Conception Church and School, was one of the last neighborhood grocery stores to close in the city. Mr. Montella stocked Isaly's chip-chopped ham, Italian hot peppers, winemaking supplies, and Cotton Club soda pops. He was fluent in English and Italian and knew enough words in other languages to conduct trade. His starched white apron and hat were always spotless and he was coldly polite.

The original Scarsella Furniture Company was founded in 1937 by my father Alfred, known as Al, and my Uncle John, known as Jake. Two other uncles, Sam and Armand, also operated this pioneer home furnishings store. Located at Oak and Albert Streets, the store was readily identifiable by the Sealy Posturepedic logo featuring a barebacked woman. Apparently, the good sisters at the Immaculate Conception School had their students avert their eyes when passing this advertisement.

This well-known store specialized in all-wood handcrafted goods. Broadloom carpets were stocked on 12 and 15-foot rolls and a full line of modern appliances were introduced to families still using iceboxes and hand-ringer machines. At this firm, a man's word was good enough to get credit and customers became extended family. To this day, retirees tell me they still have furniture they purchased when they got married.

Few now know that many prominent families were rooted on the gritty East Side. Both the DeBartolo and Cafaro clans once called this working class part of town home. Old East High School, home of the famous award-winning golden bears, educated entire generations of East Siders whom later went onto positions of importance.

The Italian wines, Irish songs, German beers, Greek pastries, and Jewish humor, all of which made the East Side enclave memorable, have been absorbed by a less personal homogenized suburbia. Although the MVR Club still operates in Smokey Hollow in the shadows of Youngstown State University and Oak Street still leads out of town, the East Side, like most of the city, is now strangely silent. It's as if a page in history has been turned.

Easter Parade

by Richard S. Scarsella

In the Mahoning Valley, holidays were once always lavishly observed. Ethnic families hung onto old world traditions in America. Foods, music, and religious rites made greater Youngstown a colorful metropolis.

During Eastertide, throngs of consumers would flood area merchants eager to celebrate the church holiday and throw off the wintertime blues. Purchases of food and clothing dominated their lists. In years gone by, Kroger, Century, Loblaw, A&P, Acme, Fisher Fazio Costa, and United grocery stores featured fresh dressed, locally grown turkeys and hams. These choice meats were the focal points for huge dinners planned by those exhausted by Lenten fasts and duties. Barth Farm eggs were bought by the case by families baking and coloring eggs. Isaly's, Lawson's, Borden's, and Sealtest's dairies all delivered extra orders of creamery butter, sour cream, milk, and frozen confections right to our doorsteps.

Fanny Farmer and Fron's candy parlors sold thousands of pounds of sweets. Easter baskets were filled year after year with either homemade or locally made chocolate rabbits, chicks, jellybeans, and marshmallow eggs. Licorice, caramels, bonbons, lollipops, lemon drops, taffy, mints, fudge, and sweetmeats delighted both young and old as the long somber Lenten calendar concluded with festive celebrations of the Resurrection and the long awaited springtime.

Homemakers and bakeries alike produced a dizzy array of pastries, lamb cakes, pies, tarts, tortes, cream puffs, custards, and puddings. Anise bread, iced in powdered sugar and appointed with hardboiled eggs, were local delicacies. Of course, sugar cookies of bunny figures and crucifix themes were jewels to behold.

Great churches, made of stone and brick, once anchored ethnic enclaves in a city filled with bars, taverns, and cocktail lounges. Robed youth and adult choirs enveloped the air with rich liturgical music. Pipe organs boomed with resonance and added dignity and authority to the services of all faiths and congregations.

Well into the 1960's, radio shows hosted by famous personalities aired special programs during holy week. Bing Crosby, Frank Sinatra, Perry Como, Lena Horne, Ethel Merman, and Mary Martin entertained living rooms across the nation with old standards and newly released tunes. Judy Garland's immortal song "Easter Parade", which was the name of movie starring Judy Garland, seemed to sum up our affection for a holiday that once had a mystique unrivalled by even Christmas.

When the trees blossomed, flowers bloomed, robins returned, and the days lengthened, we knew Easter was on its way. The arrival of spring happily coincided with Easter. Buying a new lightweight outfit for church and visiting was a time-honored ritual. Strouss', McKelvey's, Livingston's, Hartzell's, and Lustig's dressed us like "city slickers". Indeed, even rural folk came to town to buy at least an Easter bonnet. Mill workers, more accustomed to donning overalls than to wearing suits, could be seen all over town "dressed to the nines".

Although Easter and spring were a virtual parade of sights, sounds, tastes, and fragrances, we never forgot those that had passed before us. Florists sold mums, carnations, lilies, and wreaths for the well-tended graves of our beloved. Long processions could be seen between Good Friday and Easter Sunday enroute to cemeteries. Families always paid their respects during the holidays. Oftentimes, they would light votive candles in memory of the dead. Invariably, indomitable widows could be seen, dressed in black dresses, hats, and veils, grieving amongst the headstones and markers, as if they had just been widowed. For those tempted to forget, Easter was very much about death as it was about life.

Today's modern world has commercialized, sanitized, and compartmentalized life and death to a degree that we oftentimes pay little attention to the passing of the seasons. Fractured families and those of little or no faith do not celebrate Easter with great gusto if at all. Few folks plant spring gardens. It is truly an unrecognizable world in some respects.

Still, I fondly recall with great acuity the not so distant years when Easter and the arrival of spring were most special times in our lives. Contemporary youth can only guess what it was once like to welcome spring and acknowledge Easter as in days of old. They have lost more than they will ever know.

Eastertide Reflections

by Richard S. Scarsella

The large number of Christians in the Mahoning Valley can be traced to early settlers from Connecticut. Strong Protestant roots were transplanted to the Western Reserve territory and flourished. Mainline faiths such as Presbyterian, Episcopalian, Methodist, and Lutheran established "mission" churches in the vast lands west of the Appalachian Mountains. Naturally, Easter time was a major holiday.

Huge waves of European immigrants, seeking livelihoods as farmers, artisans, or tradesmen, were primarily of Catholic and Orthodox stock. Unlike thrifty Yankee Protestants, these newly minted American Christians openly reveled during the most solemn of Christian holidays. Merchants soon took notice of the ever-increasing popularity of Resurrection Sunday in the Mahoning River settlements.

Through the early 1970's, both Christians and non-Christians were courted with an endless array of special goods and services for the secularized Easter season. Buying a new Easter outfit became a tradition with people of all faiths. Many specialty shoppes, such as Betty Goodman's, Esther Cooper's, and Peg Kish's, held private trunk shows of designer attire for discriminating clients. Many shoppers envisioned themselves as trendsetters for the spring season. Like Judy Garland in the film "Meet Me In St Louis", the Easter parade of finery was all-important for certain members of society.

McKelvey's, Strouss', and Livingston's were beacons of style, sophistication, and subtlety. Their large show windows were authentic reproductions of displays from New York's Macy's, Gimbel's, and Sak's department stores. Summer furs, full petticoated dresses, dyed pumps with matching gloves and handbags, and feathered hats all were exhibited boldly to enrapture buyers. Easter was a time to shed frumpy winter wear and to make a fashion statement. Ironically, most did so at church.

Lustig's, Baker's, and Thom McAnn's all did a brisk trade in spring footwear. Children loved to buy Buster Brown, Red Goose, and U.S. Keds shoes. All were made in America. Boys favored penny loafers. Girls fancied patent leather slip-ons.

Millinery shops were busiest near Easter. Many women justified a large investment in a hat since they would also wear it on Mother's Day. Jackie Kennedy's continental pillboxes began a fashion revolution in millinery. She contrasted sharply with Mamie Eisenhower's British inspired creations. For those on a budget, Woolworth's, Murphy's, McCrory's, Grant's, and Kressege's all offered special Easter bonnets, complete with matching accessories. Favorites included straw hats and half-bowlers with ribbon streamers and bows attached. Few women in the valley went to Easter services without a new head covering.

Downtown Youngstown was the hub for holiday shopping. Bakeries featured hot-cross buns, minced meat and raisin pies, and coconut frosted lamb cakes. Florists advertised hand and lapel corsages. For a dollar, one could buy an orchid, tea roses, or gardenias for a mom, wife, or sweetheart.

Fanny Farmer Candies, in the Paramount Theater building, was headquarters for milk chocolate rabbits, butter cream eggs, and pectin jellybeans. Pink, peanut butter, white, and semi-sweet chocolate confections could all be found here packaged in holiday wrap. One could literally smell the shop a block away.

While on spring break, most everyone "took in a movie". Hollywood always premiered blockbusters during Easter vacation. Huge spectacles, such as "Ben Hur", "Spartacus", and "The Robe" were typical crowd pleasers. It was a common sight to see ticket lines spanning several city blocks, in front of the brightly lit marquees of the State, Palace, Warner, Paramount, and Regent Theaters. No one knew that one day no movies would be shown downtown anymore.

Local cemeteries became magnets for activities as well. Families and friends of the dearly departed earnestly began to plant and decorate for Holy Week. Carnations, lilies, chrysanthemums, and forsythias all enlivened area graveyards. Crucifixes and wreaths, made of all manner of materials, dotted headstones as silent sentinels. Decorating graves was as much a tradition of Easter as shopping and family dinners were.

Times change. We are all "modern" in lifestyles and tastes. Fewer people "dress up" for the holidays as in years past. Easter is no longer viewed by some as a primarily religious holiday. However, every year as Easter draws near, I cannot help but hear echoes of another time.

Ebb Tide

by Richard S. Scarsella

An ebb tide is the flowing back of the tide as the water returns to the sea, according to the Random House Dictionary. A civilization is referred to as "on ebb" when it is seen as in a state of decline or decay. Many find solace in the past when confronted with the harsh realities of the present and the uncertainties of the future.

Why do we look longingly to days gone by? It could be that the loose pages of memory never really close in our minds. Dim remembrances persist, blunted by time and embellished sometimes beyond credulity. Our present lives are a world removed from happier days of old. Yesteryears beckon us from the outer reaches of our subconscious. For some, the shadows of the past become more livable than reality.

Some older folks act as if the past is still alive and with us. Tales of downtown Youngstown's glittering bustling Federal Street still capture the imagination. Stories of opulent movie theatres, with names like the Palace, State, Warner, and Paramount, seem as magical as the films once shown in them. Recollections of grand hotels, such as the Pick Ohio and the Tod House, recreate a period in our valley's history unrivalled for many inhabitants.

Our surroundings have morphed into an almost alien world. Omnipresent steel mills have been ignominiously silenced. Stately urban neighborhoods have been abandoned or leveled. The important thoroughfares of Youngstown—Market Street and Oak Street and Belmont Avenue and Mahoning Avenue—are ghosts of what they once were. The once pulsating central city has become an impoverished shell encircled by anonymous suburbs. Is it no surprise we look backwards to a gentler more familiar era?

It's true, as poet B. H. Fairchild stated, "In memories and in dreams it stays, always, the same." I can still vividly recall the sight of sunrises and sunsets over the downtown skyline, with an industrial haze as a picture frame. I can still hear the plaintive throaty whistles of locomotives pulling trains through rail yards groaning with manufactured products stamped with the "Made in the U.S.A."

imprints. I can still taste the sweet custard pies made fresh daily in the bakeries of Strouss', McKelvey's, and Isaly's. I can still smell the fragrant W. W. II vintage "victory gardens" boasting yields of radishes, turnips, beets, and rhubarb. I can still feel the barber's hot lather, sharpened blade, and stinging aftershave lotion on my clean shaved neck.

To this day, area folks repeat instinctively well-honored traditions and rituals. Families still gather for backyard picnics and barbecues. Couples still cruise Mill Creek Park drives in search of romantic hideaways. Survivors still decorate graves in the familial cemeteries of their forefathers. Cicadas still create a melody of harsh lament both mornings and evenings. These things have never changed.

In a sense, the past never truly dies. It is always with us in memories. B. H. Fairchild was correct when he claimed, "Memories hang in the air—barely noticeable—like flecks of dirt." We cannot escape the past. It is within us. As we age, these reminiscences become invaluable anchors in chaotic unrecognizable modern times.

Probably the most heartfelt symbol of erstwhile years is historic Idora Park. Founded in 1899, it epitomized gaiety, style, family values, adventure, culture, and the fine arts until an untimely fire in 1984 closed its gates forever. The grand ballroom, midways, wooden roller coasters, hand-carved carrousel, and Americana foods, attractions, and games of chance still have a firm grip on our psyches. In fact, Idora Park—like Federal Street, downtown movie palaces and department stores, and the Mahoning Valley steel corridor—has attained an almost mythological stature in local folklore. It has become representative of the best years of our lives.

Younger generations do not understand nor heed this morbid curiosity with the past. When their world undergoes radical changes they will experience their own ebb tide. Like their ancestors, they will have to find comfort in what little remains of their times, beyond memories, beyond faint rememberings of those that have outlived their times.

Eclipse

by Richard S. Scarsella

The Mahoning Valley was once a hotbed of rich, thriving, progressive institutions. Rural folks regularly "went to town" to seek out expertise and entertainment not readily available in farming districts. Suburbanites had to venture into the city as well. Youngstown, as the county seat, was a natural magnet for those needing anything. No longer did one have to travel to the "big cities" of Cleveland or Pittsburgh to satisfy one's needs. Trains, streetcars, buses, and taxi fleets all used the city as a hub for services to outlying areas.

Both farmers and urban dwellers alike relied heavily on Youngstown's once diverse medical facilities. St. Elizabeth's, North Side, South Side, Cafaro, and Woodside Receiving Hospitals at one time delivered a cornucopia of state-of-the-art treatment and care. Cleveland and Pittsburgh health care professionals oftentimes set up second practices in local facilities, giving valley residents cutting edge technology and diagnoses at local prices. Staffed by our neighbors, these facilities were considered by many to be of first-rate caliber. More than just buildings, these living, breathing complexes were very much a part of community life. Generations frequented their halls. Our babies were born, broken bones set, surgeries performed, and our loved ones were made comfortable before they departed, at these locally owned and managed health centers.

Unbelievably, only St. Elizabeth's and North Side Hospitals survive today. The decentralization of medical care has meant the dismantlement of much trusted, cherished establishments. Ironically, both urban and rural populations now increasingly travel to Cleveland and Pittsburgh in search of remedies, consultations, second opinions, and pioneering procedures. History has come full circle.

The arts are one of the oldest institutions worldwide. The Butler Institute, Youngstown Symphony Society, and Ballet Western Reserve continue to grow, prosper, and expand their offerings. However, many purveyors of art have not fared as well. Locally, downtown Youngstown was once a slice of New York's

42nd Street. Music halls, vaudeville houses, and movie palaces all once vied for patrons.

The Keith-Albee Palace Theater was the grande dame of them all. Unrivaled with its marble staircases, ornate fireplaces, and box seats, the Palace hosted legends such as Frank Sinatra, Jimmy Durante, and Ted Williams. The country's best entertainment graced its stage. After the "show", having a soda or a banana split at the nearby Palace Grille was a much-relished custom for those "out on the town".

The Warner Brothers Theater, before its rebirth as Powers Auditorium, was a showplace of imported rare woods, fine art, and beveled mirrors. Many moviegoers snuck in Jay's hot dogs, under their coats, when attending matinees there. For a quarter, one could view two movies, newsreels, cartoons, and live acts. We learned about life, love, disappointment, family values, war, honor, and patriotism in the shadow of the silvery screen.

The State, Paramount, Hippodrome, Park, Capitol, Cameo, Princess, and Regent Theaters all catered to particular audiences. Lavish musicals, gritty westerns, heartbreaking melodramas, gentle comedies, Biblical extravaganzas, adventure films, animated features, teen flicks, gothic thrillers, and "art" motion pictures attracted thousands of customers per day to Youngstown's once bustling downtown. Sadly, only the Warner Theater survives. A way of life disappeared when the last movie was shown downtown.

Probably the most loved and missed institution of all is fabled Idora Park. First opened in 1899, these twenty-seven acres of magic thrilled all ages for nearly a century before its untimely demise. This amusement park was a fundamental part of local culture. The grand ballroom, Wild Cat, Jack Rabbit, Baby Wild Cat, Kiddieland, Fun House, Rapids, picnic grounds, botanical gardens, minor league ball field, and midway all were familiar to child and adult alike. Idora was the heart of the valley.

Weddings, graduations, reunions, class days, political events, balls, sock hops, roller-skating exhibitions, trade shows, and more were all held at "Youngstown's Million Dollar Playground". In many ways, Idora was the crossroads of the valley. Here, one could find urbanites, agrarians, rich, poor, native-born, foreign-born, liberals, conservatives, and people of all ages freely intermingling in their pursuit of leisure. Custard, corn dogs, freshly roasted peanuts, caramel apples, blue cotton candy, fresh lemonade, buttered popcorn, vinegar-drenched French fries, salt water taffy, and walnut fudge all seemed to unite inhabitants at Idora, if only for a while. When it was shuttered, nothing came close to replacing its egalitarian prominence in our area's culture.

Memories and Melancholy: Reflections on the Mahoning Valley and Youngstown, Ohio

It is said institutions, like people, have lifespans. Perhaps they have souls. They definitely leave legacies. This might explain why we grieve for those places that have disappeared forever from our lives. Their absences leaves a void that only time can dull.

End of Summer

by Richard S. Scarsella

In the Mahoning Valley, like everywhere else, seasons came and went regardless of our wishes. After the July 4th holiday, the inexorable countdown began for school reopenings. As the seemingly endless days shortened in length, we knew the sunny hot days of bliss were numbered.

Area farmers busily cut and baled hay. Housewives frantically jellied fruit and canned vegetables. Men folk doggedly patched rooftops and repaired storm windows. Children of all ages began to shop for uniforms.

Well into the 1960's, busloads of families "heading into town" in ninety-degree weather were a sight to behold. Women were attired in "I Love Lucy" cotton housedresses, complete with matching hats, shoes, gloves, and jewelry. They had in tow reluctant offspring, all of who bitterly complained endlessly that summer was not over and questioning why they had to shop for back-to-school clothes.

Strouss' and McKelvey's, the landmark anchors of the once bustling downtown business district, both featured New York styled show windows. These elaborate displays were tableaus of academic Americana, usually evoking New England traditions. Picturesque scenes of all-American girls and boys, impeccably outfitted in wools, tweeds, cashmere, angora, penny loafers, and saddle shoes, surrounded by colorful faux leaves, made the end of summertime almost palatable.

A trip to a local barbershop or beauty salon was mandatory for all area youth. Boys would receive a trim or "butch" haircut. Girls would have their hair styled, with pipe curls, a la Hayley Mills, a favorite choice. Buying a new pair of Red Goose, Stride Rite, Buster Brown, or Keds shoes was a real treat.

When Labor Day approached, the Canfield Fair—one of the largest county fairs in the country—reawakened after a long slumber. City dwellers marveled at the wide array of livestock, agricultural products, farm machinery, arts, and crafts. Horse shows, milking contests, baby pageants, and bandstand variety productions all took our minds off the passing of the season.

Labor Day was the grand finale of the Lake Erie beach life many Youngstowners enjoyed. Ashtabula Harbor was a beehive of yachts and speedboats seeking refuge from increasingly choppy water. Geneva-On-The-Lake began to shutter cottages and mothball the boardwalk. When the wind shifted, old-timers would claim they could feel cool Canadian fall air from the north.

On Labor Day night, historic Idora Park put on a spectacular fireworks show, which illuminated nearby idyllic Mill Creek Park and the entire south side of the city. When the last firecrackers exploded, the antique carrousel stilled, and the neon lit midway darkened, we knew summertide was over. We dutifully returned to school the following day, with our memories burning bright.

Foolishly, we thought every following summer interlude would return us to these languid golden days of lore. If only this were so.

Environs

by Richard S. Scarsella

In the Youngstown area, the growth of the suburbs can be traced to post—World War II affluence. The war effort had turned the Mahoning Valley into a prodigious beehive of production. Mills and factories buzzed with purpose, pride, and prosperity, as they churned out armaments and goods for the Allied troops. The region literally became "an arsenal for democracy".

The end of the war left a peacetime population hungry for consumer goods and a higher standard of living. In pursuit of the American dream, local residents began building their dream homes in the outskirts of town. Boardman, Canfield, Austintown, Poland, Liberty, and Lincoln Knolls were all transformed from rolling farmlands into housing tracts and commercial strips, in the late 1940's, l950's, 1960's and 1970's. The metropolis would gradually undergo a significant demographic and social metamorphosis, with the central city losing its luster to its country cousins. Life would never be the same.

As the new communities grew, landmarks such as the Palace, State, Paramount, Park, Regent, and Hippodrome theaters, the Tod House and Pick Ohio hotels, the Isaly Dairy West End anchor ice cream parlor, downtown Strouss' and McKelvey's department stores, Idora Park, the Elms Ballroom and Rayenwood Auditorium were either closed, demolished or unceremoniously abandoned. Collectively, these historic structures represented the once vibrant, varied culture of the Mahoning Valley.

Meanwhile, in booming suburbia, new symbols of progress became our everyday reference points. Neighborhood cinemas and drive-ins became the rage. The Schenley, Belmont, Newport, Boardman, Liberty, Lincoln Knolls, and Wedgewood Theaters all became first-run movie houses, at the expense of the once legendary downtown movie palaces. The West Side, North Side, Boardman, Ski-Hi, and Mid-Way drive-in shows catered to car loads of young, growing families in search of affordable, wholesome, and convenient entertainment. They revolutionized the leisure habits of everyone.

Strip plazas featured variety stores all under one roof, with free storefront parking. The Mahoning, Boardman, Liberty, Austintown, Lincoln Knolls and Wedgewood Plazas were enticing with their new, slick, air-conditioned variety stores. Woolworth's, Grant's, Kressege's and Murphy's all targeted the "baby boom" households in their sparkling, streamlined suburban emporiums. Art Deco styled, chrome laden curved lunch counters and soda fountains, "hi fi" departments and aisles of "scientifically developed" cosmetic counters made suburban patrons loyal to these contemporary five and dime merchants.

Plaza locations of Gray Drugs, Livingston's, Abrahams, Hartzell's, Richman Brothers, Lustig's, Strouss' and McKelvey's Loft boutiques made trips to traffic congested, pigeon infested downtown Youngstown unnecessary. These familiar names were only minutes away by car for most families in the outskirts. A drive downtown became an option and not a necessity. One felt very modern living, shopping, and working in the burgeoning "bedroom communities" which now ringed Youngstown. The building of super highways, such as Route 80, Route 680 and Route 11, now allowed one to circumvent the city entirely. A trip to town became a rarity and was not part of one's routine. One hardly noticed the fadeout of historic surroundings once known intimately.

Giant branch stores of the A&P, Kroger, Loblaw, Century, and Fisher supermarkets were anchors for other businesses. Trend setting Red Barn and Burger Chef fast food restaurants, Howard Johnson's orange facaded roadside eateries, Dog House lunch stands and flea market styled Bargain Port, Consolidated, Al's & Paul's, Atlantic Mills and Hill's pioneer discount department stores all became integral parts of our uptown lives.

Buses and walking became increasingly obsolete in these newly built communities. Owning an automobile was a must. Service stations on four corners offered S&H, Top Value, Plaid and Gem trading stamps if one would fill one's car up with Atlantic, Sinclair, Pure, Sohio or Amoco fuel. For a refreshing treat, suburbanites would frequent Fron's Candies and Confections, the Dairy Isle, Isaly's, or Lawson's. On payday, one could drive up to the windows of Dollar, Peoples, Union National, or First Federal banks to cash one's checks and pay bills.

Unbelievably, all of these well-known business names of suburban life have vanished. Like so much of what was once dear in the Mahoning Valley, they exist only in one's memories now. These once standard icons and trademarks of suburban sprawl have all disappeared into local history and lore. New names and businesses seek one's allegiance. Suburban America has come of age in our own midst. In one of the glorious ironies of history, the future has become our past.

Epitaph

by Richard S. Scarsella

The recent demise of Youngstown's legendary Idora Park ballroom cruelly ends an era in local history. This once glittering dance hall, complete with Art Deco suspended cloud ceiling, rainbow hued flickering lights, and rotating mirrored sphere, was literally Mahoning Valley's social and cultural hub.

Built in 1910 to replace an earlier dance pavilion, it hosted balls, proms, sock hops, concerts, receptions, political events, and special events for several generations. At one time, trolley cars and buses all daily disgorged thousands of patrons to this cathedral of sophistication and romance.

Idora's grand ballroom was the largest between Chicago and New York City. Its fame was nationwide Lawrence Welk, Guy Lombardo, the Dorsey Brothers, and Sammy Kaye, to name a few, all created magic with their distinctive big band repertories. Gliding across the multi-layered wood dance floor was an experience on could never forget.

A victim of a 1984 fire that destroyed part of the Wild Cat coaster and closed the park, the ballroom was also vulnerable to changing tastes and the flight to the suburbs. In 1986 it closed its doors for good. It languished for fifteen more years before it reached its ignoble fate. Structurally sound, no individual, corporation, foundation, or government entity came forward to rescue this priceless landmark.

Although the Idora ballroom and twenty-seven acres of the former amusement park were listed on the National Registry of Historic Places, its owners inexplicably neglected it. Its gates were never secured. The crown jewel of "Youngstown's million dollar playground" was abandoned and left to the mercy of nature, vagrants, and arsonists. Its likes will never be seen again in our midst.

When the Idora ballroom literally burned to the ground one helplessly watched one's legacy disappear into the annals of time. The smoldering ruins are a biting repute to all those that could have prevented this senseless callous avoidable tragedy. The mortal loss in our collective consciousness will forever be felt.

Thankfully, memories endure. Idora's ballroom will never truly die. It has simply passed into an urban legend.

Faces of Poverty

by Richard S. Scarsella

In my youth, the poor were bit players in the production called life. They were ever-present, in the shadows of the mainstream, and "without voice". Poor folks were expected to "know their place" and to "keep their peace". And for the most part, they did.

Urban poor were easily avoided. They lived in obscure enclaves down near the river or in the warehouse district. Sometimes they could be seen on the bus or in the courthouse. No middle-class person spoke to any of them. "Respectable" folks just did not socialize with these unfortunates unless there was a reason to do so. This informal "caste system" was observed well into the 1960's in the Mahoning Valley. We did not question it. This was just the way things were.

Of all the less privileged, the itinerant indigents were the most interesting and perceived to be the most threatening. Migrant workers, from down South and Mexico, followed the crops into the Ohio Valley like clockwork. These "hillbillies" and "Moors" were of concern to residents because they were not known and not as submissive as the hometown poor. The police followed them closely when they came to town, merchants let them in their stores one-at-a-time, and theaters made them sit in the balconies so as not to disturb the townies.

Gypsies were examples of the industrious poor. Cursed by history, rich in heritage, doomed to travel from town to town, they relished their freedom and resisted attempts to become middle-class. Being "poor" was very much a part of who they were and they were proud of their ancestry. Identity was all they had and no one was going to take their identity away from them. Their resistance to Americanization made them suspects in our eyes.

The fact that gypsies lived "off of their wits", could out-talk those of the educated class, and knew things about nature and magic made them symbols of a world unknown to us. They earned our grudging respect. Their home remedies, fine fabrics and laces, and Old World wisdom greatly enriched our lives.

Carnival workers were treated with a combination of fascination and dread. Roustabouts, roughnecks, "foreigners", and those avoiding the long arm of the law made up the bulk of this non-traditional disenfranchised population. The so-called "freaks" captivated audiences when performing. Off the midway, however, they were treated with a mixture of curiosity, suspicion, and denigrating humor.

When colorful personalities such as the turtle boy, the bearded lady, or Tom Thumb imitators left the carnival grounds to do business, merchants and professionals required payment "up front" before services were rendered. Some places of commerce would not allow them to enter, since their mere presence would be upsetting to others. They were denied common courtesies well-off people took for granted. The fact that they were allowed to entertain us but not mingle amongst us seemed not to matter to those enforcing the prevailing social order. Christians and non-Christians alike discriminated against these and other downtrodden groups at will. In the land of the free, some were apparently more equal than others.

The tumultuous 1960's reversed long accepted practices and prejudices. Government programs, equal rights laws, and a philosophy of inclusion, not exclusion, took roots during this memorable era. President John F. Kennedy, Martin Luther King, Senator Robert F. Kennedy, and President Lyndon B. Johnson collectively challenged a nation to "do the right thing". The result? All classes were to be treated fairly, regardless of income, race, creed, nationality, or disability. The rest, as they say, has become history.

Fading Idora

by Richard S. Scarsella

Sadly, more pieces of local history disappeared recently, with further demolition at Idora Park. In the final weeks of 1999, the owners of this landmark leveled the Kiddieland Colonnade Building, the Baby Wildcat Coaster, concession stands, and picnic pavilions. With their demise, valley inhabitants have irretrievably lost invaluable symbols of an era that is still dear to our hearts.

Idora Park was founded in 1899. It was shuttered in 1984, after fire, changing tastes, competition, and mill closings rendered it unprofitable. In 1999, Idora was widely remembered in its centennial year with celebrations, memorabilia, video presentations, lectures, and a book. Its 100 years of warm memories make Idora a continuing presence in our lives. Unfortunately, Idora is fading away, piece by piece, courtesy of the wrecking ball. In 1998, the arcade and carrousel edifices were destroyed. A l986 fire was even more devastating to this fabled amusement park.

The Kiddieland Colonnade Building was a striking neo-classical, Greek Revival horseshoe shaped structure. Before becoming the signature children's playground pavilion, bathed in Coney Island rainbow hues, it was the Olympic pool bathhouse.

This grand complex of changing stalls, concessions, and offices once hosted lavish aquacade extravaganzas. Esther Williams inspired swimmers once performed Busby Berkeley based aquatic feats in the Idora Pool not usually found inland. The salt-water spring under the pool gave swimmers buoyancy only found in oceans. With genuine sand surrounding the pool, two-piece beauties in repose and loudspeakers blaring Big Band sounds, the Idora Bathhouse decks were a touch of Atlantic City, Hollywood, and Tahiti, all rolled into one.

The filling in and conversion of the Idora Pool into a baby boom mecca of miniature rides transformed the bathhouse into a pavilion of child-centered delights. Games of chance tickled youngsters. Favorites included fish, darts and rifle ranges. Nearby, the Idora Limited Depot transported families around the upper park, through the gardens, and around the picnic grounds and ball field.

The Kiddieland Colonnade Building was an oasis, where grandparents and parents could stand in the shade, under the archways, to avoid the scorching summer sun. No one knew, until recently, that it may have very well been located at the base of the reputed Native American burial/ceremonial grounds.

The Baby Wildcat was the smaller, younger sibling of the sprawling Jack Rabbit and menacing Wild Cat coasters. Children felt very grown up, when they rode this junior coaster solo. It was considered a bridge ride into the adult rides, which were located outside of Kiddieland on the midways. Once atop this spunky coaster, riders could clearly see, from a bird's eye view, the antique automobiles of Hooterville Highway, the bump cars, and the Ferris Wheel. When in operation, squeals of delight could be heard every five minutes, as the Baby Wildcat gave its trusting passengers the biggest thrills of their innocent lives.

When fans speak of Idora, they talk food. The infamous French fry stand, which literally collapsed upon itself and was recently cleared, helped make Idora legendary. Over a half-century before McDonald's arrived on the scene, Idora onion rings, fresh egg cream custard, roasted peanuts, caramel apples, blue cotton candy, snow cones, and lemonade were purveyed at privately owned stands throughout the park. For many years, hungry valley residents would drive to Idora just to buy "fast food" and listen to the free concerts. Our area has had nothing to rival these visceral experiences, thereby making these Idora memories cherished.

The mighty picnic pavilions once accommodated huge, catered factory picnics, class day activities, and extended family reunions. Before church festivals drained Idora's vitality, the Idora picnic pavilions were booked years in advance. Overlooking the minor league ball field, the grand ballroom, the midways, Mill Creek Park, and the botanical gardens, the picnic areas were beehives of ethnic foods, song, dance, and games. On any given day, the Idora picnic grounds were a veritable Tower of Babel, with diverse languages freely spoken amongst broken English. Idora's exotic mechanical attractions, animal acts, and carnival displays made picnics here unique.

Idora's firm grip on our emotions bears testimony to the magic that once existed in our midst. Preservation attempts have all failed to save Idora from a rapidly approaching ignoble end. Only the eerily silent grand ballroom, weed-ridden botanical gardens, deserted ball field, and derelict Wild Cat and Jack Rabbit coasters remain on the once pulsating midways. Combined, they echo another much missed time of our valley's history.

It is hard to fathom that this 27 acres, "Youngstown's Million Dollar Playground", designated a National Historical Registry Site by the United States

National Park Service, will be allowed to die such a needless, tragic death. Idora would seem to deserve better treatment.

We tend to forget that Volney Rogers fought hard to preserve and protect Mill Creek Park and that the Powers family literally saved the Warner Theater from dismantlement in the eleventh hour. It is unimaginable what our valley would be like without either facility.

The total, merciless loss of the physical remains of Idora Park will leave an unthinkable mortal gash in our local culture and psyches. The old axiom is true. We are our history.

Family Helpers

by Richard S. Scarsella

As a child, I remember well all the unofficial extended family that made my childhood memorable. Many urban families employed "day help" to run the households. For children, these domestics were a wealth of wisdom and friendship. I still have fond recollections of these hardworking men and women.

Our elderly gardener appeared like clockwork in early spring to assess what we would be "plantin" come springtime. His name was Saltasty. He raked, pruned, cultivated, mulched, and fertilized with great care and dignity. He answered my many pesky questions patiently and always gave me gardening projects to do. He didn't even get mad when I pulled flowers instead of weeds. He took real pride in my modest achievements and enjoyed chilled pink lemonade with a relish seldom seen in other adults. Unlike my younger companions, he was a reliable friend I could count on. Mother would scold me often to "Let the man get his work done peacefully," to no avail.

When our gardens were invaded in the 1950's by the dreaded Japanese beetles, our gardener was philosophic about the violation of our tiny Garden of Eden. I had no doubt he would handle the situation well. After trying all manner of home remedies, including "old Injun tricks", our gardener discovered a most efficient remedy for the blight, much to my delight. The answer? Praying mantis.

We watched diligently as these noble, graceful, and voracious green terrors rid the garden beds of all types of bugs. The gardener told me many times that all the cures one needed could be found in nature. The twinkle in his eyes made me believe he knew a lot more about life than horticulture. As it turns out, he did. After he passed away, the rose gardens, in particular, never bloomed fully again. He was irreplaceable.

Our housekeeper was a solid, tall, broad, fundamentalist Christian Baptist woman from deep down South. Her name was Carrie. She always smelled like lilac cologne and wore her coarse hair in a bun, wrapped tightly in a hairnet. She arrived by the "bus line" and walked stoically to our home, carrying her change of clothes and shoes in a shopping bag. Using a skeleton key, she would let herself into the backdoor. Mother would pour her a cup of coffee, indulge in chitchat, and before long, the house was a buzz with string mops, Electrolux sweepers, Milsek furniture polish, and white vinegar and water mixture odors. Calling me "child", she watched me like a surrogate mom, as she cleaned with speed and determination.

Come lunchtime, our housekeeper would not take her meals with the rest of the family. "It wasn't proper," she would say. She always said a prayer of thanks before eating. I would rush through dinner and join her for conversation, whenever I could. She would tell me tales of how she was raised in a mountain shack, with many sisters and brothers, and how her folks "lived off the land". Her stories of eating fresh honey out of a honeycomb, making homemade elderberry wine, and catching catfish in nets for a fish fry were captivating for me. I can still hear her say to "Do right and live right and you're sure to go to heaven."

The milkman, dry-cleaning man, yardman, meatman, and farmers selling fresh produce and vegetables out of trucks all were regular fixtures in my formative years. Along with the postman, itinerant knife sharpener, Fuller Brushman, Avon lady, and the mysterious gypsies, these colorful individuals were once standard contributors and advice givers for my family's well being. From them I learned much about the world outside the confines of my front porch and yard.

As I cruise suburbia, I sometimes think of these unforgettable characters in my life. How alien this modern world would appear to them. They all inhabited a time when people knew one's name, one took pride in one's craft, and one was seen and treated not just as a worker or paid laborer, but as a trusted friend of the family.

How long ago it all seems now. It's hard to say goodbye to yesterday.

Family Matters

by Richard S. Scarsella

Many of us look back fondly to the years when extended families were commonplace. It was not unusual for aunts, uncles, first and second cousins, as well as grandparents, great aunts and great uncles, to live in the same neighborhood or on the same part of town at one time. We felt sorry for friends who did not have relations in the area. Life without the colorful personages we knew as kin was unthinkable.

Being raised in a mature family, with most members well beyond child-rearing years, allowed me to experience the thrills and drawbacks of an old-fashioned upbringing, with surrogate parents aplenty. Elders were respected, right or wrong. Children were respectful, regardless of the circumstances. Traditions were honored. Everyone knew his or her place.

Birthdays were always a grand celebration. Getting together to "break bread" and witness the passage of milestones was of paramount importance. Gifts ranged from silver liberty dollars, savings bonds, family heirlooms, and vintage books. Older generations were hell-bent not to spoil the youngsters with frivolous presents. A pampered child was thought of as an embarrassment to the family.

Christmas, Easter, and Thanksgiving were gala affairs. Relatives from across the country came by car, bus, train, and plane for communal get togethers. Cherished stories of the "olden days" would be retold over and over, causing some to blush, some to cry, and some to laugh. You could let your hair down with your own kind and learned not to take yourself too seriously. To put on airs was met with scorn. Great aunts and uncles admonished children not to get to big for their britches. Rebukes were fast, final, and forgiving. You could always count on family to come to your defense with outsiders.

Photographs were the lifeblood of tribal ties. Antique, dusty albums, filled with dated, yellowed pictures, torn newspaper clippings, and folded telegrams, were a living chronology of family social and cultural history. Weddings, baptisms, and graduations all were lovingly catalogued, preserved, and presented for viewing. The commentaries that accompanied the snapshots were rich in detail, imagery, and pathos. Every family, I came to understand, was like a novel. Fame, fortune, illness, tragedy, romance, war, and heartbreak all were part of the family tree. Both faith and fate seemed to be twin determinants of our futures and pasts.

Funerals were an odd combination of fierce mourning and intense socialization. The onus of burying your loved ones was somewhat softened by the presence of the clan. The insidious retreat of well-loved acquaintances to their graves was an inevitability of nature. World-weary scions spoke assuredly of seeing their beloved in the afterlife. Survivors knew that with each internment, they themselves were drawing closer to mortality. One could not but help notice that each black Cadillac limousine entombment procession was shorter as the years progressed.

Family burial plots, marked by crypts, markers, and urns, were lavished with attention. The pride and honor of heredity would not allow for memorials to be ignored. Mother's Day, Father's Day, Veterans' Day, and all other major holidays required flowers, plants, wreaths, flags and candles be set up by family members for those who had "given up the ghost". Marble tombstones, engraved with names, dates, and images of ancestors, were strangely comforting and unnerving. Old-timers would wisely mutter "No-one gets out of this world alive." Unlike the real world we lived in, cemeteries seemed frozen in time.

When I think back to not so distant years of the past, the images, songs, jokes, stories, and embraces of long gone familiar faces are quickly rekindled. At dusk and at dawn, I especially feel kinship with those that have passed ahead of us. Dorothy, in the Wizard of Oz, said it all when she plaintively exclaimed, "That there is no place like home!"

Fifty Some Years Ago

by Richard S. Scarsella

The years come and go quickly. They tend to blend into one another. Calendars, diaries, almanacs, and encyclopedias mark time effectively for those too busy to notice. Our minds make silent notes on things deemed memorable. Historians document the rest.

In 1949 Peking—now spelled Beijing—fell to the Communists. Chinese Nationalists failed to keep this ancient imperial city democratic. The rest of China would later succumb to the "red menace". From this date on, Americans would fret about "Who lost China?" World geopolitics would never be the same again. Only recently has China emerged from international isolation to rejoin the family of nations.

NATO, the North Atlantic Treaty Organization, was founded in 1949. This coalition of Western European countries included France, Italy, Great Britain, and West Germany. The United States was the senior partner. The aim? To contain Communism to Eastern Europe at all costs.

A Greek civil war ended this same year. By the narrowest of margins, this cradle of democracy was spared the heavy hand of totalitarianism by a Communist defeat. To many, it seemed surreal that the land of Socrates, Plato, and Aristotle was threatened by anti-democratic forces.

Ominously, George Orwell's Nineteen Eighty-Four was published in war-weary England. This gloomy tome predicted an autocratic state with the rights of the individual obliterated. The Soviet Union's grasp on its captive nationalities seemed to be credible evidence that Orwell's vision of the future was perhaps more possible than many cared to acknowledge.

Arthur Miller's 1949 Pulitzer Prize for Death of a Salesman was a warning and a wake-up call for many concerned about the American way of life. His poignant play seemed to be a metaphor for a nation in danger of forfeiting its soul to capitalism. Were we all to become like Willie Loman and lose touch with reality in our quest for material wealth and success? Was a type of socialism the answer?

72   Memories and Melancholy: Reflections on the Mahoning Valley and Youngstown, Ohio

The 1950 invasion by North Korean forces into South Korea shocked an America awash in post-World War II prosperity and peace. Were the "reds" even more evil than the recently vanquished Nazis of Hitler's Germany? Were atomic weapons impotent against enemy infiltration? The world waited in anguished anticipation as two conflicting political cultures grappled for world dominance.

Diners' Club cards, considered to be the first modern charge cards, were first issued in New York this same year. The Rodgers and Hammerstein musical South Pacific wowed 1950's audiences with Polynesian romance and wartime adventure. In this same year, Charles Schultz's irreverent cartoon Charlie Brown both soothed and unnerved once complacent Americans about a rapidly evolving world. Were adult-like philosophical children the wave of the future and consciences for the present?

In 1951, the advent of the first 33 R.P.M. long-playing record brought music to the ears of a wider marketplace. Shockingly, President Harry Truman dismissed hawkish General Douglas MacArthur. Later this year, a truce was agreed upon between South Korea and North Korea. Many sighed in relief. Few people paid attention to another Asian country named Viet Nam.

Although world events oftentimes seemed remote, they impacted our lives in the industrial heartland called the Mahoning Valley. When American troops went on alert in reaction to Chinese, Greek, Soviet, or Korean hostilities, local steel mills hummed with armament orders. Although many overly sentimentalize the heydays of the downtown Youngstown shopping district, magnificent motion picture houses, and historic Idora Park, these now faded places were welcomed retreats in a world that seemed both increasingly alien yet oddly familiar. Though few can accurately recall events of some fifty years ago, what did and did not happen still influences our lives. Memories serve as mute monuments for the milestones of time.

Fine Dining from the Past

by Richard S. Scarsella

In the not so distant past, the Mahoning Valley boasted many fine dining, full service establishments. Downtown Youngstown not only had private club dining rooms, hotel ballrooms, grilles, coffee shops, cafeterias, soda shops and bars, it also had nationally known restaurants. These eateries catered to industrial barons, retail/wholesale executives, traveling salesmen, tourists, socialites and natives, that were "out on the town".

Up into the 1980's, many gourmands went south, up Market Street, past the colorful Amoco signature sign, into the pricey Uptown district. Adjacent to Mill Creek and Idora Parks and close to Volney Road and Newport Glen upper income residences, the Uptown area offered both designer retail boutiques and Epicurean delights in renovated, impressive, former residences. These stately mansions now were open to the public. To this day, residents speak of the "restaurant mile".

There were three restaurants of this era that set the pace for their competition. Their names? The Mansion, Colonial House and the original Antone's. All were the epitome of taste, decor, gracious dining and expert service. Patrons from Akron, Cleveland and Pittsburgh frequented their dining rooms. Fabric tablecloths and napkins were standard, as were full place settings. Valet service, of course, was available. Luxury cars in the lots and on the neighboring avenues all bore testament to the exclusive clientele. What was it, you ask, did these dining halls offer?

The original Antone's was closest to downtown Youngstown, near the Market Street Bridge, in a Greenwich Village type atmosphere. Its main attraction? Home cooked Italian and European main courses. Long before Americans "discovered" ethnic foods as specialties, Antone's was serving locally grown tomatoes in sauces, garnished with rich, creamy, cheesy toppings on their Old World favorites. Fettuccini, eggplant, and chicken Parmesan were all made famous here. The formally dressed servers presented the food with flair, just like in an old Audrey Hepburn film. Sadly, this great landmark closed, after it moved to Boardman. However, food buffs can still partake of its original recipes, by visiting the smaller, less formal Antone's Family Restaurants.

A sophisticated, big city nightclub atmosphere could be experienced at the Mansion. Live talent entertained in the lounge, while diners sampled dishes and appetizers from a Club 21 styled menu. Known for fine, dry Martinis, served in elegant long stemmed glasses, the Mansion attracted a late night crowd. Theater-goers from the Playhouse and Uptown Theater nested here, discussing what they had just seen around the corner. The mirrored dance floor was filled with women dressed in cocktail dresses and gentlemen dressed in suits. Regrettably, this grand institution disappeared in an untimely fire.

The Colonial House closed briefly in the 1990's, but reopened as elegant as ever, under the name Colonial House II. Its Central Park townhouse style, characterized by leather booths and crystal chandeliers, echoes a time when folks dined unhurriedly. The wide, white, expansive entrance, with canopy and Greco-Roman pillars, welcomes hungry, hassled customers into its dimly lit, intimate dining rooms and gentlemen's bar. American favorites, like steaks and chops, are served here in generous portions. Rich, delicate pastries and after dinner drinks complement the meals. The legendary Uptown dining tradition lives on here, like a window into another period of time.

Flashbacks

by Richard S. Scarsella

We have all become decidedly modern. Our technologically advanced insular worlds include computers, cell phones, and a dependency on air-conditioned comfort. Sadly, it is now common to not know our neighbors. Many have all but forgotten that it was once not always this way.

Until the 1970's, summertime was not a period of hibernation. We lived outside and enjoyed the heat. Those that retreated into their homes, anchored to fans and air-cooling systems, were thought to be anti-social or puny. Summertide was a short-lived season of communal get-togethers and sharing. No one wanted to be left out of backyard picnics, block parties, and front porch gatherings.

Legendary urban neighborhoods—in all parts of Youngstown—once were known for festive cookouts. Ethnic enclaves would barbecue freshly dressed foul, pork, lamb, and beef and feast through the gloaming most every day. Frozen dinners, convenience food, and take-out meals were considered unhealthy and to be avoided.

Block parties featured baked pastries, backyard fruits and vegetables, and home-brewed spirits. Brier Hill and Lansingville residents prided themselves on their family recipes and secret ingredients. Friendly competition existed between those who sought to serve the ultimate potato salads, sausage links, chiffon cakes, and rice custards.

At one time, even working-class homes had expansive porches. High-end residences featured screened decks. They were the scene of many afternoon and late night hospitalities. Ladies oftentimes served tea or punch outdoors—utilizing bone china plates and leaded cut glass punch sets—for club members, church guilds, and acquaintances. Large canvas tents and the shade of elm trees were favorite locations for light refreshments. These civilized socials involved ladies dressed in feathered hats, cotton gloves, and silk hosiery.

Gentlemen were known to invite men folk over for a smoke after dinnertime. Verandas were aromatic with the fumes of Lucky Strike cigarettes, Cuban cigars, and cherry tobacco pipe smoke. Watching and listening to men "chew the fat" in a haze of smoke until the sunset was a typical pastime of area youth. The World War II, Depression, and union strike yarns they retold were wildly entertaining for those not worldy-wise.

In the years before health clubs, spas, and diet centers existed, "walking around the block" was a favored form of exercise and health maintenance. You could literally set your clocks by the routine appearances of many sidewalk denizens. The arrival of strangers in our midst was greatly remarked about and subject to close scrutiny. We knew our own.

Long established Mahoning Valley communities once boasted vibrant, friendly, and welcoming environs. Stray dogs and cats were readily given sanctuary. Tramps and hoboes were given meals. Door-to-door salespeople were offered iced pink lemonade. Missionaries were eagerly invited to Sunday suppers. Of course, family reunions were gala affairs and the subject of conversations for months.

When I drive through our picture-perfect suburban subdivisions, my images of days gone by come back in a series of flashbacks. Did we really listen to the radio on front gliders until sign-off time? Did we really sing songs of Americana, with parlor piano accompaniment, until we were hoarse? Did we really catch fireflies in glass jars in large enough quantities to create natural lanterns? Did we ever think this way of life would end?

I oftentimes have to guard against embellishing past memories. Polio scares, Sputnik hysteria, nuclear bomb drills, simmering prejudice, religious intolerance, politics of division, and repressions of all sorts temper my views of previous times. However, when I hear the hooting of an owl, smell a bonfire, taste hot elderberry pie, feel fresh cut spearmint leaves, or see a group of children blowing bubbles on a driveway, I am easily transported into a twilight zone of the soul.

Good-bye Five and Dimes

by Richard S. Scarsella

Up into the 1960's, downtown Youngstown's Federal Street was lined with posh boutiques, classic tailor shops, and brightly lit theater marquees and grand department stores. Names such as Livingston's, Bond's, Warner and McKelvey's were proudly pitching their products. One whole segment of popular retail stores had a cachet all their own. What were they? Variety stores.

Fondly referred to as five and dimes, these vendors of bazaar-like, inexpensive notions were anchors in the once bustling downtown business district. Trolleys, and later buses and cabs, all once lined up, disgorging throngs of willing buyers, into the doors of W.T. Grant, S.S. Kressege, G. C. Murphy, Woolworth's, and McCrory's. These early day discounters competed fiercely for the patronage of housewives, businessmen, professionals and society matrons. Their appeal? Wide selection and reasonable prices.

Strouss-Hirschberg's, McKelvey's, J.C. Penney Co. and Sears, Roebuck and Co. were all higher priced than the variety stores. The full-line department stores usually did not compete directly with their homespun cousin stores, when it came to name brands, styles or prices. The five and dimes concentrated on merchandise that the department stores had vestiges of in their basement budget departments.

Five and dimes could provide one a bit of satisfaction for only a nickel or a dime. Candy, thread, thimbles, pencils, cards, goldfish, and fishing line all were sold side by side. Holiday items for Halloween, Christmas and Easter were always first displayed in these middle-class, Mid-Western orientated, wholesome emporiums. A weekly trip to a variety store was part of one's regular shopping routine.

Why do these stores still linger strongly in our memories? For many reasons. Variety stores had a smell of a penny candy factory. Bridge mix, licorice sticks, candy dots, fresh roasted mixed nuts, circus peanuts, and cotton candy all assaulted your senses. Who can't remember buying or receiving a box of turtles, non-pareills, multi-colored party mints, or Valentine heart candy from one of these confectioners?

Children loved variety stores for two reasons. Pets and toys. Thousands of children, over years past, would bring home their first pet from these eclectic stores. Who can't recall a child bringing home an "exotic" goldfish in a plastic bag or a cup? Parakeets were always "on sale" at one of these stores. For the more daring, one could buy a salamander or a chameleon. At Easter, the pet departments were a riot of color. Why? One could buy a dyed blue, pink, orange, or yellow chick (peep), rabbit, duck, or turtle.

Children thrilled to shop the toy department aisles, while parents bought mundane things in house wares or the garden centers. The five and dimes changed American social and cultural history by featuring Barbie dolls, G.I. Joe's, and Japanese made novelty toys and electronics. Intricate models of World War II ships and fighter planes, Easy Bake Ovens, and Tinker Toys all were on display for eager hands to touch and test drive. Even older folks found fun things to buy at these stores. Favorites included puzzles, with thousands of pieces, glue crafts, and woodworking kits, complete with wood.

A couple of dollars went a long way in these stores of dreams and necessities. Santa Christmaslands were a veritable orgy of red velvet, white cotton trim, gold and silver foil, and plastic tree ornaments. A portrait, taken with an ever ebullient Santa and his elves, was a tradition in most homes. A child could buy gifts for the whole family, for fewer than five dollars, and have change left over. Christmas has never been the same with the passing of these quintessentially kitsch American merchants.

Back to school meant a trip to the five and dimes. These one stop-shopping stores featured uniform clothing, shoes, notebooks, pencils, and gifts for the teachers. Many a science project were constructed with purchases from the five and dimes. Whenever in doubt, a trip to one of these stores would surely furnish ideas and tools for any student.

Like so many American landmarks, the five and dimes slowly disappeared from our lives. The downtown anchor stores, which featured sleek escalators, live organ music, and do-it-yourself photography stalls, closed first. Five and dimes found refuge in the Uptown district, Mahoning, McGuffey, Liberty, Boardman, Austintown, and Lincoln Knolls plazas. However, these stores began to close in the 1970's and 1980's. First, Grant's went bankrupt and closed. Murphy's became Murphy Mart, Woolworth's became Woolco, and Kressege's became K Mart. Only K Mart survives. McCrory's was the last sole survivor downtown, until a few years ago. Woolworth's shuttered their last mall location in Boardman a year ago. A few small Ben Franklin stores survive outside of Youngstown, but they are mere tokens of a dynastic variety store epoch.

In their heyday, the five and dimes boasted serpentine chrome lunch counters, topped by revolving, glass enclosed desert towers, full of crème pies and chiffon cakes. Elegant do-it-yourself make-up counters were once displayed, with tubes of Max Factor, Maybelline, and Cover Girl cosmetics, complete with directions for pubescent girls and fading matrons. Record counters reigned supreme, with their "Top 40" lists, indexed to neatly rowed 45-RPM records and albums, all adorned with teen idol posters. Teens would gather in awe, immersed in the luxury of hi-fi, stereophonic sound.

The flannel nightgowns, support hose, corduroy slippers, pipe cleaners, plastic flowers, and be-smocked sales "clerks" all gave variety stores an aura that today's super-discount stores do not have and will never have. These stores were crude cathedrals of American consumerism yet to come.

Wooden floors, fans twisting overhead, the smell of fresh popcorn, cheap perfume counters, battery displays, fan magazine racks, and pinball machines all were part of the five and dime mystique. We relished the experience of shopping in these flea market like retail stores. These institutions dotted great American cities, towns, and suburbs alike. They were the McDonald's of their times. Seemingly, there was one of these stores right around the corner, as predictable, reliable and familiar as an old family friend. They were integral parts of our lives.

When I visit a small town, I always head for the local five and dime. Why? Where else can you find linoleum, oil cloth, contact paper, wrapping bandages, liniment, styptic pencils, post-cards, all wool socks, American made underwear, party mix, and a copy of the Constitution under one roof? Our metropolitan area is much the poorer for not having these oasises of Americana. Luckily, memories of these colorful establishments tenaciously live on, as threads to another much missed time. Good-bye, five and dimes.

Gothica

by Richard S. Scarsella

Gothic culture pertained to the middle ages of Europe. Some referred to these years as the "dark ages". Writers characterized gothism as an epoch of gloom, mystery, and the grotesque. An aura of degeneration prevailed. A preoccupation with death was considered the norm.

Locally, many folks of certain maturity refer to the 1900-1940's as America's dim past. On cable television, the History Channel has mined days of yore for images and tales that still hold interest today with cosmopolitan audiences.

At the beginning of the century, the Mahoning Valley was fairly primitive. Nature was still feared and resisted taming. Sagas of vicious timber wolves and howling coyotes abounded. Encroaching civilization and entrenched wilderness were in a desperate struggle for dominance. Communities such as Youngstown and Boardman were once outposts of civilization, encircled by virgin forests and beasts of the wild.

Native Americans represented many things. Some saw them as noble redmen. Others viewed them as idol-worshipping savages. Their foods, songs, and medicine infiltrated Christian society gradually. Indian folklore centered upon evil spirits troubled many. Modern settlements ignored the fact that primitive indigenous people had a comprehension of life, death, and after death unknown to early pioneers.

Those living west of the Appalachian Mountains lacked the education that those in the east took for granted. Belief in luck, omens, and the unexplained colored the lives of westerners. The early years of Boardman were concentrated on surviving an oftentimes-inhospitable environment. The advent of paved roads, electricity, indoor plumbing, and mechanized industry transformed the valley. Immigrants from around the world now called the area home. Despite municipal advancements, free available schooling, and organized religion, belief in the preternatural continued. Things existing outside the ordinary course of middle class or working class existence were objects of fascination and dread.

Roving bands of gypsies excited morbid interest in old world customs, superstitions, and the occult. Reaching Boardman via Route 224, the nomads found residents eager to buy charms, amulets, and potions to ward off bad luck and to insure prosperity. The Roma, as gypsies were called, oftentimes encamped near Midlothian Boulevard. Why? They were close to Youngstown to peddle their wares and magic but were outside of the city police boundary. When local authorities received complaints about the vagabonds "working the area", the gypsies were told to leave town or risk imprisonment. Leaving under the cover of darkness, the gypsies crept out of the county only to return later in the season.

Carnival freak shows routinely came through the valley on the Cleveland to Pittsburgh entertainment circuit. Some were booked at Idora Park. Others worked at the Canfield Fair or at festivals. Disfigured performers exhibited birth defects and traumas for a price. Siamese twins were a favorite attraction. Turtle boy, devoid of any limbs, was also popular. When these human oddities traveled through Boardman on their way to an engagement, they were the subject of much ridicule, revulsion, and pity. Some thought they were cursed by god or possessed by the devil. Others deemed them less than human.

Contemporary life has sanitized society and perpetuates a collective amnesia concerning our roots. There are still some who remember a different era when we were not sophisticated, logic-based, technologically dependent, and skeptical of the unknown.

King Tut's curse, Bigfoot mythology, and UFO sightings all are veiled expressions of a Gothic-like deep-seated curiosity with the abnormal. Is it a death wish urban dwellers cannot deny or camouflage? Our infatuation with the macabre is alive and well and living in our midst. Somehow, I am not surprised.

Grandmother's China

by Richard S. Scarsella

In every family, you will find a set of dishes, stemware, glassware, candlesticks, or figurines proclaimed to be "good" or "special", regardless of price. Children are warned to be careful when handling such precious items. My grandmother jealously guarded her beloved possessions, though they were things not held in high esteem by other family members.

In grandmother's household, she had the inevitable Lenox chinaware displayed in her indomitable china buffet. As a child, whenever I would run through the dining room, the rattles from this sacrosanct piece of furniture would elicit loud scolding to slow down. Accidents were to be avoided at all costs. Too much time, care, and money were invested into these revered objects to expose them to everyday hazards of running children, errant toys, or curious pets.

Regularly, grandmother's china would be used for holidays and special dinners. Unfortunately, these occasions were far and few in between. No matter. Grandmother knew she had what it took to entertain in style. In this she took great pride and comfort. It's one thing to have something and not use it and quite another matter to not have something barely used, she use to exclaim.

We use to ask grandmother to bring out her bone china, along with the complementary pieces, for a birthday or to show off for friends. These requests were stonily ignored by silence. The family finery had to be spared needless use. Only grandmother could decide when and what was to be used from her collection of fine dining house wares.

As the years slipped by, the family spread out across America. Grandmother rarely was able to utilize her jewels. Only complete family gatherings were deemed important enough to bring out her best table settings. Unfortunately, these reunions rarely happened once a year.

Grandfather died. Grandmother moved into a retirement apartment. Ironically, she had no room for a china buffet. She boxed her prized possessions and kept them in her only large closet. Someday she would surely need them again, she always told me. Someday soon.

When grandmother became an invalid, she lost her apartment to a hospital bed. Her things were all put into storage for her. When grandmother passed away, no one wanted to go through her things or to settle her affairs. I offered, since I was the only one in town to do so.

The storage warehouse was dark, damp, and musty. Several large cartons had my grandmother's name and code number marked on them. The furniture had been disposed of long ago. Papers, books, clothing, household items, and odds and ends all brought back almost forgotten memories. What a mess it was, I thought, as I tried gallantly to sort out everything. The boxes seemed to have been tossed around, with their contents showing the results.

One last container was marked "Fragile-Do Not Drop/Breakable Items Inside." Yes, it was grandmother's finery. Safe as usual, I thought.

I opened up the packing case with great anticipation. To my shock, the china and stemware were all broken, with the exception of one cup and matching saucer. The linens, including imported lace tablecloths and napkins, were mildewed beyond belief. The gold candlesticks and silver settings were missing. "Stolen", the warehouseman casually told me. Gold and silver always were stolen, I was told, since they could easily be pawned.

Somewhat depressed by my unexpected findings, I returned to my home. As usual, I made some tea. I poured the tea into all that remained of grandmother's china—the cup and saucer—and ruefully reflected on life's ironies.

For the rest of my life, I have repeated this simple ritual. Grandmother's china legacy proved useful, after all.

Hardware Memories

by Richard S. Scarsella

Up into the 1960's, downtown Youngstown was the hub of the valley. Streetcars, trains, buses, and cars all converged on the central business district. They provided a steady stream of patrons for stores of all kinds, on and around East and West Federal Streets. Millineries, haberdasheries, pool halls, ethnic restaurants, and first-run movie houses all serviced the newly affluent post—World War II consumers. One type of establishment thrived in good times and in bad times, since it specialized in do-it-yourself items. Its name? The all-American hardware store.

Both immigrants and long time families frequented hardware stores to buy basics that any homeowner or home renter needed. The king of premier local hardware stores was the original Stambaugh—Thompson Company. Located between Fifth Avenue and Central Square on West Federal Street, this emporium was a virtual palace of implements.

This anchor store boasted marble floors, wrought-iron interior balconies, elevators and several floors of state-of-the-art house wares. Uniformed, professional sales "clerks" were walking encyclopedias of hardware facts and lore. They could easily diagnose your problem, lead you to the proper department, use your measurements to select a replacement part and ring your purchase up on a bronze cash register with unflappable efficiency. If they were stumped by your request, they would disappear behind oak counters and refer judiciously through piles of manuals, before rendering their advice.

The old Stambaugh-Thompson's was the first home store to open branches in neighborhoods. Its Uptown and West Side stores were harbingers of the movement towards the outskirts of town. After opening locations in the strip plaza, built in the 1950's and 1960's, the downtown Stambaugh's landmark headquarters was sold and leveled, in keeping with a then aggressive urban renewal policy of the times. Like Livingston's, Lustig's, the Palace Theater, and the Tod House Hotel, the downtown Stambaugh's disappeared from our lives.

Cleverly Hardware was located on the West Side at Mahoning and Hazelwood Avenues, down the street from the old Schenley Theater. Here, the owner knew everyone by name. An informal ambiance reigned at this establishment. The staff wore overalls, chewed tobacco and reeked of cigarette, cigar, and pipe smoke. They knowingly selected, sorted and weighed screws, bolts, nuts and washers on huge, antique, iron scales, which looked like they could decapitate unwary shoppers. Chisels, planes, Swiss army knives, wiring, fuses, picket fences and window screens all were on display for discerning browsers to inspect. Old-timers could always find parts for aged furnaces or machines here, if one had the luxury of time to help the salesmen locate what was needed in a huge, Byzantine, gulag-type inventory of miscellaneous items. This store closed in the 1970's, when new owners could not harness the mystique of a hardware menagerie.

In Poland, The Johnston Hardware Company, at Rt. 170 and Rt. 224, serviced both farmers and urbanites, in its authentic turn of the century Western Reserve styled storefront. A small town feeling welcomed buyers here. An ornate tin, tiled ceiling, overhead fans, and creaking wood floors mixed with the smells of turpentine, paint thinner, mulch, litter, and grass seeds. Wood barrels, custom-mixed paint, wallpaper books, Burpee seed packets, and battery displays all mesmerized children. Hardware stores were really like adult toy stores, full of strange wonders that only grown-ups could understand and master. This mercantile mainstay was closed in the 1980's, razed, and replaced by a similar structure, which now houses various businesses.

These venerable storehouses of light fixtures, kitchen supplies, drains, pipes, faucets, showerheads, mailboxes, bird feeders, unfinished furniture, and glass doorknobs still linger on our minds. Why? Where else could one find linoleum, contact paper, flypaper, pedestal sinks, over-sized toilet seats, beveled mirrors, Tiffany-like shades, and radio tubes under one roof?

Whenever I have a new key made at the giant modern home centers, my mind drifts back to these archetypal merchants that once sold such Yankee staples as pumpkin seeds, lime, Christmas tree stands, windmills and birdbaths. These stores truly helped make memories of the best years of our lives, which for the most part, were made up of everyday things, such as shopping at the nearby, friendly, reliable, and colorfully hypnotic hardware stores of times past.

Harvey Firestone: Neglected Native Son

by Richard S. Scarsella

The Mahoning Valley is the home of many notable personages. William Holmes McGuffey, author of the Eclectic Readers, William McKinley, 25th President of the Unites States, and the Warner brothers, pioneer motion picture studio founders, all called this part of the Connecticut Western Reserve Territory home. Few now know that legendary tire magnate Harvey Firestone also came from our midst.

Firestone was born on a rustic farm in 1868 in Columbiana County, right over the Mahoning County border. His parents were sturdy mid-western settlers, who believed in God, country, hard work, and Protestant thrift. Their son loved and worked the land in the shadows of the emerging industrial colossus down-river called Youngstown.

Harvey frequented the village of Columbiana, the town of Salem, and the county seat Lisbon. A trip to the "big city" meant traveling north on what is now Route 7, later called Market Street, through Boardman Center into the Mahoning County seat named after founder John Young. Here, the young Harvey found goods, books, and diversions not readily found closer to his farmstead.

Raised after the conclusion of the Civil War, Firestone led a typical farm boy's life. He tended livestock, planted fields, and did his studies during inclement weather. The Bible, an almanac, and McGuffey Readers augmented his formal schoolhouse education. Upon graduation from Columbiana High School in 1887, Firestone found employment with the Columbus Buggy Company. Drawing upon his agrarian background, he got the idea to create rubber wagon and carriage tires.

An entrepreneur at heart, he first opened his own business in 1900, specializing in solid rubber tires for carts and buggies. America's fascination with the "tin lizzy" automobiles, made by Henry Ford, convinced Firestone to concentrate on the emerging car and tractor markets that would eventually transform both urban and rural culture. When Firestone inked a deal that gave him exclusive right to provide Ford Model A tires, the name Firestone became a nationally recognized trademark. His innovations include mass production of pneumatic tires, nonskid tire treads, low-pressure "balloon" tires, and refined farm tractor tires.

Firestone never forgot his boyhood roots. Local lore holds that Harvey intended to open his first rubber tire factory in Youngstown. However, after meeting with resistance from bankers and iron tycoons, the former, afraid of risk, and the later, fearful of losing their workforce to the higher paying Firestone Tire Company, he made Akron his headquarters. Despite the lack of faith and snubs he encountered locally, Firestone never severed his native ties. Up until his death in 1938, he graciously hosted the graduating classes of his alma mater for a plant tour and dinner at his country club. He endowed his hometown with funds to build and operate the still existing Firestone Park. This beautiful facility includes woods and an Olympic pool, both named after their benefactor. His generosity bears testimony to the loyalty he felt for his hometown.

Sadly, when the Henry Ford museum of Michigan dismantled and relocated Firestone's farmhouse, local residents did too little too late to save this rich piece of local history. Although the Firestone Tire Company experimental farm survives on what is left of the family estate, few citizens know that Henry Ford and Thomas Edison were once guests there at family picnics that Harvey so relished.

There is an old proverb that says that no one is really dead until they are forgotten. Let us hope that the Firestone legacy is preserved in his old stomping grounds. After all, he is one of us.

Historic McGuffey Letters Donated to Butler Institute

by Richard S. Scarsella

The William Holmes McGuffey Historical Society of Youngstown has announced that the McGuffey Archive letters have been donated to the Butler Institute of American Art of Youngstown. Never viewed by historians, researchers, or local residents, the letters have been previously stored in a safety deposit box, awaiting a permanent home.

According to society president and Boardman resident, Richard S. Scarsella, "The McGuffey Archive family letters are a rich source of social and cultural history, both for the community and the nation. They are unique and full of details characterizing another era." A circa 1960 portrait of the famed educator, painted by society member Mildred Garver, was also donated to the Butler Institute. The letters act as support material for the painting. Combined, the letters and portrait document the life and work of the author of the famous Eclectic Readers, which were first published in 1836 and remain in print today.

William H. McGuffey, 1800-1873, was raised on a large farm in Coitsville Township, which is now known as the McGuffey Wildlife Preserve. Donated in 1998 by the W. H. McGuffey Historical Society to the Mill Creek Metroparks, the homesite is a National Historic Registry Landmark site. The Department of Interior National Parks Service granted this designation in 1966. The facility is located on McGuffey Road, which was a path to downtown Youngstown made by McGuffey's father.

McGuffey lived and taught in the Youngstown area until young adulthood. He was a prolific correspondent, being both an educator and an ordained Presbyterian minister. His letters were collected by society member and McGuffey great niece Helen Bair Owen of New Wilmington, Pennsylvania. A total of four McGuffey relatives live in the Youngstown area and are active in the society.

"Our society purchased the McGuffey family letters five years ago in an effort to keep them in the valley," stated Scarsella. "We did not want them to be sold and lost to the metropolitan area. Luckily, the director of the Butler Institute, Dr. Lou Zona, accepted the McGuffey letters and portrait into the Butler catalogue. A precious bit of local history is now guarded for posterity."

A major part of the McGuffey Archive resides at the Melnick Museum, located in the Mill Creek Metroparks Fellows Riverside Gardens Davis Visitor and Education Center. Generational photographs, vintage Eclectic Readers, and family genealogies are part of this collection. Richard Scarsella, Helen Owen, and others are now cataloguing the contents.

During McGuffey's lifetime, letter writing was considered an art and a necessity. Literacy was considered a privilege, usually achieved by only the wealthy. His seven readers educated millions and provided instruction in reading, writing, ethics, and religious instruction. McGuffey was instrumental in the establishment of free public schools in the western and southern regions of the United States. He was nicknamed "The Schoolmaster of the Nation".

On Christmas Day, 1865, McGuffey wrote from the University of Virginia to sister Harriet Love concerning the freed slaves. "They do not know what to do with themselves now that they are free and very many of them will (I fear, must) die for want of food and clothing and fuel and medical attention. Their former owners are for the most part trying to do for them all they can, but this but little." McGuffey concluded, "Thousands will be in their graves before next Christmas! No power can help it—at least none on earth!"

The W. H. McGuffey Historical Society of Youngstown is the last chapter of the National Federation of McGuffey Societies existing in the country. The federation once numbered one hundred thousand and included auto magnate Henry Ford as a member. Today, a group of fifty local members toils endlessly to keep the McGuffey heritage alive in a world McGuffey would scarcely recognize. The letters and portrait are a bridge back to another time.

(For more information about the above, contact Richard S. Scarsella at (330) 726-8277 or write to the William Holmes McGuffey Historical Society, P.O. Box 9561, Boardman, Ohio, 44513)

Historic Restaurants Still Linger on Our Minds

by Richard S. Scarsella

The Mahoning Valley is a virtual patchwork of clashing ethnic religions, customs and traditions. All cultures have one thing in common. Food. They love to cook it and love to eat it. Food became the common language for diverse people, forced to live and work in close quarters in the steel valley.

Families in the old countries of western, central and eastern Europe brought their cherished recipes to the "new world". They made them part of the pan-American cuisine. Bagels, pizza, kielbasa and tacos are just some of the important foods Americans now call their own.

In the Youngstown area, many immigrant families opened sandwich counters, cafes, bars, saloons, grilles, delis and tearooms that later become full-fledged restaurants. Some have survived into the present day. Most disappeared in time, due to changing tastes, demographics or increased competition. Their legacies live on.

In downtown Youngstown, on West Boardman Street, near the new Vindicator building, the Mural Room once reigned supreme. This New Orleans eatery had a Southern charm that bespoke gentile, languid, ante-bellum civility. Diners were entertained with ceiling to floor murals of tasteful, calming scenes. Here, time felt frozen. Discreet, unhurried and romantic, this dimly lit establishment, replete with back smoking rooms and ladies' lounges, bowed to urban renewal demolition. Our area has never had anything take its place.

On Youngstown's once elegant North Side, blocks from posh Wick Park, a sleek, curved, chrome trimmed Art Deco styled eatery catered to the after-theater crowds and night owls. The 20th. Century Restaurant, on Belmont Avenue, made salad famous and chic by perfecting an incomparable "spinning bowl salad". Desserts, inspired by Schraffts of New York City, tantalized one's taste buds. Rich, dark, creamy, buttery, pecan garnished German chocolate cake attracted patrons from the tri-county area. This landmark closed in the 1980's, to make room for a strip plaza. People still talk about its Friday fish fries and macaroni salads.

In Canfield, the Parkview Restaurant catered to patrons out for a country drive. Home cooking, served family style, was the big attraction here. Located in a once grand Connecticut styled mansion, right on the Village Green, this antique-filled dining hall served up wholesome, Yankee foods, like beef stew and fresh fruit pies, in which both farmers and city folks delighted. Reaching its peak in the 1970's, it closed, after national restaurant chains began to fiercely compete for clients along the Rt. 224 corridor, between Canfield and Poland.

Shott's Restaurant, on Market Street, in Boardman, was a classic steak and chop dining spot, very popular in the 1950's and 1960's. Tufted leather booths gave Shott's a New York uptown ambiance, right in suburbia. Businessmen had many long luncheons here, despite the fact that the restaurant was "dry", as was all of Boardman at one time. It was later razed for a church parking lot.

In Niles, high atop the Eastwood Mall, the legendary Cherry's Supper Club brought a touch of Las Vegas to the valley, in the 1970's. Here, national acts sang, danced or joked, as locals sampled clams on the half shell, pate, "fresh" lobster or imported wines. With its semi-circular stage and state of the art sound and lighted, mirrored dance floor, the king of the legendary "strip" of restaurants on Rt. 422 was replaced, in the 1980's, by a series of succeeding "theme" restaurants. None ever equaled this early pioneer of popularly priced dining.

Dining out has become a national past time. Fast food purveyors account for the majority of the dining expenditures. However, when many area gourmands get into their cars and go out for the evening, to "make a night of it", they wistfully recall the grand old restaurants of a not too long ago time, when dining was extremely fine.

Historical Perspectives on Mahoning Valley Labor

by Richard S. Scarsella

To an out-of-towner, the name Mahoning Valley conjures images of solid men, covered in soot, toiling over open-hearth blast furnaces, with fire lapping at their heals. To these men and their families, the national holiday of Labor Day was a much-needed break from bone-grinding, muscle burning work.

The term labor means toil, for economic gain. Those in the white-collar professions, such as banking and retailing, labeled those that sold their bronze, in the mills, for a living as "day laborers". Why? These salt of the earth workers were employed for a day, a week, a month or for a lifetime, as long as they could perform daily, almost superhuman feats of strength and endurance on the job. Should they fail to accomplish their given tasks, many strong men were in line to take their places. The Mahoning Valley was a literal Darwinian community, where the strong survived and bred a like kind. The others, less fortunate, less hardy, less adaptable to inferno-like work conditions, who could not compete with these mighty brutes of industry, were winnowed out.

Although Labor Day in the Youngstown area is synonymous with the agrarian spectacle of the Mahoning County Canfield Fair, this holiday had its roots deep in the native iron, steel, and manufacturing soil along the Mahoning River. The Mahoning Valley was blessed with an abundance of raw materials, ideal for the Industrial Age. Like the Native Americans, who once mined salt, for curing and cooking purposes, the burgeoning industrialists in the 1850's moved away from salt mines, grist and saw mills, into "heavy industry". No more did the day begin at dawn and end at dusk, like on the valley's idyllic farms. The growing mills were open twenty-four hours a day, making workers at the mercy of schedules. A paid day off was a luxury, one scarcely hoped for. It was a long time in coming.

Here, in Appalachian foothills, coal was the basis of the Mahoning Valley's transition from agriculture to industry. Ideal for crude blast furnaces, coal was used to make iron. Railroads and canals rushed to capitalize on the new coal-based industries. Jobs were plentiful, unskilled, and quickly snapped up by local men. Coal mining peaked in the 1870's, leaving the countryside pock-marked with holes and shafts, much to the chagrin of farmers and cattle. Miners and foundry men dreaded the prospect of returning to farm-life, which was dependent on weather, infestations, and fluctuating prices. Retail and professional positions were hard to secure, for uneducated men untrained in more gentile careers, such as accounting and wholesaling.

The shipping of coal and iron into the valley secured most industrial jobs at this time, to the great relief of thousands of blue-collar workers. The valley shifted its previous allegiance and dependence on coal to gas for heating, lighting, and manufacturing purposes. Employment in gas conversion and gas producing companies increased dramatically.

By the 1880's, throngs of immigrants flooded the valley, seeking out the emerging heavy industry jobs. Tensions oftentimes came to a head, between local men and newly naturalized Americans. However, they were all brothers and sisters of industry. When the mills suffered slowdowns and strikes, all suffered.

Valley politics were increasingly determined by the votes of the "great unwashed". Prejudices based upon religion, ethnicity, party affiliation, or class were blunted by the new found affluence, to which valley residents were becoming accustomed. Working families needed places of rest, relaxation and rejuvenation, as well as stores. Their wants began to shape the future of the valley. By 1894, most of the states celebrated Labor Day, in recognition of the needs and contributions of the working class and their building of the prosperity and well being of the country. Grand festivities were held yearly to remember the "working man". Downtown Youngstown's Central Square had the largest such event in the area.

Downtown Youngstown underwent a building boom in the late 1800's, with stores, theaters, and saloons all built to service the men and families of the emerging labor class. Strouss-Hirschberg and G.M. McKelvey Company built flagship stores, which anchored the bustling central business district. Families of labor had to buy things, which farmers could make for themselves. Food and work clothes were major consumer items for working families, hard pressed by low wages and high housing costs. A whole newly enlarged mercantile class of workers, such as clerks and managers, prospered off of their heavy labor class cousins. Fewer people were self-employed now, since they were opting to work for the sprawling mills or large downtown concerns. Youngstown was fast becoming a modern city, with new neighborhoods being built for the mill workers.

In 1891, Volney Rogers created magnificent Mill Creek Park, using his own funds to acquire property. Rogers envisioned an oasis of green for the hard-working, time short urban dwellers of industry. Mill Creek Park became the major summer retreat for area workers. Its mixture of manicured gardens, man-made lakes, waterfalls, trails, and untouched woods became a haven for the residents of mill towns. This park system became Ohio's first park district.

In 1899, a streetcar company founded Idora Park. Idora was an early "theme park", complementing its neighbor, Mill Creek Park. Idora's owners envisioned this family spot as a resort destination. It even boasted a hotel, at one time, for city folks, which could afford to spend a couple of days away from the grime and noise of area factories. Working families found brief refuge from their hard lives by frequenting the Idora botanical gardens and lagoons, animal acts, dance contests, open-air concerts and plays, athletic competitions and midway attractions. The demise of the area's industrial base in the 1980's heralded the final years of "Youngstown's Million Dollar Playground", where Labor Day was annually observed in high spirits.

Laborers and their families knew, if they were to improve their positions in life, they needed more education. This realization led to the eventual founding of a neo-classical "cathedral of learning" on Wick Avenue, named the Reuben McMillan Free Library. This new facility, replete with hand-carved paneled walls, marble floors, and vaulted ceilings, became an instant success with working men. They voraciously read the newspapers for career opportunities, housing, do-it-yourself tips, and news from the "old country". Their families came to the library as well. Wives read family, medical, recipe and craft texts, while their children read fairytale books and American classics, such as "Tom Sawyer".

U.S. Steel, Carnegie Steel, Republic Steel, and Youngstown Sheet and Tube were some of the many heavy industrial firms that made Youngstown famous. In the 1900's, it was considered one of the top steel-producing regions in the nation. This achievement was based upon the backs of the average laborers, who hoped for better things for their families. Pipe, tinplate, sheet metal, limestone, slag and molds were all the products of local men, intent on making the Mahoning Valley an industrial giant and a good place to call home.

Youngstown natives were concerned in the 1900's that American culture might be engulfed by cosmopolitan, pedestrian, working-class, foreign-born culture. In response, the Butler Institute of American Art, the Mahoning Valley Historical Society, and the Stambaugh Auditorium were founded to "illuminate" and refine the newly defined middle-class working families. Ironically, an emerging American culture was being shaped by the very people it hoped to Americanize.

World War I, between 1914 and 1918, oftentimes called the "Great War", brought huge orders of war related purchases to the valley. Unions began to increasingly organize area workers, leading to the turmoil of 1915-1916. Strikes, mob violence, $1.5 million destruction of property and state troops showed that the workingmen of the valley were not to be taken for granted. They were frustrated with unsafe work and housing conditions, low pay and long hours. Area industrialists responded grudgingly with labor concessions, planned housing communities, and increased social services. In unity, came strength. The unions kept pressing for more of their demands. Youngstowners began to join and support the unions in record numbers.

The Industrial Workers of the World (IWW) and the American Federation of Labor (AFL) both changed the lives of workers, by promoting an 8-hour workday, as opposed to the common 12-hour workday. The Y.M.C.A., Y.W.C.A., and local church groups galvanized these working class families to improve the valley's quality of life. Temperance movements, anti-KKK rallies, and Community Chest drives all sought to make the Mahoning Valley a pleasant, safe, equal place for all to live and raise families. Self-help groups, youth clubs, and ethnic culture clubs wanted the valley to be more than just a strip of mills. Local laws began to change to reflect the growing interest in safety, health, and morals.

The scourge of the Great Depression, beginning in 1929, mortally ravished working class families. The great American industrial machine slowly ground to a halt, until World War II revived its engines. The war years ushered in the resurgence of prosperity. The Valley hummed, twenty-four hours a day, to produce goods for the Allies. The defeat of the Axis forces in 1945, left the workingmen and women with newfound confidence in their worth as productive, necessary components of the American century.

The G.I. Bill allowed the sons of working families to return from the war and obtain higher education. America was becoming more technological in nature, and less industrial. Electronics, aviation, space, and computers were the new growth businesses of the 1950's. Workers now needed higher education to secure these higher paying, more intellectually challenging occupations. Now, brainpower, not muscle power, would be the standard for increasing numbers of working families.

Youngstown College morphed into Youngstown State University to meet this new economic imperative. Kent State University, with two branches in the valley, and neighboring Western Pennsylvania colleges, all competed amongst themselves for the children of working class families. Technical and trade schools, such as ITT Business School, also educated and re-educated today's modern workers.

Youngstown Sheet and Tube's closing of aging mills in the 1970's, echoed the trend elsewhere in the valley, of old line industrial jobs moving out-of-town or overseas. The General Motors' plant in Lordstown is the newest and possibly last, giant industrial complex the valley will ever have. Representative of the 1990's, this facility has robots doing tasks men once did. Each car made here has more computer chips in it than any of the NASA moon modules had aboard. Women make up almost half the workforce and minorities are well represented here, unlike the iron and steel factories of old. Today's workers are no longer agents unto themselves. Rather, they are wed to technology and have become agents of change.

The unionization of nurses, teachers, and librarians, in the 1960's and 1970's, seemed odd and threatening at one time. Now, even physicians are considering unionizing. Workers and professionals of all kinds are drifting towards each other, as the demands of technology, managed growth, capital driven market economies, the New World order, and world economies take their toll on the old American industrial system, which was based upon the division of labor and services.

Today, retail salespeople, computer analysts, elevator operators, health care providers, assembly men and women, and oxygen furnace technicians all have a level of education, wages, benefits, and rights that the groundbreaking laborers of old could ill conceive. We have now witnessed skilled craftsmen, such as carpenters and plumbers, earning more salaries than a college professor or police officer. Using one's hands is no longer a mark of social inferiority. In fact, the ever-expanding service industry jobs are excellent opportunities for transition into management—a dream most laborers of the past never attained.

Labor Day no longer is solemnly celebrated. At one time, stores, offices and factories closed to honor the "common man". It was once typical, on this day, to attend church, listen to speeches, watch parades and have a picnic with the family. These traditions have ebbed. Today's wealthier, better-educated working populace observes Labor Day in the comfort of air-conditioned, cable connected, computer networked homes, far removed from the Mahoning River post-industrial remnants.

Historians and the media keep alive the sweaty turmoil and legacy of the millions of working people, who made this country preeminent. As stewards of this heritage, we must preserve the "can do" spirit of those admirable men and women of mortal flesh and their immortal dreams of a better life, in a better land, for all workers, for all time.

Holiday Thoughts

by Richard S. Scarsella

Holidays bring a rush of memories to mind. For both Christians and non-Christians alike, the triad of Thanksgiving, Christmas, and New Year's days brings a welcomed relief from everyday routines.

I recollect the local bus and taxi companies adding rolling stock to their fleets to accommodate increased traffic to the downtown retail district. The lack of affordable and accessible parking lots downtown made bus and taxi travel sensible and necessary.

I recollect colorful Thanksgiving Day parades and exciting football games between local high school powerhouse teams. Before television captivated our lives, Thanksgiving Day activities outside of the home were commonplace. Of course, attendance at church was the primary social function next to family dinners.

I recollect area stores not being decorated with Christmas decorations until the day after Thanksgiving. This practice made the Christmas season special and less commercial.

I recollect the grandiose Santa workshops at the venerable Strouss-Hirshberg and McKelvey's department stores. These toy departments were true wonderlands of porcelain dolls, wood soldiers, and electric trains. Having a photograph or portrait made with Old Saint Nick was a rite of childhood repeatedly yearly.

I recollect the lighting of the Central Square Christmas tree in downtown Youngstown. For many, this ritual was the official beginning of the Yuletide season.

I recollect purchasing fine chocolates at Fanny Farmer and Fron candy shops. Their indescribable confections were unsurpassed and distinctive in taste, texture, and presentation.

I recollect families selecting formal holiday clothing for society events. Ladies would purchase long gowns or cocktail dresses at Livingston's, Esther Cooper, or Betty Goodman boutiques. Gentlemen would buy tuxedos or dress suits at Bond's, Glasgow, or Shy Lockson tailors. Children would be clothed in classic velvet Shirley Temple or Buster Brown outfits from Strouss-Hirshberg's Uptown store, Lerner's, or Hartzell-Rose & Son's Red Beam Rooms.

I recollect Isaly's delivering Yule-time ice cream logs, with tiny green Christmas trees inside each slice.

I recollect Paradise fruitcakes packed in Wedgwood blue round tin containers. I still see these angel-decorated receptacles at flea markets.

I recollect earnest Salvation Army volunteers, dressed in uniforms, stoically ringing bells over huge red kettles, while they solicited alms for the poor.

I recollect grand film debuts at our luxurious downtown motion picture palaces during the gala holiday months. Going to the movies was a welcomed relief for our tired feet after a long hard day of shopping.

I recollect the ringing of bells at area valley churches on Christmas Eve, Christmas day, and New Year's Eve. The metropolitan area literally was alive with the majesty of Westminster chimes.

I recollect couples "stepping out" on New Year's Eve to ring in another year in style. The Elks, Moose, Mason, and Odd Fellows lodges all hosted elegant dinners with live orchestral entertainment. The Youngstown Club, high atop the old Union National Bank building, had the best view in town to watch area fireworks displays.

I recollect the romantic grand ballroom of historic Idora Park featuring big band music on New Year's Eve. This beloved dance hall was as timeless as time itself.

I recollect dutiful relatives removing wreaths, candles, and ribbons from area gravestones. Thoughts of departed loved ones hung heavy on our souls as we concluded the season of joy.

Looking back, it is hard to believe how things have changed and stayed the same. Though many familiar faces and places have long passed the scene, I still find a measure of comfort in what remains.

Hollywood Eulogy

by Richard S. Scarsella

Americans love movies. The early silent films, such as D. W. Griffith's "The Birth of a Nation" and Charlie Chaplin's "The Tramp", entranced audiences, hungry for entertainment. Pipe organs, full of sound effects, would majestically rise from the stage floors and flood the theaters with such exotic sounds as cymbals and harps. They hauntingly gave life to motion pictures. Youngtown's legendary Palace, State, Warner, Paramount, Park and Hippodrome theaters all once had professional organists create breathtaking moods for expectant fans.

"The Jazz Singer" of 1927, with Al Jolson, was Hollywood's first "talkie". It revolutionized the film industry. Silent stars such as John Garfield, Norma Shearer, Mary Pickford, and Gloria Swanson were pushed aside by this new technology. A growing studio system, with names such as MGM, Universal, RKO Radio, Paramount, Warner Brothers, Columbia, and 20th Century Fox, efficiently developed the star system. Young men and women were chosen from the heartland or lured away from the bright lights of Broadway stages. In Hollywood, they would be transformed into American royalty.

Bigger than life figures were spawned during the "golden age" of Hollywood. In the 1930's and 1940's, Tyrone Power, Cary Grant, Gary Cooper, Spencer Tracy and Clark Gable all represented American masculinity, ingenuity, patriotism and values. However, it was the movie actresses that best defined this era of melodrama, romance, and elegance.

Joan Crawford reigned supreme with her padded shoulders and piercing stare. Her film "Mildred Pierce" is a classic. Bette Davis chewed up the screenplays with her haughty demeanor and affected style of smoking. Her "All About Eve" performance still is riveting. Mae West combined both humor and sex appeal in her star vehicles. Her double entendres were a breath of fresh air in a conservative Depression scarred nation. Her depiction in "She Done Him Wrong" crackled with the spirit of women's liberation from convention. Katherine Hepburn was a trailblazer for women's rights. Her "Desk Set" role prophetically portrayed women as both indispensable and accomplished in the world of work. Greta

Garbo's fragile persona and translucent vulnerability made her captivating and elusive. Her portrayal in the star studded "Grand Hotel" made her a symbol of all doomed heroines. Her real life mirrored her characters and she became the archetype of a public recluse. All these screen goddesses molded American tastes, styles, culture, and attitudes.

The decline of the studio system in the 1950's was the beginning of the end for America's legendary Hollywood dream machine. Television sapped ticket sales. Television lured icons such as John Wayne and Loretta Young to the small screen. Movie specials were now made for this new medium at the expense of the big screens. Movie palaces closed and were supplanted by drive-in theaters and neighborhood cinemas. Elizabeth Taylor, Grace Kelly, Bridgette Bardot, Marilyn Monroe, Marlon Brandon, Paul Newman, James Dean, and Montgomery Clift were considered by many to be the last "stars". Television personalities now became the rage.

With the recent death of Hedy Lamar, who was arguably the most stunning of the gilded Hollywood faces, the Hollywood legacy grows dimmer. Hedy's "Sampson & Deliah" role epitomized the refinement and fantasy of escapism. Her show stopping beauty, comprising of porcelain complexion, coal black hair, hourglass figure, and regal composure, coupled with modest talent, demonstrated Hollywood's alchemy. The "look" became the message.

We sought emotional release and satiation in bigger than life dramas, epics and comedies. The stars became our celluloid idols and alter egos. We lived vicariously through the films and their leading men and women. For a small fee, we were temporarily admitted to another world made courtesy of Hollywood. Our theatrical experiences made indelible impressions on our psyches. The movies and their lustrous personalities became firmly embedded in our lives and collective memories of what was, is and could have been. The history of the silver screen became our histories. With Hedy Lamar's death, another star has fallen from the Hollywood firmament. As Bob Hope says at the end of all of his shows, "Thanks for the memories."

I Sometimes Recall

by Richard S. Scarsella

I sometimes recall former times. Over the last forty years, the Mahoning Valley has greatly changed. However, the memories linger on.

It's hard to believe that downtown Youngstown once attracted thousands of shoppers per day to fashionable department stores, stylish specialty shops, and grand movie theaters. The parades held for St. Patrick's Day, Veterans' Day, and the Christmas season were legendary. Rural families would plan a day "in town" months ahead to take advantage of these public spectacles. Holiday decorations, high school marching bands, and verbose politicians all made these gay celebrations memorable. Downtown grilles, clubs, pubs, and restaurants were hard pressed to service the crowds of revelers. Today, deserted Federal Plaza gives nary a hint of what once was.

Newcomers to the area cannot fully appreciate the once prevalent "steel city" culture. The mills were the soul of Struthers, Campbell, and Youngstown. Gritty men, dressed in overalls, literally earned a living in the bowels of iron and steel blast furnaces. Neighborhood bars, called "beer gardens", cashed their checks and let them run up a tab. Ethnic churches, with names such as Holy Ghost and Immaculate Conception, baptized their young and buried their elders. Few of these laborers ever left their provincial worlds. Nonetheless, for the most part, they were happy, in their own way.

Old-timers retell with relish how city folks made an annual summer trek to the shores of once pristine Lake Erie. Presque Isle, Put In Bay, and Geneva-On-The-Lake were at one time considered chic vacation spots. Before Lake Erie was prematurely proclaimed "dead" by the press, fishing fleet excursions and private marinas attracted anglers and boaters in throngs. Sun worshippers loved the panoramic view of ore ships, flocks of seagulls, and Canadian sunsets. Only recently has Lake Erie been rediscovered as the forgotten jewel it has always been.

In years past, every home had a brick chimney spewing out trails of smoke on winter mornings. The soot would gently alight over neighborhood cars and yards. Glistening white snow looked even more magical with its black dustings.

Occasionally, snow was tinged with yellow, orange, or red hues, as a byproduct of industrial complexes. Only in Youngstown did it snow in colors.

Generations of inhabitants fell in love with and at fabled Idora Park. This "Million Dollar Playground" seduced lovers of all ages with the romantic Tunnel of Love, the dreamlike Grand Ballroom, and the picturesque Botanical Gardens. An area institution for over a century, it slowly is receding into the annals of local history, like so many other once common landmarks.

When daybreaks and the nighttime gloom disperses, I sometimes recall these things and many more. Truly, there is nothing so final and merciless as time.

Ice Kingdom

by Richard S. Scarsella

In the gritty Mahoning Valley, wintertime oftentimes brought a touch of magic into our lives. Long before modern weather broadcasts announced with any certainty a chance of snow flurries, it was not uncommon to awaken to a totally unexpected fairyland like blanket of snowflakes.

The generous dusting of smoke-belching mills, stern North Side stone mansions, Gothic-inspired Mill Creek tree stands, and ethnic neighborhoods precipitously hugging the banks of the muddy Mahoning River, was a sight to behold. Arctic Canadian air, mixed with Lake Erie precipitation, regularly turned our cityscape into a picture postcard tableau of Dickinsonian proportions, replete with snow-covered architecture.

Children loved to make snow forts out of drifts. Sparkling icicles, hanging dramatically from pointed rooftops and elegant eaves, were knocked down with brooms and brandished as swords in this storybook setting winter provided. Whole streets became snow chutes, with youngsters hurdling down avenues precariously atop trashcan lids and milk crates. Hoboes, bums, and all matter of bag people gaped in wide-eyed wonder of the transformation of our metropolis into a frozen amusement park.

Most neighborhoods had an empty lot or woods with a pond to skate on. If not, one was easily created by using a garden hose to flood low-lying areas. Once frozen, these man-made bodies of water were focal points for ice-skaters of all ages.

Those with transportation frequented Lake Glacier, Lake Newport, Lake Cohassett, Lincoln Park, Crandall Park, Pemberton Park, or Borts Field for recreation. At these locations a bonfire, hot chocolate stands, and/or piped-in music awaited those brave enough to take to the ice.

Small children on double-bladed wood skates, teenagers wearing leather English racing skates, and older couples skating Austrian waltzes and two-steps were once familiar scenes in our midst. Possible Olympic contenders would stage impromptu performances, complete with white fur trimmed capes, skirts, and muffs, much to the delight of the watching crowds. Images of Sonja Henning abounded. It was as if a spell of white magic briefly descended into our environs.

The popularity of ice-skating reached its apex some thirty years ago with the opening of the Mill Creek Metroparks' Wick Recreation Centre refrigeration rink. Skate rentals were available, a repair shop and professional instruction were on-site, and the shelter had large picture windows, allowing the less hearty to stay warm as they viewed those on the rink. Weekends and evenings allowed thousands of families to partake in the Alpine past time for a nominal fee. Regardless of location, ice-skating was a very much a part of area lives for generations. Many residents met their first loves and spouses while partaking in this wholesome American diversion.

Perhaps, it is only my memory playing tricks on me, but I can still envision endless winter days when our industrial landscape appeared enchanted. When first falling to the ground, the blinding white snow overlay was pristine and cleansing. All the black soot, decomposed leaves, and unsightly litter were temporarily vanquished from sights. The downtown office towers, overhead telephone lines, and flora and fauna all were encased in reflective frozen coverlets. On quick inspection, the surroundings looked like an ice kingdom from another time. To skate with abandon with such a stunning backdrop was invigorating, indescribable, and memorable as only dreams can be.

To this day, as I travel Rt. 224, I sometimes think of the long closed indoor Boardman Ice Rink, where I once took lessons. The Mill Creek Metroparks' artificial rink is now shuttered as well. When I pass long known haunts of intrepid skaters, I am perplexed that skating has now been eclipsed, despite the recent opening of a year-round hockey rink. No, the once dominant frequent gatherings of ice skating enthusiasts are long gone. However, when the snow first settles to the ground, I look longingly into the moonlight, and I can almost see ghostly images gliding cheerfully in the shadows of time.

Idora Ballroom

by Richard S. Scarsella

Into the year 1986, two years after the Idora Amusement Park closed, the Idora Grand Ballroom still played a major role in valley social and cultural history. This huge, all wood, turn of the century Coney Island style dance pavilion once acted as a magnet for all sorts of glittering society events, raucous political gatherings, and business trade shows.

Idora Ballroom, the biggest remaining ballroom between Chicago and New York City, once was booked years in advance for a wide variety of affairs. High school and college reunions, sorority and fraternity socials, cotillions, union socials, factory dance marathons, and polka parties all filled this venerable facility to the rafters. Seating over 2800 patrons, this landmark was and is still unmatched in size and amenities. The unusual Art Deco suspended cloud ceiling, with its rainbow hued colored lights and flickering stars, made this venue the ultimate in sophistication and romance.

In the 1920's, l930's and 1940's, callow young men would buy tickets at the ballroom to dance with equally shy maidens. If one was lucky, a young man would have the girl of his dreams fill her dance card with his name only. Magic was created here, with the help of big band music from such greats as Guy Lombardo, Lawrence Welk, and Jimmy Dorsey bands.

In the 1950's, the American Bandstand Top 40 record hops swept the ballroom floor. Rock and Roll became popular locally, due to radio stations, such as WHOT, promoting the likes of Elvis Presley and Buddy Holly. Our country would never be the same again.

The 1960's brought the Motown Record sound to the Youngstown area. The music of the Supremes, Smokey Robinson, and Stevie Wonder brought all races and socioeconomic groups to the Idora dance floor. This in turn promoted integration and equality.

The 1970's at the Idora Ballroom were dominated by polka. Local favorite Frankie Yankovic went onto national fame, due to thunderous support from grateful Idora audiences. Picnics and ballgames were also held in the shadows of the ballroom, in keeping with the very wholesome setting of Youngstown's "Million Dollar Playground".

Both Democrats and Republicans trotted out their favorite sons at lavish, smokey, conspiratorial rallies and dinners at the ballroom. Idora's imposing size, historical ambiance, and convenient location made it the natural hub of politics. National figures, such as President John F. Kennedy, were feted here in splendid manner.

The yearly Home and Garden Show and national car shows were once immense regional attractions, generating thousands of dollars into the local economy. The ballroom was turned into a wonderland of color, style, technology, and performance, making us feel like we were at a large city convention center. This grande dame of a ballroom was truly an anchor for our lives.

Oddly, the Idora Ballroom now stands vacant, abandoned and derelict. Tragically, it is faded by the ravages of time, neglect, and the elements. It is grim testimony to a more prosperous era, when the valley hummed with growth, employment, pride and purpose. The Idora Ballroom evokes memories from many generations. It still haunts our psyches. It refuses to die quietly. If not saved now, it will not easily be forgotten. Idora Ballroom is an integral part of the essence of our valley.

The Idora Century: 1899-1999

by Richard S. Scarsella

Mahoning Valley residents celebrate Idora Park's 100th. Anniversary this year. Looking back at old Idora photographs, newsreels, and memorabilia reminds us how much this grande dame of an amusement park means to us all. Shockingly, the Idora we knew and loved now stands vacant, abandoned, left to the mercy of vandals, weather, and the march of time.

Luckily, Idora fans will find a book in area stores by the end of July, titled "Idora Park: The Last Ride of Summer". Authored by Youngstown native, Professor Rick Shale, Youngstown State University English Department, and co-authored by Pennsylvanian Charles J. Jacques, Jr., amusement park fans and historians will find this book a treasure house of vintage photographs, historical narratives, and statistics, which illuminates the Idora mystique.

Idora had its start in 1899. Founded by the Youngstown Park and Falls Street Railway Company, this "trolley park" was located at the terminus of a railroad line and first named Terminal Park. Why? Idora lured passengers onto the motorized railway, all whom paid fare to escape the steel city's smog, heat, and congestion. Later, many patrons bought property along the line. Interestingly, to this day, the Youngstown area continues to grow south, towards Boardman.

Idora's neighbor, spectacular Mill Creek Park, positioned Idora as the garden spot of the valley. Lush botanical gardens, lagoons, and fountains complemented Idora's picnic grounds. Pony rides, bear acts, monkey cages, and Atlantic City diving horses entertained "city folks" for a small fee.

As the Industrial Revolution picked up steam in the 1900's, Idora began adding mechanical attractions. An arcade advertised penny pinball-like machines. The first merry-go-round captured the hearts of infants and adults alike. A dance pavilion played phonographs, in between band performances. Idora's first roller coaster was added in 1903. With this attraction, Idora now competed with parks in Akron, Cleveland and Pittsburgh. It was now a regional park.

Music and memories define the Idora era. With the 1910 opening of the "Grand Ballroom"—a Coney Island, Moorish, Victorian inspired edifice, replete with gingerbread towers, topped with cupolas—Idora now booked national big bands and orchestras. Guy Lombardo, the Dorsey Brothers, and Lawrence Welk all graced the Idora bandstand. Along with the Idora "Casino Theater"—a vaudeville/summer stock open-air arena—this park was Youngstown's social and cultural showplace. Even downtown Youngstown's theaters could not rival the depth and breadth of Idora's entertainments.

The 1920's and 1930's witnessed Idora's greatest expansion, mirroring the growth of the greater Youngstown area. The Jack Rabbit roller coaster, Olympic-sized swimming pool, a larger carousel and the Wild Cat roller coaster turned Idora into "Youngstown's Million Dollar Playground". Steel mills, churches, schools, and organizations packed the midways, with special days reserved for them only. People, desperate to escape the scourge of the Depression, the World War II rationing, and the restraints of middle-class/working-class conventions, found a sense of freedom, adventure and joy at Idora. Attending the park was truly a right of passage in our increasingly homogenized common culture. Idora, in the 1940's, was a veritable beehive of attractions, attended by all, regardless, of class, race, or age.

The 1950's post-war affluence fueled Idora's prosperity. The ballroom thrived with sock-hops. Kiddieland was built over the Olympic pool and became an instant hit with "baby boom" families. Modern roads and highways made Idora more accessible, to a larger market, than ever before.

The 1960's ushered in the infamous WHOT radio station "hot days" and rock concerts. Psychedelic music, hippie styles, and social unrest began to concern middle-class families, which were the mainstay of attendance. Expansions at Kennywood, Cedar Point, and Geauga Lake parks began to hurt gate receipts. Television also kept people away from the park. The ball field no longer hosted minor-league teams. Idora's allure began to wane, in the wake of suburban competition.

Steel mill closings in the 1970's, the proliferation of church festivals, the emergence of mega-parks—such as Kings Island and Disney World—further weakened Idora's appeal. The park, frozen in time, was hemmed in by a residential neighborhood and Mill Creek Park. Regrettably, the maturing Idora owners could not expand the park, to meet increasing competition and changing tastes. When advertised for sale, no bidders came forward to buy this unique piece of local Americana.

Without doubt, the 1984 fire—which leveled the Old Mill/Lost River water ride and one-quarter of the Wild Cat coaster—was the determining reason why Idora closed. Robbed of its number one attraction, Idora held an auction, that same year. Generations of dreams and pleasures—represented by Idora's antique rides, tasty concessions, and kitsch souvenirs—were sold to the highest bidders.

The park, that officially began and ended summer in the Mahoning Valley, was shuttered. The ballroom closed about a year later. The result? Idora is slowly slipping into the abyss of history.

"Idora Park: The Last Ride of Summer" does not cover Idora's history after 1984. Die-hard Idora fans may be interested to know about attempts to save the park. Briefly, half-hearted efforts by the Mahoning Valley Preservation Club to get Youngstown to buy the ballroom led to the creation of a more activist group, called the Idora Park Historical Society. This association put the 27 acres of Idora Park on the National Registry of Historical Places and had a signed purchase agreement to buy the park. Infighting amongst the historical society founders weakened their efforts to gain financing for their project. Remarkably, Mount Calvary Church repurchased the property—after a previous foreclosure—for a second time. Tenacious efforts of the Idora Park Institute to garner public support for the preservation of all or part of the park seems to be the only viable hope of saving some semblance of Idora Park, as it once was. Hopefully, Mill Creek Park's mild interest in acquiring or leasing Idora—under certain conditions—will lead to serious dialogue about Idora's perilous future.

The Native-American ceremonial/burial grounds, reputed to be under the Idora picnic-grounds, which are built on a large mound, are also not mentioned in the new book. According to the Native American Council of Ohio, tribal oral history pinpoints Idora as ancient tribal land. History buffs will recall Lanterman's Falls used to be called Idora Falls, until recently. No such tribe, by the name Idora, ever existed. However, Native American encampments in nearby Mill Creek Park—with projectile points as evidence of inhabitation—seem to add some credence to this urban lore of Idora Park. The park's present owners have denied permission for a Youngstown State University archaeological dig to be conducted at Idora.

Shale and Jacques do capture the essence of Idora in their book. Over 250 photographs of rare and dated tableaus tug at your heart. Scenes of vintage rides, luxuriant foliage, summertime confections, ballroom extravaganzas, screaming roller-coaster riders, happy families, and fire charred remains bring back a rush of memories for Idora aficionados. Graphically, one can see a paradise lost.

"Idora Park: The Last Ride of Summer" will be an asset to and become an heirloom for any household interested in the rich, varied, scandalously neglected Mahoning Valley history. Perhaps, another book will commence in the year 1984 and bring us forward into Idora's second century. Hopefully, by then, the sad remains of Idora Park will be rescued from oblivion and regain there rightful places in our daily lives as symbols, landmarks of the best years of our lives.

Happy Birthday Idora Park!!

The Idora Century Mark

by Richard S. Scarsella

As a local preservationist, I am oftentimes asked to speak about area history. The top two subjects? Idora Park and William Holmes McGuffey. Both names continue to influence our social and cultural history. Idora conjures up the most vivid memories.

Founded in 1899, when horses still trotted around neighborhoods with produce and ice, Idora was erected by a trolley company. Why? Idora's purpose was to sell tickets and land along the train track out in the wilderness—Youngstown's South Side! To this day, the city continues to grow towards Boardman.

Your ancestors could tell of lush botanical gardens, spring fed curative fountains and live animal exhibits at the Idora picnic grounds. Caged bears and horses jumping off of scaffolds, an Atlantic City tradition, intrigued city folk, as they ate their salt-water taffy. The primordial smells of nearby Mill Creek Park made Idora even more exhilarating. The remains of exotic flora and fauna not native to Eastern Ohio still survive, according to Youngstown State University biology professor, Dr. Carl Chuey. Like the Idora dance hall, these plants stand as mute testimony of another era.

Until it closed, Idora was in competition with nearby Kennywood, Cedar Point, Geauga Lake, Euclid, Westview and Cascade Parks. To survive, Idora added mechanical attractions. A carrousel, Ferris wheel and coasters joined arcade amusements on the tree-lined, terraced midway.

An open-air vaudeville theater, with retractable canvas walls, along with a grand ballroom, anchored Idora as a family entertainment complex. Later billed as "Youngstown's Million Dollar Playground", Idora became a coaster mecca. It boasted the Jack Rabbit, Baby Wildcat and Wildcat—the later, dubbed by the American Coasters Enthusiasts Association, one of the top ten wooden coasters in America. A victim of the slumping economic times, changing tastes and a devastating fire, Idora folded in 1984. Only Kennywood, Geauga Lake and Cedar Point outlived it.

So, you ask, why does Idora persist in our psyches and in urban legend? Because Idora was much more than rides and games of chance. It was color, sounds, smells and tastes that imprinted this grand dame of a park upon each generation. In the ballroom, an Art Deco, suspended cloud ceiling, with flickering rainbow hued lights, created the ultimate romantic scene for young lovers. The lilt of the merry-go-round lulled babies to sleep and calmed tired parents. Greasy French fries and hot, sweet cotton candy made patrons salivate like Pavlovian dogs. Fresh egg and cream custard and ice-cold tap beer quenched parched throats, as the breeze off of nearby Idora Falls, at the Old Mill, cooled sweaty brows.

Idora had something for everyone. It was truly the meeting grounds for all ages, ethnic groups and classes. An immigrant steel laborer would wait in line for fresh squeezed lemonade, in front of a steel baron. Both would return time and again. Factory days, church revivals, polka festivals, sock hops and rock and roll concerts drew people from far around the valley and beyond. Summer began and ended with Idora Park. A century after its debut, Idora is now an abandoned landmark.

It's ironic that Idora is reverting back to nature. This is the way Native-Americans found Idora eons ago. Their ceremonial/burial grounds at Idora, still unexcavated, may be all that remains of this hallowed place, if last-ditch efforts to save the park fail. Perhaps, this is a fitting end to a great legacy. Only time will tell. Mill Creek Metroparks' overture to the present Idora owners, consisting of an offer to buy or lease all or part of Idora, providing outside funding is secured, may be too little too late, according to the Idora Park Institute. Let's hope this is not the case.

Idora Facts

by Richard S. Scarsella

*The Tunnel of Love was later called the Old Mill, The Rapids, and the Lost River Water Ride.

*The Olympic Pool featured a sandy beach, salt water (from a stream that flowed through a salt vein) and an "aquacade" show, inspired by Esther Williams's films.

*The Wild Cat Coaster was rated, by the American Coasters Enthusiasts Association, as one of the Top Ten Wooden Coasters in America, before it partially burned in 1984.

*The Jack Rabbit Coaster is the second oldest wooden coaster in America.

*The Baby Wildcat Coaster (in Kiddieland), Arcade, and Carousel buildings were demolished in the winter of 1998.

*According to an environmental impact study, conducted by Dr. Carl Chuey, Youngstown State University Biology Department, the Botanical Gardens still contain flora and fauna, not native to Northeastern Ohio.

*The Native American Council of Ohio's tribal oral history claims that indigenous people oftentimes interred the remains or ashes of the departed on high ground, in view of water, similar to the Picnic Grounds, which are reputed to be on a ceremonial/burial mound.

*Sock hops were made popular by local radio personality Dan Ryan, at the Idora Grand Ballroom, in the 1950's.

*Big bands stopped regularly in Youngstown, to play the Idora Grand Ballroom, which is the largest such ballroom still in existence, between New York City and Chicago.

*The Idora Grand Ballroom can seat 2,800 people for dinner, making this facility larger than any other Mahoning Valley facility.

*The Ballroom's suspended cloud ceiling, with rainbow-hued indirect lighting and twinkling lights, is one of the best and last such Art-Deco examples in the country.

*"Moonshine" was made under the Jack Rabbit Coaster, according to urban legend.

*Only beer was sold in the park. Patrons could bring their own "hard liquor" for ballroom events, but could not drink it elsewhere in the park.

*One acre of Idora is presently used by Mill Creek Metroparks' Old Mill Museum for parking.

*In 1993, Idora's 27 acres and structures were placed on the National Registry of Historical Places, which is a designation of the United States Interior Department's National Parks Services.

*Miniature golf was first introduced to Youngstown on the Idora Midway.

*The 1984 fire burned the park offices and the Idora archive of original pictures, advertisements, and newsreels.

*The 1986 fire destroyed the original dance pavilion, named Heidelberg Gardens, along with the Fun House and Bumper Cars.

*Concessions at the park were owned and operated by many area families.

*Favorite Idora foods included fresh-roasted peanuts, caramel apples on a stick, buttered popcorn, egg and cream custard, hot dogs on a stick, cotton candy, saltwater taffy, lemonade, and sugared elephant ears.

*Antique car shows first gained popularity in Youngstown, with displays at the Ball field and Ballroom.

*Baby Shows were a tradition, with girls wheeling their dolls in carriages at the Ball field.

*The Ball field hosted minor-league baseball teams, into the early 1950's.

*The Silver Rocket Ships replaced airplanes in the late 1940's.

*Roller-skating was featured at both an outdoor rink and in the Ballroom.

*Idora's Casino Theater featured nationally known stars of vaudeville and musical comedies up to the early 1930's.

*Idora outlasted competing parks such as Westview of Pittsburgh, Pennsylvania, Euclid Beach of Cleveland, Meyers Lake of Canton and Cascade of New Castle, Pennsylvania.

*The original Carousel was later moved to Cascade Park, New Castle, PA.

*The WHOT Radio Hot Days were later renamed Spring Things and attracted thousands of rock and roll fans to Ballroom "battle of the bands".

*The Carousel was listed in 1975 to the National Register of Historic Places.

*The 1984 fire began due to a welding unit igniting the Lost River water ride.

*The Idora auction, held in 1984, drew buyers nationwide, hungry for a piece of authentic amusement park memorabilia. The Carousel sold for $385,000 to a New York City couple.

*Mount Calvary Church bought Idora in 1985, lost it to foreclosure in 1989 and repurchased it in 1994. No definite plans for the "City of God" development have ever been announced.

Idora Park Memories Still Bright After Twenty Years

by Richard S. Scarsella

"Let's go on the Wild Cat!" was a familiar phrase once heard throughout Youngstown's famed Idora Park over the years. Believe it or not, twenty years have passed in a blink of an eye since this popular refrain has been uttered. When the park closed on Labor Day, 1984, an end of an era was upon us.

Today, area folks fondly reminiscence about the heyday of "Youngstown's Million Dollar Playground". The infamous wooden roller coasters, named Wild Cat, Jack Rabbit, and Baby Wild Cat, epitomized the thrills, adventure, and carefree abandon we enjoyed every summer at this historic amusement wonderland. Many "lost their lunch" or swallowed insects on these jolting rides. Screams of delight and horror routinely emanated from these venerable attractions and drifted into nearby Mill Creek Park and the Fosterville neighborhood.

Of course, Idora Park offered enjoyments of all kinds and endeared itself to us on many levels. The hulking Ferris wheel and elegant hand-carved carrousel anchored the midway and were major draws for young and old alike. Fun House antics, featuring distorting mirrors and air jets, were fail-safe crowd-pleasers. Bumper cars catered to the more daring. The miniature golf course serviced a more genteel clientele. Throughout the park, music could be heard, courtesy of the loudspeakers, Heidelberg Gardens—the old dance hall—or the grand ballroom.

Musical entertainment and Idora Park were joined at the hip. Balls, dance marathons, sock hops, and rock and roll dance contests all were held there. Lawrence Welk, the Dorsey brothers, Guy Lombardo, and Glenn Miller—to name a few—brought "a touch of heaven" to the Mahoning Valley year-round. Obviously, romance and marriage were nurtured by these concerts and shows and prevail until the present. These halcyon days remain unforgettable for generations.

Food was an Idora Park trademark and tradition unmatched in the area. Cotton candy, caramel apples, corn dogs, fresh roasted peanuts, homemade custard, and fresh-cut French fries all were gastronomic delights not easily found elsewhere. Indeed, concessionaires guarded their family recipes fervently and never divulged their secrets. Many still comment about the distinctive flavors and consistencies of these carnival-inspired treats.

From Memorial Day until Labor Day, the traditional end of summer, classic picnics were held at the Idora Park pavilions. Catered meals, brought in from local tearooms, fed throngs of Idora patrons. When satiated, crowds would board the Idora Limited small gauge railroad for a leisurely ride around the once exotic gardens. Unusual flora and fauna greeted our eyes, as did a panorama of the minor-league ball field and glimpses of the midway. These lazy hazy days of yore still burn brightly in our memories.

Downtown Youngstown, opulent motion picture houses, Strouss' and McKelvey's department stores, and the steel corridor all have been eclipsed during our lifetimes. Representative of another age, they linger on in our minds as ghostly images from the not-so-distant past.

Idora Park, however, still elicits brilliant recollections, as fresh and as resplendent as descriptions allow. For most of us, Idora Park was an ongoing affair of the heart. Words alone cannot do justice to a magical place that once graced our lives.

Like most love affairs, Idora Park conjures a tinge of melancholy. We knew it would never last forever. And it didn't. Yet, we find strength in what remains—the tender remembrances that the cruel passage of time cannot dim or erase.

Idora Wars

by Richard S. Scarsella

No other landmark in the Youngstown area elicits more emotions than venerable Idora Park. "Youngstown's Million Dollar Playground"—now reduced to rubble—lives on vividly in the collective memories of a populace laid low by the decimation of the steel industry. It would be an understatement to say that a genuine love affair still exists, despite the brutal passage of years, between loyal valley residents and the now vanished Coney Island styled historic amusement park, which once graced our lives.

Founded in 1899 by a trolley car company seeking to sell tickets and land, Idora Park was never meant to survive into the modern era. But, she did last and thrive, despite a catastrophic depression and two world wars. From the beginning, Idora Park had to prove she was more than a passing fad with investors and patrons. Profits demonstrated her viability as a destination spot for fun and relaxation. Few know the cutthroat economics that theme parks are subject to and must overcome to remain viable.

From the start, Idora Park was in mortal combat with Kennywood Park in Pittsburgh, Pennsylvania and Cedar Point and Geauga Lake, both near Cleveland, Ohio. Although she outlasted Meyers Lake in Canton, Ohio, Cascade Park, in New Castle, Pennsylvania, Euclid Beach in Cleveland, Ohio, and Westview Park, in Pittsburgh, Pennsylvania, Idora Park literally lived from season to season. Lavish catered picnics for industrial mills, ethnic churches, and fraternal organizations were the lifeblood and biggest profit makers for the park. Dance revenues and concession stand income kept Idora Park liquid when the valley convulsed with cyclical economic woes and rabid international conflicts. For many, Idora Park was a luxury in a tight-fisted blue-collared metropolis. She had to promote vigorously to endure. And she did so.

Idora's coasters and Grand Ballroom were her crown jewels. They were known nationally. The cutting-edge indomitable Wild Cat, the classic meandering Jack Rabbit, and the baby boom pleasing miniature Baby Wild Cat of Kiddieland put Idora Park in a class of its own. For many years, the premier wooden coasters in the Mid-West were located in Youngstown. Only when rejuvenated Cedar Point, Geauga Lake, and Kennywood Parks added new, larger attractions and coasters in the 1970's did Idora Park begin to lose ground to better-financed competitors. Landlocked by Mill Creek Metroparks and a subdivision it helped sell, Idora Park became frozen in time. This timelessness became part of her eternal appeal and endeared us to her. Like an unchanging matron, she was always present.

The Grand Ballroom was unrivalled. It was larger than any other dance pavilion in Cleveland or Pittsburgh and attracted top big bands and rock and roll groups. In fact, it was considered to be the largest ballroom between Chicago and New York City. It could hold several thousand patrons easily. With its art deco suspended cloud ceiling, replete with recessed rainbow lighting, twinkling stars, and mirrored glass revolving globe, the Idora Grand Ballroom became memorable for several generations. Inevitably, it lost the cultural wars, when radio, television, cable, and computers made ballroom dancing an anachronism.

Closed in 1984 after a devastating fire swept the midway, attempts to preserve, restore, and reopen Idora Park were met with cold silence, callous indifference, private agendas, and rancorous infighting. Local politicians and business people lacked vision, will, and expertise, all of which were needed to save this National Historic Registry site. Ignorance prevented many from assisting those intent on salvaging the remains of Idora Park. Competing interests cancelled out good will and support for Idora redevelopment. Personalities, narrow-minds, and dysfunctional group dynamics stalled plans for Idora's rebirth as a cultural center. As the years ticked by, the skirmish with time was lost. More fires, insidious decay, and broken hearts doomed efforts to safeguard Idora Park for future generations.

Even now, endeavors to immortalize Idora Park are fraught with ill will. The Youngstown Playhouse, another faded icon, and a native playwright, with strong Idora roots, have been locked into a very bitter public debate over ownership of Idora based ideas used in a play. Even though the twenty-seven acres known as Idora Park is nothing but a field of weeds and debris, Idora Park still ignites passion over its legacy. The result? The Youngstown Playhouse staged an Idora play in summer of 2002. Angela Woodhull is mounting her Idora production in May of 2003.

The Idora wars will probably never end. An institution that lasted over a century—with even the origins of its name in dispute—surely will not disappear gracefully or quickly in our midst. Nor should it. The birth of a legend is never easy. The death of a legend is even harder.

In the Day

by Richard S. Scarsella

There is a popular euphemism regularly used now meaning yesterday. One often hears someone state "In the day" when speaking of the past. Try as we might to ignore previous years, they are constant sources of reference in one's lives.

I cannot help but recall when American automobiles were longer, lower, and wider than European counterparts. The 1950's era Yankee motor coaches brimmed with oversized chrome moldings, sharp fins, and exaggerated grilles. No one ever could confuse Detroit cars with those assembled on the Old World continent. DeSoto, Packard, Imperial, and Plymouth, to name a few, once dominated urban North American cities. Sadly, these proud symbols of New World ingenuity and technology have been driven off the roadways by vehicles half their size. To add insult to injury, our roadways now are full of imported models. The new "international" sedans, with parts made in both America and in Europe, are true hybrids. They do not reflect America's distinctive style and love for motorcars.

Not too long ago, it was common practice to take a bus line downtown to see a film at one of Youngstown's magnificent movie palaces. Eating dinner in the central city and catching a 7:00 P.M. movie was quite cosmopolitan and romantic for those seeking a night on the town. During the heyday of Federal Street motion picture houses, valley residents could be found nightly sitting in these Hollywood entertainment complexes, anxiously awaiting the proscenium draperies to part and reveal critically acclaimed productions. The rush to get on the last bus from Central Square to home was part of the thrill of going to the flickers.

For the longest time, folks enjoyed making homemade ice cream and candy. It was not unusual for families to get out the ice cream maker, along with dry ice, milk, and sugar, and made a couple of gallons of frozen confections. Until Isaly's made premium ice cream affordable and easily available, store-bought ice cream was a luxury. Old-timers took great pride in whipping up batches of fudge, peanut brittle, and buckeyes. Factory-made chocolates were considered inferior to those made in the kitchen. Imported Swiss chocolates were thought of as frivolous self-indulgences, except maybe for the Christmas season. Hardtack was the typical sweet preferred and stocked in the pantry.

Believe it or not, pizza was not always popular in our area. When pizza parlors began to spread across town in the post-World War II years, many residents had to be convinced to sample this Italian delicacy. Chinese food was also not widely eaten at one time in the Mid-West. The television commercials for Rice A Roni—"a San Francisco treat"—really familiarized consumers with rice entrees and led to their acceptance.

I still remember how young children, retirees, and bums would collect redeemable glass soda pop bottles for a penny apiece. Grocery stores used to have wooden racks set up in their store windows to receive these returnable containers. Up into the 1970's, Coke, Pepsi, 7 Up, Dr. Pepper, Holly, NeHi, Golden Age, and Cotton Club all recycled bottles and provided a steady, if meager, income for those willing to return empty bottles. For many, canned pop just does not have the taste satisfaction like the venerable classic bottled beverages.

It is true, back in the days of old life seemed simpler, better, and more knowable. Today's complex modern world has increasingly become inscrutable for those of use reared in another time. Memories help anchor us during these present rootless years.

When I am ready to despair, I hear my grandmother exclaim "Twas not always so." And then I continue on to face what life has dealt me.

In the Land of McGuffey: Hope from the Heartland

by Richard S. Scarsella

Few now know or care that there was a time when free accessible public education in the United States was an unheard of luxury and, but a dream. During this period, only the wealthy could afford to become learned. The unwashed masses were on their own. Into this dim state of affairs a man from the heartland compiled an anthology series that offered hope and literally educated generations of Americans. His name was William Holmes McGuffey. And he is from my hometown. His legacy? Salvation and hope through education.

After matriculating from Boston College, I returned to Youngstown, Ohio and began to search out my roots. My studies in the East, down South, and abroad awakened a keen interest in comparative cultures and civilizations. Little did I appreciate that a scholastic giant was raised in my backyard. In my youthful ignorance, I associated the name McGuffey with a local plaza, a community center, and a street leading out of town across the Pennsylvania border. Upon further inspection, my enlightenment revealed that the "schoolmaster of the nation" was more than just a purveyor of children books. He was an archetypal tireless cheerleader for the rags to riches philosophy that fueled the growing wealth and optimism of the American republic. McGuffey told every man that he could be prosperous and go to heaven! McGuffey knew this to be true. Why? Because he lived the kind of life he promoted.

Born in 1800 in Washington, Pennsylvania, at age two his family crossed the nearby Ohio line and settled in Native American country. Living on an isolated rustic farm on the outskirts of industrial Youngstown gave the McGuffey clan the benefits of town life minus the seductions. Anna McGuffey, his mother, loved books and revered the Bible. They gave her great joy. Her desire—like so many mothers of her era—was for her son to become literate, successful and respect the Almighty. The concepts of hard work, fear of damnation, understanding God's will, and perseverance were all imbued in her offspring. Alexander McGuffey, his father, was a rough-edged man of the soil. He worked the land diligently, respected it, and taught his son to become a steward of nature.

Love of God and country were standard in pioneer homes west of the Appalachian Mountains. Religion and family held scattered settlements together as they met the onerous challenges of everyday existence. A hope for a better life—here and in the thereafter—anchored the McGuffey family and their neighbors.

William McGuffey's mother wanted her son to become an ordained Presbyterian preacher. The circuit riders traversing Ohio sometimes stopped at the McGuffey homestead for fresh water or to break bread. Young McGuffey marveled at how these men of the cloth seemingly appeared from nowhere on horseback with little than a change of clothes and a Bible in their backpacks. Formal religious training for the McGuffey children entailed walking through thick woods, on a path their father cleared, several miles to the parson school in Youngstown operated by Reverend William Wick. This famous Connecticut Western Reserve Territory clergyman boarded his wards in harsh weather and made them part of an extended family. Under the minister's tutelage, McGuffey was exposed to another way of life. He discovered gentile society and institutionalized faith in the hub of gritty iron producing Youngstown. While there, he also discovered he had a calling to become an educator. McGuffey vicariously experienced a closer relationship with God while becoming an accomplished reader. Anyone could be saved, he concluded. His mission was to share the good news.

At age seventeen, McGuffey became an itinerant preacher around Youngstown, graduated from Washington College, Washington, Pennsylvania, and acquired a reputation as an acclaimed professor of ancient languages at the newly opened Miami University, Oxford, Ohio in 1826. In this college town, he married a judge's daughter and became decidedly affiliated with establishment stock. However, he did not forget the common man. Indeed, he preached not only at the university chapel but also at other area churches and assemblies. By 1825, Ohio had become the fourth most populated state in the union. Educational reform and progress were percolating, regardless of entrenched opposition. Voluntary societies, comprised of elite men and women, endeavored to "guide society." The general mood of the ruling class was that men needed to be lifted up, given social purpose, and taught to refrain selfish passions. The alternative was certain suffering and doom.

By joining the Western Literacy Institute—an association devoted to building a system of superior public schools in Ohio—McGuffey became friends with Lyman Beecher, a prominent nineteenth century minister, and his daughter, Harriet Beecher Stowe, author of the controversial Uncle Tom's Cabin. The result? In 1836, he published the first McGuffey Eclectic Reader. The rest, as they say, is history.

Next to the Bible and Webster's Dictionaries, the McGuffey Readers have been read by more Americans than any other book. His self-help tomes conveyed solid Yankee values: patriotism, individualism, morality, and piety. McGuffey feared that materialism, minus these key elements, would lead to barbarous secularism, debauchery, and eternal condemnation. The early success of his readers was based upon the promises that interventions could stem the forces of darkness and economic servitude. He rejected notions of Calvinistic predestination and the elect.

McGuffey had a mission to reconcile the needs of civil society and the requisites of religion. He seamlessly and fortuitously used focus groups of children to determine their interest level and reactions towards selections in his constantly revised series. Belief that children and common schools would lead to expanded boundaries of democracy motivated McGuffey to spread the word. Namely, that an educated man could not only save his immortal soul but could become a model citizen as well.

McGuffey spread this mantra during his terms at Cincinnati College, Ohio University, and the University of Virginia. Representative of his era, both the man and his readers were resolutely self-righteous and oozing moral rectitude. Although McGuffey steered clear of the abolitionist movement, national politics, women's suffrage, and growing liberalism, he remained immensely popular. Why? He unrelentingly emphasized the importance of personal character. Once acquired, he felt one could be both enriched in the temporal world and rewarded with heavenly favor. McGuffey was a self-appointed steward of morality and made no apologies for his championing a better way of life. It was his duty. His texts popularized his personal credo that property and sanctitude were cornerstones of American society. He galvanized fundamental Christian tenets into powerful social forces. One could self-determine, by judicious exercising of free will and good conscience, one's destiny.

Obedience, hard work, honesty, sobriety, a sense of obligation, "right living', industriousness, self-reliance, fear of God, love of country, and social obligation wedded Christian beliefs to the emerging bourgeois society. The readers were efficient, entertaining, and didactic vehicles. Their cargo? Homogenized culture and palatable parables. From the Great Lakes, west to the Dakotas, and down to the Gulf of Mexico, the readers' religious and moral conservatism struck a chord in an expansive nation. McGuffey, like fellow Ohioan, John Chapman, better known as Johnny Appleseed, literally became a pied piper. He sold an elixir for self-improvement.

McGuffey portrayed America through a rose-colored lens. Nasty tensions between immigrant groups, rich vs. poor, Protestants vs. Catholics, workers vs. managers, and urban vs. rural interests were little alluded to in his offerings. However, McGuffey did advance the premises that Native Americans should be dealt with in a kindly fashion, that women needed to be educated, and that nature was not to be merely subdued but rather managed responsibly. The readers artfully reconciled the hard-driving American market economy and individuals' needs and aspirations in a noble attempt to forestall a rapacious national implosion.

The McGuffey Eclectic Readers totaled seven, including a primer. By the 1879 edition, they included more humor, drama, and selections from "great authors". The aim was to infuse "high" culture, arts, and literature into those seeking admittance into the middle class. McGuffey, like his peers, strongly believed that education bred gentility. Once possessed, status and power, in addition to common sense and virtue, would follow. In this worldview, both society and the individual were beneficiaries. Refinement and inner cultivation all became integral parts of America's social structure. McGuffey made it all available in carefully prescribed lessons.

McGuffey employed word lists, grammar, memorizing, reciting, crude phonics, and closed-ended questions as pedagogical techniques. Bible tracts, excerpts from Shakespeare and Edgar Allan Poe, poetry, speeches, and short biographies, along with elocution instructions also were utilized, with directions given for both student and instructor. All were marshaled in McGuffey's attempt to give students a lingua franca for life. Those who meticulously used the readers invariably were improved in some way. For McGuffey, this was the aim of his publications. To his death, he remained adamant that one could overcome all obstacles. His pioneer childhood days had taught him well.

Although we know well that McGuffey's America was fractured, the myth of pastoral unity still prevails when we speak of early America. Victorian culture enthusiastically embraced McGuffey's themes. He standardized and sanitized mores and traditions. The readers in effect were literally snapshots of the times they helped to mold. Actually, they were a wish list of how some thought everyone should act and live. As a road map for success, they were unrivaled in their influence. Ironically, McGuffey was not enriched financially by his prodigious toil. Towards the end of his life, his only royalty was a couple of hams per year. His younger brother, Alexander McGuffey, continued revising the anthology series for a variety of publishers, allowing McGuffey the freedom to pursue a variety of interests.

Exact figures of sales are unavailable. Fifty million copies sold are considered by many to be a viable number. Like the Bible, the leather-bounded readers were handed down within families and schools and were used in churches as well. Henry Ford referred to the readers as his alma mater; he paid for the 1857 reprinting. This captain of industry and proponent of mass-production ironically was enamored with and sustained by an idealized vision of a bucolic America, which never really existed in the large urban areas he helped to transform. Despite Ford's delusion, to McGuffey he owed his achievement. America was radically changed as a result.

Clarence Darrow, raised outside of Youngstown, in the nearby village of Kinsman, Ohio, was also a student of the indefatigable readers. He attributed to them solid morality tales, all of which formed his imposing personality, both inside and outside of the courtroom. Like other admirers of the readers, President Harry S. Truman praised McGuffey's stress of ethics. The readers, it would seem, expressed heartfelt sentiments of a people building a new culture out of the wilderness. Like invisible glue, the McGuffey's compilations helped cement an American ethos.

Although the readers have never gone out of print and sold 150,000 in 1980, they are now viewed as cultural curiosities and historical artifacts. Still used in rural and Bible-belt Southern school districts, Amish schoolhouses, Sunday schools, and mission programs, they have long ago ceded leadership to modern specialized texts. No longer can one find a series like McGuffey's, which attempted to educate mind, body, and spirit. For those over the age of sixty, the name McGuffey is easily recognized and much admired. Despite his critics, McGuffey long ago became synonymous with the hope of Americana. He helped millions realize the classic American dream.

As I re-discovered my hometown in my post-collegiate years, I joined the local William Holmes McGuffey Historical Society. It is the sole surviving chapter of the National Federation of McGuffey Societies, which was once 100,000 strong. I have been president of the society for the last five years. During my tenure, I have become friends with three direct descendents of the famed schoolmaster. Recently, I was able to purchase the remnants of the McGuffey family archives—Henry Ford persuaded one of our McGuffey members to donate the bulk to his Michigan museum—and have arranged for never before seen letters in McGuffey's handwriting to be catalogued. They will be put on display in a new metropolitan park's visitors and education center, where the archives will reside. Echoes from the past, some call them.

The path the McGuffey children took to school is now called McGuffey Road. One has to travel through a cheerless ghetto and past a state-of-the-art prison to reach the McGuffey home site. There, one can see the drumlin, an unusual depository of glacial rock on a plain, which the McGuffey family used as an Indian lookout. This serene seventy-eight acres of pastures and woods, renamed the McGuffey Wildlife Preserve, was deeded in 1998 to a local park district by my historical society in memory of our native son. Occasional visitors make a pilgrimage to this property, which was dedicated in 1966 as a Registered National Historical Landmark by the United States Department of the Interior National Park Service. This small tribute for an American legend survives in a world McGuffey would scarcely recognize.

McGuffey's belief in literacy as a change agent has been sustained. Today, the acquisition of an education is portrayed by many as a magical cure for societal ills and inequalities. When I piloted a character based storytelling program, using excerpts and adaptations from the McGuffey Eclectic Readers, both streetwise urban and sophisticated suburban children responded enthusiastically. Who would have guessed McGuffey's approbation of Twinkle Twinkle Little Star would still gladden hearts after all these years? McGuffey knew everyone enjoys a good story. He also knew hope was the opposite of despair. His mother would be proud.

Interdependence of Local Communities Based in History

by Richard S. Scarsella

Metropolitan Youngstown comprises many communities. Villages, towns, townships, and small cities are all in the orbit of the Youngstown-Warren census district. Many folks wrongly assume that outer and inner suburbs were once totally independent of the industrial corridor, which Youngstown anchors on the Mahoning River.

Boardman, Poland, Canfield, and Austintown residents routinely traveled to Youngstown for a myriad reasons. There were services and attractions that the central city offered that could not be found outside of its borders.

Many youth of yesteryear looked forward to a day at the Youngstown Y.M.C.A. and Y.W.C.A., which were located one block from each other. Indoor pools, courts, clinics, and leagues attracted youngsters, teens, and young adults from many miles around. These venerable institutions not only promoted strong civic and moral values and sportsmanship, but also nurtured friendships amongst children and adults in Boardman, Poland, Canfield, and Austintown, many of which endure today.

The "big city" of Youngstown once boasted a full slate of entertainment establishments. For a long time, one had to go to downtown Youngstown to attend a first run Hollywood or foreign film release. Matinees were favorites of patrons living in the "outskirts", which Boardman, Poland, Canfield, and Austintown were once named. Why? Suburban viewers liked to be home before dark since the roads leading out of Youngstown were not well lit in the evenings and night driving could be hazardous.

When Boardman, Poland, Canfield, and Austintown were agricultural and raw material producers, going "to town" was once considered quite a big deal. Through the 1960's, rural intrepid travelers "dressed up" in their Sunday clothes, so they would not stand out as non-urbanites on downtown Youngstown sidewalks. City denizens once had the idea that those living outside of Youngstown were less sophisticated than themselves.

Youngstown College, founded in the Y.M.C.A. building, and later renamed Youngstown University, drew many students from the county environs. Fraternities, sororities, and service clubs all had membership from families across the Mahoning watershed. Social events were magnets for huge crowds and were indeed "mixers." Attending an institute of higher learning in the heart of an infamous city was considered both an adventure and a necessity for those enrolled. Many prejudices towards the city were challenged by those coming to town regularly. "Little Chicago", as Youngstown was once known, had many attributes that those living elsewhere could not fathom.

Old Youngstown was once home to numerous splendid ethnic neighborhoods, dynamic houses of worship, progressive schools, cultural landmarks, and almost endless career opportunities. Many Boardman, Poland, Canfield, and Austintown workers made their "marks", honed their professions, and gained job experiences in Youngstown. Later, they used the same in their native stomping grounds.

Youngstown State University, the Youngstown Symphony Center, Stambaugh Auditorium, and the Youngstown Playhouse, to name a few, still are patronized by populations living over the "city line." The Mahoning County Courthouse, mass transit, and highway systems all connect and interconnect Youngstown to Boardman, Poland, Canfield, and Austintown seamlessly.

Of course, memories are the invisible glue in any civilization. Collective remembrances of "hard times" and better days live on wherever we reside. Idyllic picnics on the shores of Mill Creek Park's Lake Glacier or leisurely walking the colorful midway of beloved Idora Park are shared experiences which unite us in spite of our differences or where we call home.

Mahoning Valley contains a wide diversity of customs, beliefs, and commonwealths. Like it or not, we have all had a direct or indirect impact on each other's lives.

History does not unfold in a vacuum.

Intermigration of Mahoning Valley Has Long History

by Richard S. Scarsella

There is an old adage that all roads led to Rome. In the Mahoning Valley, it was once said that all roads led to Youngstown, the county seat. This was of course an exaggeration. However, it had a ring of truth. Why? Many necessities of life could be found and found cheaply in downtown Youngstown.

Residents of Boardman, Poland, Canfield, and Austintown routinely traveled to "the big city" for personal, business, and government reasons. Youngstown offered a huge selection of items, values, and novelties not found in their own stomping grounds. City folks journeyed to the "outskirts", as these rural communities were named, for seasonal produce, farm-fed meat, fuel, Christmas trees, and hand-made crafts. This intermigration of disparate populations oftentimes led to the development of deep friendships, marriages, and relocations of whole clans.

Citizens of the inner suburbs had easy access to the dirty, busy, and colorful Youngstown. Greyhound metro liner buses once stopped along country roads and delivered passengers from the outlying areas to the hub of the Youngstown shopping district. Inner-city trolley lines extended throughout the environs and allowed rural consumers to patronize vendors regularly without losing a whole day when "doing business".

Farmers from surrounding communities once earned dependable extra income by bringing fruits, vegetables, and dressed meat to the legendary Pyatt Street Market on Youngstown's south side. This open-air market, replete with sawdust on the ground and poultry in cages, advertised "right from the farm" food to city denizens. Urbanites "went to market" several times a week in search of natural grown food. Displayers, once paid, would many times buy furniture, appliances, or hardware with their proceeds and load the same on the beds of their trucks before they headed across the city limits.

Boardman, Poland, Canfield, and Austintown families enjoyed "going to town" to purchase special things. Brides to be were enamored with the posh bridal salons located in Strouss', McKelvey's, and Livingston's department stores. New York designer gowns were displayed with oriental rugs, velvet wallpaper, and crystal chandeliers as backdrops. Grooms to be were dazzled and well treated by the old world diamond jewelers of Federal Street. Convenient lay-a-way plans made payments affordable. Newlyweds trekked to the mortgage departments of Youngstown's commercial banks and savings and loan institutions. Headquartered in skyscrapers, these venerable financial concerns tailored credit for agrarian borrowers, mindful of the fact that harvests were at the whims of Mother Nature. Fred Evereth Furrier catered to those "that had made it". Those owning vast spreads were considered a local version of landed gentry. In search of estate quality fur, large landowners selected "sensible" fur for warmth and not flash.

Many provincial inhabitants were intimidated or repulsed by the noise, grit, and pace of industrial Youngstown. Some chose to take their business elsewhere, at times. Poland shoppers favored nearby New Castle, Pennsylvania. This sister city of Youngstown was nestled in the rolling foothills of the Appalachian Mountains. Troutman's, an affordable family friendly emporium, was a popular destination. The absence of a clothing tax appealed to those whom valued thrift.

Boardmanites were drawn to the scenic village of Columbiana. It's cinema, banks, car and tractor dealerships, and feed and seed supply stores were "just down the road" for those not fond of large cities. The Harvey Firestone Experimental Farm attracted many growers to this area. Many would "make a day of it" and walk around the Columbiana rotary for a stroll, after eating at one of the storefront eateries.

Canfield customers oftentimes headed out to Route 62 and gave their business to Alliance merchants. This bucolic college town, with tree-lined streets, gated yards, and Western Reserve architecture, appealed to those that sought a leisure day of window-shopping. Alliance was a veritable intellectual enclave amidst fields of grain and was as welcoming as Youngstown was not.

Austintown purchasers liked "to do business" in historic Niles, Ohio. Home to the impressive President William McKinley Museum, this small city had a disarming urban aura that townships did not possess. Horse trades could be made in the shadow of the National Historic Landmark named after the slain president. First-run films played at the Robbins Theatre, for the pleasure of viewers wanting to "catch a matinee" before heading home.

It's true; there has always been an uneasy relationship between Youngstown and its neighbors. The fast paced, impersonal, and multi-cultural metropolitan

Youngstown seemed alien to the more conservative populations of Boardman, Poland, Canfield, and Austintown. Yet, scions of both agricultural and cosmopolitan families intermarried, prospered, and re-established themselves in non-native locales, much to the alarm and astonishment of previous generations.

Our non-descript strip plazas and mall culture has not eliminated a collective nostalgia for days of old. Even now, when I venture out to buy something, I can vividly recall fleeting images of how things once were on "shopping days". These warm memories make today's shopping experiences bearable.

Ironically, Youngstowners now find themselves heading out of town to suburban retail and professional centers. The faded city now beckons out-of-towners with culture, higher education, and entertainment not found elsewhere. Intermigration continues.

Isaly's and Me

by Richard S. Scarsella

Long time valley residents can easily remember the once ubiquitous dairy stores named Isaly's. These white facaded shops, with elegant black italic signs and butcher paper window signs proclaiming specials of the day, were forerunners of today's convenience marts. We patronized them for many reasons. They are still missed today.

Isaly's ice cream was advertised as "dairy fresh". And it was, made from the milk of local farms. Area farmers sold their milk exclusively to Isaly's and had to meet high standards to do so. Before the days of dependable refrigeration, out of town frozen confections oftentimes melted or suffered freezer burn while in transit to Youngstown. Therefore, Isaly's had a captive market and expanded aggressively to nearby Pittsburgh, Canton, and Akron. At its peak, Isaly's operated 396 stores. This was a far cry from the modest 1902 beginnings of founder William Isaly who first opened a plant in Mansfield.

Morning milk and cream deliveries to the home cemented our loyalty to the Youngstown plant, first opened in 1918. The sounds of jingling glass bottles being placed into milk boxes on our front porches throughout the city was a common daily ritual. The Isaly's milkman was a trusted family friend and very much a part of our neighborhoods.

Although many families were suspicious of "store bought" ice cream, Isaly's became a local legend. It combined old-fashioned ingredients with state-of-the-art technology to bring us quality products at affordable prices. Kids loved the skyscraper cones, which gave the illusion of more product for a nickel than conventional scoop cones. A rainbow skyscraper cone, which included a medley of colorful flavors, was a hometown favorite not found elsewhere. Savoring an Isaly's block of ice cream at the holidays, with a Christmas tree or pumpkin in the middle of a slice, was an indescribable treat no longer found.

Isaly's specialized in creamy shakes, thick malts, phosphate sodas, and root beer floats. No one in town had the range of flavors and toppings that Isaly's featured. The Whitehouse sundae, topped with genuine whipped cream, freshly chopped nuts, real chocolate syrup, and Maraschino cherries was the choice of children, teenagers, and grandparents alike. Isaly's bridged the generation gap and gave great pleasure at "popular prices".

Lunch counters at Isaly's were social magnets for different parts of town. Having a cup of percolator coffee, dipping a freshly fried doughnut, eating pie a-la-mode, or snacking on a grilled cheese sandwich while sitting on a revolving red leather stool at a chrome horseshoe shaped counter was a right of passage for us all. The jukebox at Isaly's could also be counted on to have the newest "top 40" records available for listening. The cost? Three plays for a quarter.

When I think back to the hundreds of times I bought chipped chopped ham, the Vindicator, a loaf of bread, penny candy, a quart of ice cream for twenty five cents, or a Klondike bar at these now vanished landmarks, I shake my head in wonderment. The long fadeout of Isaly's in the 1970's seems unreal. To this day one can still see an occasional storefront with the sun-damaged name Isaly's painted on it. These pathetic reminders of a once proud dairy dynasty serve as milestones for a world rapidly disappearing in front of our disbelieving eyes.

Die-hard Isaly's fans still curse the day in 1969 when it was announced the Mahoning Avenue plant would cease to make ice cream. The later abandonment of the architecturally elegant Art Deco signature regional office, complete with penthouse apartment and auditorium, was yet another dark day in local history.

When I travel east on Mahoning Avenue over the Mill Creek Park Bridge that intersects with Glenwood Avenue, it's comforting to view the old Isaly's complex. At dusk, when the lengthening shadows swallow the receding light, the outline of this cherished trademark seems timeless and mute. It nobly stands as a silent sentinel to an era in our lives irrevocably lost. Memories can truly break your heart.

For more information about Isaly's, refer to "Klondikes, Chipped Ham & Skyscraper Cones: The Story of Isaly's" by Brian Butko)

Isaly's Neighborhood Memories

by Richard S. Scarsella

For generations, Mahoning Valley residents enjoyed frozen confections from a legendary company that produced and distributed them locally. The name? Isaly's.

With a corporate office at the intersection of Mahoning Avenue and Glenwood Avenue, Isaly's was unmatched in its offering of sundaes, banana splits, shakes, malts, and cones. Its signature skyscraper cone endeared Isaly's to every child in town. Available in standard cup or sugar cone, the skyscraper was a long, tapered, pointed sword of high butterfat ice cream. Favorite flavors included banana and Whitehouse.

The Isaly's headquarters was a striking art-deco complex, complete with a semi-circular tower. Inside, one could find state-of-the-art mixers, coolers, and freezers, as well as a Radio City Music Hall styled auditorium. Isaly family members lived high atop the complex, in a penthouse apartment. From its terrace, one could see a stunning panoramic view of Mill Creek Park or an eye-opening vista of the Mahoning Valley industrial hearth.

Area inhabitants could always depend on a neighborhood Isaly's dairy store for glass bottles of milk or juice, quarts and half gallons of ice cream, and a variety of deli meats. Only Isaly's and drugstores were open on Sundays for many years. Therefore, Isaly's became a natural gathering spot for neighbors and gossips.

Isaly's was a big part of our lives. In the wee hours, Isaly dairy trucks used to cruise neighborhoods daily, delivering milk, cream, butter, and ice cream to doorsteps.

Patrons regularly perched at Isaly coffee counters, sipping freshly ground coffee and munching on deep fried donuts. Isaly's was a place to pick up a newspaper or buy a loaf of locally made bread. Riding your Schwinn bike to Isaly's to buy penny candy was a sure sign of growing up. Drinking a phosphate, with a date, while playing the jukebox, was a virtual rite of passage for teenagers at Isaly's.

Isaly's could not meet the crushing competition of out-of-town national dairy plants or chain food stores. Slowly, Isaly's began to shutter its distinctive shops. Eventually, it closed its home office and licensed out its name. Sadly, the Isaly's logo was taken down from its main office building, plants, and retailers.

Like Strouss', McKelvey's, Lustig's, Livingston's, Hartzell's, and many others, Isaly's name passed into local history. Its legacy? Full stomachs, good feelings, and priceless memories.

John Kennedy, Jr.: A Profile in History

by Richard S. Scarsella

The immense national, grim fascination riveted upon the John F. Kennedy, Jr. disappearance and death is remarkable. Why? The pull of history still grips a very ahistorical, supposedly modern nation. Like Greek gods of old, the young Kennedy was a mirror of the past and future.

This paradox of contemporary America is graphic evidence that history still matters in our lives. The Kennedy clan of Boston has long been our national royalty. Ambition, power, fortune, fame, scandal, glamour, and tragedy—lots of tragedy—have all been part of the Kennedy heritage. And ours. The assassination of iconic President John F. Kennedy in 1963, on television, was a wake up call for our innocent nation that prosperity could not insulate anyone from the forces of fate. As in empires of antiquity, death would forever shape history, as the Kennedy family proved many times.

The Kennedys evoke a Shakespearean tale, with a distinctive American twist. Joseph Kennedy, Sr. was a archetypal self-made first generation business tycoon. His rags-to-riches dynasty was passed onto his sons. Public service was the fullest expression demanded of a Kennedy. President John Kennedy picked up the torch of leadership. His short life was remembered best by his visions for a dynamic country, his challenge of a moon space program, his gracious, fashionable wife, Jacqueline, and the promise of his children.

Even though Senator Robert Kennedy was slain and Senator Ted Kennedy was mortally disgraced, America always felt that some part of the Kennedy Camelot magic still lived on in President John F. Kennedy's son. His scion was a living link to an American golden age of possibility, before the bleakness of Viet Nam and Watergate blighted the nationscape. We all hoped that the alleged Kennedy family curse would not touch this gilded successor.

John Kennedy, Jr. was enigmatic and embodied the dash, dare, intelligence, and charisma of his matinee-idol like father. He also personified the elegant, decorous, cosmopolitan, sensitive nature of his statuesque mother. Born in Washington, D.C., with roots in Boston, he lived in Greece, with his stepfather Aristotle Onassis, and in New York City, with his mother and sister Caroline. As a thirty-something new husband, he and his wife, Carolyn, settled into the Empire City as young professionals. America's "sexiest man alive" and "most eligible bachelor" transitioned into adult life with the world as his oyster. He had not yet claimed his legacy.

John Kennedy, Jr.'s founding of a politically irreverent magazine called "George" was seen to many as a testing, and a tease, of the political waters. Democrats dreamed of and Republicans dreaded the advent of the "crown prince" making a run for the presidency. At age 38, this Kennedy commanded almost mythic attention from admirers and the media alike. Lionized by the press, yet very down to earth, he was a celebrity of merit, humor, talent, reserve, tradition, and great potential. Jackie was rightfully proud of her prodigy. Truly, he was his father's son, America's heir apparent.

Students of history will confirm that one person, in the right time and in the right place, can define an era. Napoleon, Churchill, Hitler, and Franklin Roosevelt are all evidence of how an individual can singularly shape a nation's fortune. The pages of history are full of the exploits of bigger than life figures. John Jr. seemed destined for some type of greatness.

John Jr. now belongs to the pantheon of greats and near greats. Like Princess Diana, he will live on in celluloid and in print. He will be larger in death, like James Dean, Elvis Presley and Marilyn Monroe, than in life. Taken from us at his prime—like his father—we will always wonder what could have been, had he lived. The political and national arena are much poorer for his untimely exit. His sudden, violent departure leaves a giant wound in the nation's psyche. He epitomizes a type of American tragedy.

Perhaps, Caroline Kennedy or one of her children will continue the Kennedy mystique. This is doubtful. At long last, the endearing Kennedy saga may be nearing its end. Without a strong Kennedy contender in our midst to anchor us, we will look back wistfully and painfully at the melodramatic Kennedy years. History will treat "John John" kindly. This is little consolation for a fallen star. Like his father, John Kennedy Jr. now belongs to the ages. History marches on.

Labor Day Facts

by Richard S. Scarsella

President Grover Cleveland, in 1894, signed a bill, creating a national Labor Day, six days after the Pullman Car strike was broken by federal troops.

Skeptics viewed the creation of Labor Day, by President Grover Cleveland, as an election year move. He lost the election.

There is still doubt as to who proposed Labor Day first. Both Peter McGuire, Secretary of the Brotherhood of Carpenters and Joiners and Matthew Maguire, of the Internal Association of Machinists, have been credited with the concept of a workingman's holiday.

New York City celebrated the first Labor Day in 1882.

Labor Day is always observed on the first Monday in September.

Summer does not end on Labor Day. It ends on Sept. 22. Most summer resorts close their doors after Labor Day.

Labor Day was once celebrated with parades, speeches, picnics, contests and fireworks in all American villages, towns and cities.

The Sunday before Labor Day was once called Labor Sunday. It was reserved for spiritual and educational labor movement expressions.

Union members once marched, hand in hand, in the streets, on Labor Day, wearing banners and holding placards and American flags, to show their "solidarity".

Labor Day is one of the few national holidays not connected with war or conquest.

Labor Day is seen as the penultimate display of American workers' contribution to national well-being, prosperity, strength and democratic ideals.

In Europe, May Day has taken on the characteristics of the American Labor Day.

In the 1950's, almost 50% of American workers were unionized. In 1995, less than 15% are card-carrying members.

Unions are increasingly trying to get more of the service industry workers to unionize.

Lake Erie Recollections

by Richard S. Scarsella

In years past, valley residents looked north to escape the steamy, smoky, acrid, gritty, smog-filled summer air. Their favorite destination? Lake Erie.

Before Lake Erie became the object of national pollution jokes on the Johnny Carson Tonight Show, Geneva-On-The-Lake, Ohio was a veritable summer mecca for Youngstown natives. Steel executives, retail merchants, professionals of all kinds and union men all were attracted to this slice of Coney Island—Ohio style.

Why? Geneva was a casual, family orientated, wholesome Mid-Western resort that was both affordable and accessible. Fudge shops and donut stands catered to vacationers, hungry for a summer treat. Genuine salt-water taffy, available in many flavors and colors, echoed Atlantic City, as did the sanitized Geneva Burlesque Theater, which featured swimsuit competitions. Geneva's fresh egg and cream custard, made with natural ingredients from shoreline farms, delighted children, as they licked their sugarcanes, while watching the brilliant Lake Erie sunsets.

Parents would sip vintage wine, made from now famous Erie concord grapes, as they watched the tide go out. Teenagers preferred sugary, fried elephant ears and NeHi pop, as they flirted in the pinball machine arcades. Senior citizens would nurse freshly squeezed lemonades, while fireflies flitted over their benches.

Long before McDonald's was originated, Eddie's Grille—still open—flipped steak burgers and served foot long hot dogs, until they became a summer ritual. Seafood restaurants all featured "fresh white perch" platters. For dessert, strawberries, hand dipped in milk chocolate, satisfied one's appetite. Toasted marshmallows over bonfires ended many a summer evening.

Youngstowners found Erieview Park a miniature Idora Park on the beach, complete with ballroom. Still surviving, it evokes the spirit of turn-of-the-century parks, which have become symbols in time of a slower paced, innocent era. Ravaged in the late 1960's and 1970's by changing tastes, motorcycle gangs, rebellious youth and increasing water pollution, Geneva dimmed in popularity.

Surprisingly, Lake Erie has gradually become cleaner. Both fishing and tourism have revived. The result? New generations of sun worshippers have rediscovered Geneva-On-The-Lake.

Modern condominiums now dot the sand dunes, alongside Art Deco "motor lodges". New marinas attract yuppies—and their money. Imported European sedans park next to Chrysler vans. Kids and adults alike snack on penny candy and bottled water. Interestingly, all visitors become enraptured by the wail of seagulls, the smell of crisp, moist Canadian air and the sight of a foggy, misty, primordial Lake Erie.

Lamentations

by Richard S. Scarsella

In years gone by, there was always a group of folks fixated upon grief, sorrow, or regret. They expressed heartfelt hurt or disappointment concerning things and events that had irrevocably transpired.

Through the 1960's, the World War I generation oftentimes bitterly discoursed about "The Great War". Lost husbands, fathers, brothers, and sons were mourned daily with tributes of prayers, flowers put upon graves, and public memorials of all sorts. Many still felt the Americans should not have fought in this European war to the death.

The flu epidemic that swept across the heartland during the war years seemed by many to be an omen that Americans should refrain from foreign entanglements, despite President Woodrow Wilson's crusade to "Make the world safe for democracy."

Those that survived the wretched Depression and the ensuing cataclysmic World War II were even more morose. Lost fortunes, broken families, ethnic animosities, and prematurely ended lives left scars that never completely healed. Veterans did not regret defending their nation but regretted their lost of innocence. Parades were gilded affairs that concealed the horrors endured by both combatants and survivors. Stony faces that lined the parade route were mute testimonials to the appalling cost paid.

When the American dream became harder to obtain, blue-collar working class families looked wistfully back to simpler times when a high school diploma was not needed to earn a decent living. Modernization, mechanization, standardization, and international competition were dirges for this backbone of America. It came to past that honest hard labor was no longer enough to get and keep a living wage, despite union protections and concessions. This implacable reality cast a pall over industrial communities and shows no sign of lifting.

Church groups always had a portion of their congregations bewailing the hand of death and the misfortunes it brought. Bereavement committees were trained to offer aid and solace in times of grief. Vigils sought to grapple with the immutable.

Ensuing fellowship acted as salves. Rituals gave some level of comfort for those bemoaning their fates.

Today's culture is decidedly upbeat. Those focusing upon death, ill fortune, plague, or war are considered eccentric. Such topics are now the province of the media. America has become a civilization hell-bent upon securing wealth, health, youth, happiness, and hedonism. Attendance at parades is down. Veteran groups are dwindling in numbers. Regular church participation has tapered off. Even cemeteries show signs of neglect. The younger generations do not fret over the past as their elders once did. To do so is considered morbid.

Few could identify with memories of black clad widows riding public transit buses with purple funeral wreaths and diminutive commemorative American flags in their hands covered with cloth gloves. These silent vigil-keepers would murmur softly the names of their beloved in soft sighs. Decorating the graves was both a private and public gesture of reverence. Graveyards were places of great lamentations. Relief could not be found within the gates. Plaintive cries could not be muffled.

Memories keep yesteryears alive, like it or not. Those that believe otherwise are oftentimes haunted by that which they hope to forget.

Land of Promise

by Richard S. Scarsella

The Mahoning Valley is rich in varied history. Sagas of pioneers settling untamed terra firma still survive. Some of the early settlements founded two centuries ago are now in eclipse. Others still shine with vigor. History does not stand still.

Elijah Boardman, born of sturdy Yankee stock, ventured forth from austere Connecticut into the rugged Western Reserve Territory and purchased acreage in 1798. Easterners were both alarmed by and captivated with the primitive environs in the Native American ancestral haunts west of the Appalachian Mountains. Mr. Boardman and company were "fortune seekers" willing to migrate and take risks. What they found was almost biblical.

Old growth forests and fields of fragrant wild flowers were truly mesmerizing. White-tailed deer and web-footed beavers were plentiful. Cardinals, blue jays, and meadowlarks were commonplace. Stealthy cougars and diminutive rattlesnakes were dreaded. These characteristics were apt descriptors for a land of promise named Boardman, Ohio.

Today, this bedroom community of Youngstown bears little resemblance to a frontier commonwealth. Vestiges of its Eden-like origins remain. Mill Creek Park and Boardman Park are enclaves of nature amidst a veritable concrete maze of housing developments and commercial strips. Perennially popular, these near pristine preserves speak to our longings for the unadulterated roots of a once agrarian-based culture.

Many still remember vast verdant farms and gentile country estates in the Boardman of yore. There was a time when Boardman rivaled other rural districts in the production of fruits, vegetables, and lumber. Indeed, city folks from Youngstown oftentimes went for "rides in the country" in search of ripe produce, fresh-dressed meats, and handmade crafts. In fact, the famed Pyatt Street Market on Youngstown's lower south side once featured many Boardman vendors hawking their wares at open air displays several days a week.

Few speak of the tribes of Native Americans, which once called Boardman their own. The Mahoning Valley was considered neutral hunting and foraging grounds by the indigenous people. Salt was a big draw and highly prized by both the so-called "reedmen" and the white interlopers.

Generations of Boardman boys and girls sought and found Indian projectile points (arrowheads) in the many streams and woods, which traversed the township. Boy Scouts, Girl Scouts, Cub Scouts, and Camp Fire troops all retold ancient Native American tales about the much-maligned Boardman forerunners. Sadly, this heritage is endangered by a modern society, which gives scant attention to its forbears.

To this day, an exodus from Youngstown heads south towards Boardman in search of a better life. The allure? Well-kept neighborhoods, effective schools, low crime rates, and a range of stores unparalleled in the metropolitan area. Ironically, as the population of Boardman grows its desirability begins to wane. Calls for planned growth and conservation requirements strike many as being restrictive, unnecessary, and anti-business.

Some old-timers still think of Boardman as a bucolic rural haven situated atop a dirty smoky industrial river valley corridor. To them, the mall, shopping plazas, franchise restaurants, apartment complexes, and Route 224 traffic snarls still seem unreal. In their homes and in their memories they seek solace. What do they yearn for? A more unspoiled realm where the pace of life is pastoral, where nature is abundant, and where cardinals are a common sight.

The Native American influence still lingers after all.

Legacy

by Richard S. Scarsella

Unbeknownst to most area residents, a local man literally changed the course of American social and cultural history. A scion of the gritty steel valley and surrounding picturesque farmland, this singular man of accomplishment embodied the American dream. His mission? To spread a recipe for self-betterment. His name? William Holmes McGuffey. His creation? The McGuffey Eclectic Readers.

Born across the Pennsylvania line, in nearby Washington County, he moved in 1802 at age two to Youngstown's east side. His pioneer family homesteaded over seventy-eight acres in Coitsville Township. Here his mother taught him Bible lessons at her knee by candlelight. His father, being an outdoorsman, shared his love for nature with the precocious boy. The result? A youth captivated by "right" living and respect for mother earth.

Being born, reared, and educated west of the Appalachia Mountains allowed McGuffey to evolve into a polished Western American man of letters. His down to earth tales of good and evil, right and wrong, and love of family and country made him the number one purveyor of self-instruction textbooks. To date, he has never been rivaled.

McGuffey's anthology series, an early predecessor of Readers Digest magazine and G.E.D. programs, consisted of six readers and one primer. Native-born farmers and hordes of immigrants relied on these basal tomes for the 3 R's of reading, writing, and arithmetic. However, these venerable tracts encompassed much more than academic instruction. They offered hope for a better life here on earth and in the afterlife. And this precious ingredient insured their success and endeared them to generations.

Soundly rooted in the rich Judeo-Christian traditions, the Eclectic Readers advocated the benefits of an organized, disciplined, God-fearing society, grounded upon strong family units. Although his reliance on the Bible was representative of his times, these books encompassed the best of western civilization literature. This accounts for their incredible popularity between 1836, when first published, until the early 1950's. Americans, then and now, were not satisfied with material things alone. McGuffey knew this intuitively. His selections from Shakespeare and writers such as Bret Harte nourished the mind and spirit. His success was based upon the wisdom of the ages that the total man must be educated for life as well as for death.

McGuffey was both a teacher in one-room schoolhouses and at prestigious universities. An ordained Presbyterian minister, he preached in clapboard barns and in gothic college chapels. Once known as "the schoolmaster of the nation", Ivy League East Coast universities and a secularized press have overlooked his prominence. Although tens of millions of Americans were educated by the famed Eclectic Readers, McGuffey has never been honored with his image on a stamp. In his own hometown, no public or university edifice bears his name. No statue honors his memory.

However, his name and influence continue in the collective national consciousness. His readers have never gone out of print. Rural, Christian, Amish, and mission schools routinely utilize the McGuffey texts across varied subject areas. Urban school districts are rediscovering their use as historical, character building, value infused cultural representatives of another American era. When vocal education critics blast American public schools, one often hears the cry to, "Go back to the McGuffey Readers."

When I travel on McGuffey Road, past the McGuffey Plaza, to the Mill Creek Metroparks' McGuffey Wildlife Preserve, a national historical landmark, I oftentimes linger at the site of the McGuffey home site. This bucolic oasis amidst urban sprawl seems strangely out of place. The Native American lookout, high above the craggy glacial formation known as a drumlin, is eerily forbidding and tranquil. Like McGuffey's legacy, it too has stood the test of time.

Legends

by Richard S. Scarsella

America's old guard film royalty is slowing receding into the recesses of time. No one, it seems, escapes the grim reaper. Not even movie kings and queens get out of this life alive.

The recent passing of inimitable Loretta Young is a painful reminder that real life invades the magical realm of Hollywood and its glittering inhabitants. This stunning movie queen, who first performed in celluloid at age four in 1917, had a career like none other. She literally grew up in tinseltown. Unlike child prodigy Shirley Temple, she matured and prospered as an adult entertainer. The very mention of her name elicited the response "star" from throngs of admirers.

Best remembered for the wholesome movie "The Farmer's Daughter", she epitomized Yankee style, class, and grace. As the leading lady in "The Bishop's Wife", a 1947 tour de force with Cary Grant, she set a new standard for American feminine beauty, intelligence, and determination. Her portrayals opposite male matinee idols Clark Gable, Tyrone Power, Spencer Tracey, and Edward G. Robinson, made her a role model for millions of adoring fans. She personified a self-possessed woman in a man's world.

Unbeknownst to many now, she was the first trailblazing actress to win an Oscar and three Emmy awards. Her television performances from 1953-1962 made her a small screen pioneer, along with Donna Reed and Lucille Ball. Not content to bring glamour alone into American living rooms, she found a creative outlet by writing, producing, and directing television series. She was truly a master of several mediums.

The "Loretta Young Show" was a kinescope milestone. Not only did the show feature Ms. Young and other Hollywood greats, it popularized anthology series drama to middle America. Her show biz gimmick? Haute couture fashions. Post World War II and Korean War consumers were hungry for the "good life". Ms. Young obliged by dazzling audiences week after week with stunning Parisian, Italian, and New York designer fashions. Even on black and white television, her flowing strapless satin gowns, billowing chiffon skirts, and layered yards of taffeta and lace enthralled television viewers. Audiences tuned in to marvel custom made creations by Edith Head, Adrian, and Jean Louise. Critics sniped that her clothes outperformed the acting. She took no notice. She was one of the few Hollywood icons to make an elegant transition from the feature films to weekly broadcasting. She was instrumental in defining the new modern American "look".

Hollywood fan magazines created a whole industry by photographing, documenting, interviewing, and exposing Hollywood celebrities. Ms. Young was not to escape unscathed. Rumors that her adopted daughter was actually her "love child", courtesy of Clark Gable, made Ms. Young seem even more mysterious, unconventional, and trend-setting. She seemed above reproach and remained popular even in retirement.

Loretta Young's heyday was shared with legends Bette Davis, Joan Crawford, Marlene Dietrich, and Greta Garbo. Screen idols Marilyn Monroe, Sophia Loren, Elizabeth Taylor, and Bridgette Bardot were part of a later Hollywood era. Only Katherine Hepburn and Olivia de Havilland remain as archetypal representatives of a time when larger than life film stars dominated our lives.

As I think back to the many hours of enjoyment I have spent in darkened movie palaces watching double feature films, these legends all seem very much alive. I will never forget the effortless charm and allure Ms. Young debuted on the "big screen". When she was on television, watching her each week glide through double doors dressed as the classy, brilliant woman of accomplishment that she was, it was easy to understand how she transfixed a nation as the persona of the ultimate contemporary American woman. She seemed almost transcendent as the muse of poise, talent, and varied emotions. She will be greatly missed. She will never be replaced. Her legacy is insured. In death, as in life, she is enshrined in Americana.

The final curtain call for the golden age of Hollywood is upon us. Old television reruns and movie tapes keep the memories alive. It's time to say to Ms. Young what she once said to us each week at the conclusion of her show. Good night and God bless.

Life at the Movies

by Richard S. Scarsella

America is littered with the remains of long abandoned theaters. Once lavish downtown movie palaces share the same ignoble fate as intimate neighborhood cinemas. Such was not always the case. Until the 1960's, the picture shows enthralled audiences with lush, wide screen, bigger than life Technicolor motion pictures.

Hollywood films mass-produced by MGM, Paramount, Warner Brothers, Universal, Columbia, 20th Century-Fox, RKO Radio Pictures, and Republic studios molded American tastes, influenced politics, and nurtured mass media merchandising. Hometown theaters were either owned, operated, or supplies by these dream factories. The allure of "being discovered" and becoming a star became a fixture of American culture. Hollywood icons became America's royalty.

There was a time, not long ago, when attending a double matinee at the local bijou was a weekly occurrence for most Americans. Newsreels, documentaries (called "shorts"), and cartoons all were part of the admission ticket purchase. Pre-1950's movie halls even featured mighty Wurlitzer pipe organs played by organists. These behemoths could be heard in the lobbies and bellowed music scores from "hit" film presentations. The sound was deafening. We loved every minute of it.

In Youngstown, stepping from the busy, dirty, loud, hazy Federal Street into the elegant lobbies of the Palace, State, Warner, and Paramount theaters was a surreal encounter. These cavernous auditoriums boasted two and three balconies, marble and tile powder rooms, oak paneled and leather tufted gentlemen's lounges, cut glass Austrian chandeliers, and swaged velvet draperies. They literally transported one from the mundane to the magical. All of these centers of popular culture were shrines of Yankee entertainment and ballyhoo. They were as familiar to one as churches. In a real sense, these grand edifices were America's living rooms. More importantly, these celluloid paradises opened one's eyes to world few could imagine. One literally lived one's life at these playhouses.

In 1931, "City Lights" premiered, starring Charlie Chaplin. The lovable tramp reigned supreme. However, this was one of the last silent films produced. The "talkies" revolutionized tinsel town. Al Jolson's "The Jazz Singer" put talking films on the map. They soon dominated. The golden age of Hollywood spanned the 1930's and the 1940's. No one thought it would ever be eclipsed. Great urban theaters became monuments to our fixation with the silver screen.

New York's Radio City Music Hall, which seats 6,000, is probably the epitome of America's love affair with the movies. This spectacular art deco styled landmark, sculpted from chrome, glass, and gilded materials, is one of the few survivors of another era. Ironically, tourists from across the heartland fill its seats daily yearning for the full Hollywood experience. Film buffs agree. There is no substitute for viewing a movie in an oversized opulent setting.

The 1939 epic "Gone With The Wind" entranced crowds with wide screen lens tableaus of graphic Civil War battles, idealized Southern cotton plantation life, and tear-ringing melodrama. Scarlett O'Hara and Rhett Butler, portrayed by stunning Vivien Leigh and suave Clark Gable, made history come alive with period costumes, realistic sets, and authentic dialects. Re-releases of the film continued to have the same effect. The majesty of the big screen presentation still prevails, regardless of television.

When I see derelict theaters, I wince. They have a certain aura shared by no other structures. Within their crumbled walls, we once discovered fantasy, adventure, comedy, chivalry, war, love, death, and the eternal. Even when shuttered, deserted theaters still evoke vivid memories of what was, can be, should be, and will be. When a theater dies, a little of the Hollywood alchemy perishes as well.

Life Without Lucy

by Richard S. Scarsella

Television replaced movies as a family friend in the 1950's. No longer did you have to dress for the theater when craving entertainment. R.C.A., Zenith, Philco, Admiral, and Magnavox made televisions for every budget. The result? Matinee idols were replaced by television personalities in our lives.

Milton Berle was dubbed Mr. Television. His satire and cross-dressing all appealed to an increasingly sophisticated post W.W. II population. Ed Sullivan perfected the variety show format to an art form. This gawkish master of ceremonies presented animal acts, Las Vegas revues, ballet, rock and roll bands, and puppet theater. Elegant Loretta Young showcased her Hollywood allure on an anthology series that featured other former tinsel town idols from the golden age of the big screen. However, when Lucille Ball debuted in 1951 on the small screen once called kinescope, our lives would never be the same.

The "I Love Lucy Show" starred Lucille Ball and her real-life husband Desi Arnaz, known to viewers as Ricky Ricardo. Her Cuban born mate was the perfect foil for her domestic woes. Lucy's longings for a theatrical career, marital equality, and self-actualization all struck a cord with Cold War affluent audiences. She became more than a gifted comedic actress. Lucy Ricardo became a mirror of the times.

Conservative Americans were aghast when Lucy Ricardo, as she was known on the show, became visibly pregnant. Up until Lucy, network writers and commercial sponsors assiduously avoided pregnancy and childbirth. Lucy changed all this, when she gave birth to her son, Desi Arnaz, Jr., while filming the comedy. An episode dealing with the birth of her television son, Ricky Ricardo, Jr., coincided with the birth of her biological son. America became captivated with the first family of television.

Lucy's smoking of cigarettes and wearing pants on television helped liberate an entire generation of women from narrow stereotypical confines. Her admitting to being a registered member of the Communist Party in her youth did not end her popularity. Fans believed her when she claimed that she was never a practicing member and only joined briefly to satisfy her grandfather's wishes. A lesser star would have been banned from the airways. Lucy went on to star and produce several spin-offs of the "I Love Lucy Show" into the late 1980's.

Her divorce from skirt-chasing hard-drinking Desi Arnaz was a wake-up call. Apparently, television's ideal couple was unhappily married, despite incredible success and fame. Lucy left her husband of almost twenty years, instead of suffering in silence. Many condemned her for the act. Many others applauded her courage. She became a pioneer independent divorced professional female in a man's world.

Lucy's talents were many. A former showgirl and B movie contract player, she possessed vaudeville, burlesque, and legitimate theater skills. Her days on radio gave her impeccable timing, poise, and confidence. With Vivian Vance and William Frawley portraying neighbor Ethel and Fred Mertz in her original show, she brought a sense of family, neighborhood, and intimacy into our lives seemingly effortlessly.

Looking back, I can't imagine a life without Lucy. She always made you laugh. Both children and adults loved her crazy antics. Seen around the world in countless reruns throughout the years, it has been said that Lucille Ball's image has been on more screens than any other image. She is still popular today.

That's not bad for a girl from Jamestown, New York.

Life Without Perry Como

by Richard S. Scarsella

In the course of a lifetime, voices become very familiar. The utterances of reassuring grandparents, the stern admonishment of a robed cleric, the steady ticking of an heirloom grandfather clock, and the friendly bark of a neighborhood dog all are sounds that speak to us on some level. Only the intonations of our parents rivaled these everyday cadences.

The world of music and pop culture greatly influenced our lives. I can still hear radio emcee Arthur Godfrey and television variety host Ed Sullivan announce our favorite personalities. Frank Sinatra, Judy Garland, Dean Martin, Peggy Lee, Sammy Davis Jr., and Ella Fitzgerald, to name a few, were vocalists well known to us. They did not need introductions. They were all very much a part of our daily lives. Without fail, these talented idols entertained, invigorated, calmed, and consoled us. In a very real sense, they were our own personal muses.

In this pantheon of immortals, one recently passed the scene and will be greatly missed. His baptismal name was Pierino Roland Como. We knew him as Perry Como.

Born in Canonsburg, Pennsylvania, in 1913, he was a haircutter by trade. He owned his own barbershop until fame came calling. In 1936, he signed a contract with then popular Ted Weems' Big Band. Years of touring ensued. In 1943, his breakthrough song "Goodbye Sue", released by RCA-Victor Records, became a smash hit. Perry Como became a "star".

Perry Como's easy going casual style and effortless delivery were a marked contrast to more formal performers. His trademark became a cardigan sweater and loafers. Although best known for love ballads, such as the 1945 "Till the End of Time", he ensured his popularity with novelty numbers like "Hot Diggity" and "Papa Loves Mambo". He embodied a wholesome "regular guy" all-American 1950's chic the likes never seen before. Though born of immigrant Italian parents, he personified a new contemporary suburban America.

While many veteran Hollywood, Broadway, radio, and vaudeville entertainers shunned television, Perry Como harnessed the new medium to cement his career.

His "Chesterfield Supper Club" and "Perry Como Show" became part of our weekly evening routines. Fans of all ages soaked up his breezy brand of sophistication. Como's smooth silky confident tunes made us feel all was well with the world, even when things looked grim.

When the 1960's became turbulent and the 1970's went disco, Perry Como regularly appeared on television with Christmas specials and headlined in Las Vegas, Manhattan, and Atlantic City revues. His popularity never waned. His haunting renditions of "It's Impossible" and "I Love You So" proved that legendary crooners could more than compete with the likes of Elvis Presley and The Beatles. He literally became a living symbol of a world gone by. Como's lush languid romantic arrangements harkened back to a time when Americans were optimistic and content. A life without Perry Como is unthinkable.

Whenever I turn on the radio and search the dial, I occasionally come across a classic Perry Como tune. He still sounds good, I always reflect. And why shouldn't he? After all, artistry is timeless.

Local McGuffey Society Sole Survivor

by Richard S. Scarsella

In 1961, the William Holmes McGuffey Historical Society of Youngstown formally organized to preserve the rich legacy of its namesake. As an affiliate of the National Federation of McGuffey Societies, it was part of an association that once numbered 100,000 members nationwide. How times have changed! Today, as this group celebrates its 40th anniversary, it is the sole survivor amongst its McGuffey peers.

Like so many ironies in history, the local W. H. McGuffey Historical Society bears solitary testament to a time that once prevailed. Few now know that "America's schoolmaster" was raised in our midst and came to manhood in the Mahoning Valley crossroads called Coitsville Township. The fact that McGuffey changed national social and cultural history seems to matter little to local inhabitants. Such was not always the case.

When McGuffey's famous anthology series, named the Eclectic Readers, were published in 1836, he was considered a phenomenon. This archetypal Western born, bred, and educated "new man" standardized the emerging American spirit, ethos, character, and culture. The mere notion that he would be almost forgotten in his own stomping grounds was unthinkable. Yet, it has come to past. History can be bittersweet.

Although Henry Ford called the inimitable McGuffey Readers his alma mater and paid for a revision and reprinting of these influential texts, the books fell out of favor by the 1950's, after selling tens of millions to receptive audiences. Why? Changing tastes, modern education theory, urbanization, and the decline of traditional American ideals all contributed to McGuffey's eclipse. In a nation of cars, television, and atomic science, his down home notions of patriotism, citizenship, character, conservation, literacy, right and wrong, and respect for religion seemed dated and unfashionable. In a land where change, youth, and modernity were adored, the solid immutable timeless values that McGuffey championed became suspect because they had remained constant and not subject to faddish revisionism.

Retired teachers and school administrators predominate amongst those that seek to keep the McGuffey philosophy alive. No longer do national figures or local leaders quote the man of letters who helped civilize the wild lands west of the Appalachian Mountains' frontier. The result? McGuffey has become a footnote in history books and educational theory, though his tomes continue to be printed to this day, only rivaled by the Bible in printing primacy.

Despite the odds, the Youngstown W. H. McGuffey Historical Society continues its work. In 1998, it deeded at no charge the 78 acres of the McGuffey homestead to the Mill Creek Metroparks. It has also endowed funds for the improvement and care of the McGuffey family farm, now known as the McGuffey Wildlife Preserve. The society also keeps vigil over this tangible link to the past and has become a historical oddity itself.

The planned unveiling of the society's McGuffey Family Archive, scheduled for a fall debut at the Davis Education and Visitors Center in Mill Creek Metroparks' Fellows Riverside Gardens, is a testimony to a man and an era that once bestrode the United States with no equal. In Youngstown, the McGuffey story continues on. Thankfully, not all has been forgotten yet.

Mahoning Valley: Home of Historical Giants

by Richard S. Scarsella

Being educated in different parts of the country and in Europe, I became keenly interested in history. Coming back to the Youngstown area, I sought out local history as a hobby. Much to my surprise, I discovered our valley rich in heritage. Even more astonishing, was the fact that three native sons literally changed the course of national political, social and educational development in the emerging New World. The names of these legends are President William McKinley, Joseph Butler and William Holmes McKinley. All three men continue to cast their shadows over their respective fields of endeavor.

William McKinley, born in 1843, entered the political arena at a tender age. Economists credit him with the Tariff Bill of 1890, a predecessor of what we now call free trade. Elected president in 1896, McKinley espoused "manifest destiny", which rationalized the colonization of Hawaii and Puerto Rico. His aggressive pursuit of the Spanish-American War laid the groundwork for intervention into Cuban affairs, a legacy that haunted President John Kennedy and tortures President Bill Clinton. McKinley's actions set the stage for President Theodore Roosevelt's popular efforts to make America a world power. Raised in Niles Ohio, McKinley met a tragic end in his assassination of 1901.

Joseph Butler, born in 1840, was a friend of the McKinley family. Butler's international business interests and travel made him a discriminating sophisticate of art. Amassing an impressive collection of early American masters, replete with Native American themes, Butler went on to found the first museum in the United States devoted solely to American art. Founded in 1919, the Butler Institute of American Art was the predecessor of larger metropolitan galleries, that to this day borrow Butler's works. The newly constructed Butler computer-generated art gallery is also considered to be a groundbreaking innovation in the art world. Butler's legacy lives on.

William Holmes McGuffey, born in 1800, was both a preacher and a teacher. His contribution to pedagogy was based upon an anthology series, named the McGuffey Eclectic Readers, first published in 1836. The first educator to employ focus groups of children, to determine high interest stories, McGuffey's texts literally educated generations of farmers and aliens alike. Still in print today, McGuffey's books perpetuated the American values of citizenship, character, conservation and morality. Henry Ford called these tomes his alma mater. The McGuffey Homesite Farm in Coitsville Township is a National Historical Landmark. Just recently gifted to Mill Creek Metroparks by the William Holmes McGuffey Historical Society, the McGuffey homestead is now called the McGuffey Wildlife Preserve.

For more interesting facts about these legends, contact the National McKinley Memorial Library and Museum at 652-1704, the Butler Institute of American Art at 743-1107 and the William Holmes McGuffey Historical Society at 726-8277.

March Memoirs

by Richard S. Scarsella

As a child, I always looked forward to March. This month broke the icy grip of winter and heralded signs of the approaching spring. The winds and showers seemed to literally blow away the frigid doldrums, if only intermittently. We all ached for warmer weather. March always obliged us.

Once the weather changed, we all rushed out to buy kites. Murphy's, Kressege's, Grant's, McCrory's and Woolworth's all displayed huge selections of affordable kites, tails, and string. Most were priced at a quarter, well within our childhood budgets. Box kites were considered hi-tech status symbols. Chinese oversized kites were luxury items and given wide berth once aloft. We all respected each other's space, when flying our airborne toys at area playgrounds, schoolyards, and vacant lots. A lost or crashed kite was a sorrowful event. In truth, these kites of youth were delicate symbols of our free spirits and search for adventure. In March, high on a hill, you could see colorful kites of all sizes, shapes, and colors throughout the valley, with majestic, belching steel mill stacks as a backdrop. It was truly breathtaking.

For Christians, March meant the beginning of Lent. Priests, preachers, nuns, and monks prevailed upon our consciences to "give something up" during this holy season of fast, abstinence, and purification. Ash Wednesday signaled the commencement of the Easter season. Luckily, St. Patrick's Day interrupted our self-sacrifice.

In once thriving downtown Youngstown, a huge parade honored the ancient Celtic in grand style. Green papered floats, covered with carnations, toilet paper, and tissue paper turned this event into a great spectacle. Marching bands, flag lines, majorettes, veterans groups, and politicians on review stands all filled Central Square and Federal Street with happy onlookers. Revelers enjoyed corned beef, green beer, and shamrock decorated pastries all during this annual celebration. The countdown to spring began in earnest when St. Patrick's Day arrived and passed.

Homeowners began to survey winter damage in March. Home repair and remodeling agents canvassed the once vibrant city environs. Free estimates were given, deposits changed hands, and contracts were signed. By the end of March, outdoor projects started. City street crews could be seen working furiously to open stopped-up sewers, in anticipation of the April monsoons.

Flower and vegetable gardens quietly showed signs of life as well. Crocuses timidly budded. Early weeds followed suit. Earnest discourses centered on when to plant seeds or bulbs. Almanacs were consulted when the last frost might be. The longer days of March were bellwethers of the even longer days yet to come.

Area cemeteries would witness an increase of visitors during March. Family and friends reverently raked up leaves, twigs, and trash around marble headstones. Plans were made to buy plantings at favorite nurseries and to transplant the same, with the aim of having blooms by Easter Sunday. Even amongst death, the March gales promised rebirth.

During March, Mill Creek Park commenced to cut dead trees, clear trails, mulch gardens, and reopen closed drives. Animals of all kinds became more visible. Hikers followed them outdoors. Migratory birds, such as Canadian geese and ducks, used the park lakes and ponds as rest stops in their Northern migrations. Nature was stirring again.

Of all the annual March practices and customs, the revival of historic Idora Park was the most riveting. The long dormant wood skeletal coasters slowly came to life. The Wild Cat, Jack Rabbit, and Baby Wild Cat emerged form their long winter naps and seemed to leap back to life, as if by magic. When we heard the melodic carrousel calliope and saw the lights of the Ferris wheel at dusk, we knew summer was not long off.

These March memories once appeared like clockwork every year to thousands of valley inhabitants. Some remain. Most have inexplicably vanished. Like March itself, they all seem timeless.

Memories of Memorial Day

by Richard S. Scarsella

It's noteworthy, that in a country that prides itself as being modern, that we still observe Memorial Day. Perhaps, we do this because of some collective sense that those before us achieved much, sacrificed more, and deserve at least a passing mention in our fast-paced world.

In years past, Memorial Day was more than a day off work and school. Families went to church services, to find solace and strength, while remembering the dearly departed. Decorating graves was an intergenerational activity. On this day, the dead's reach into our lives was renewed and honored. Like the ancient culture of Egypt, Americans acknowledged the ever-pervasive influence that the deceased have on the living.

Flags, hung outside wide, shady porches, stood sentinel for families recalling the good and not so good old days. Newspapers would offer lengthy, detailed, and patriotic accounts of prominent and common people that made selfless contributions to the defense and progress of their nation and communities. Some families put notices in the press, accompanied by pictures, poetry or prose, in an effort to immortalize their loved ones. Decoration Day gave rise to many heartfelt expressions of thanks and grief.

Colorful downtown Youngstown parades were often held. Smartly dressed military units, gaunt veterans groups, fresh-faced youth groups, and perky high school bands all turned out to display their reverence for this all-American observance. Red, white and blue American and Ohio flags lined both downtown streets and cemetery lanes. Picnics at Mill Creek Park, with lemonade and apple pie, became almost derigueur. Idora Park would officially begin summer when it opened its gates and midways to the throngs seeking holiday diversions.

Memorial Day traditionally ended with children lighting sparklers in their yards or setting off caps. Family oriented radio and television shows brought closure. Fireworks over Idora Park briefly illuminated the evening gloom. Then, throughout the valley, residents would pray, as they lay in their beds. Memories, that had been openly and publicly displayed, now became private and solemn again. At day's end, all that one was left with was memories.

Messages

by Richard S. Scarsella

The ancient practice of letter writing is now obsolete and near death. Telephones, with low priced long distance charges, began the decline. Fax machines accelerated this trend. Computers and e-mail have further decimated the ranks of those practicing communication with the stroke of a pen. Many young people do not know the thrill of receiving and sending letters. It is now a lost art.

Such was not always the case. Schools once vigorously advanced a curriculum based upon good penmanship. The Palmer method of cursive writing was deemed best by private and Catholic schools. Public schools favored the Zaner-Blosser method. Elegant, legible, and uniformed pencraft was the ideal. A "bad hand" was a disgrace. One had to be able to compose and write in manuscript a letter-perfect document for both private and career needs.

Postal workers were once very much part of our lives. The mailman was like part of an extended family. He would often be invited into the pantry for refreshments and was given a gift at Christmas. Twice a day, within the city limits, he would deliver the mail, usually on time. The morning and afternoon deliveries were closely watched by neighborhood wags. Overdue bills, calligraphy drawn invitations, printed announcements, and "first class" mail were all subjects to much conjecture, discourse, and debate. Close-knit environs relied upon the post for news from the outside, entertainment, and funds. When a child was allowed, "to get the mail", this was considered a right of passage and an honor.

It was not unusual to see homemakers go through the mail daily on their expansive front porches or in front of their picture windows. Curious neighbors would just happen to "drop by" around delivery time and make innocent inquiries about the mail. Vacationing or ill neighbors did not have to fear for the contents of their mailboxes. Friends were all too willing to "pick up the mail." Only the most trusted folks were given this weighty responsibility.

Before junk mail, computer generated mailings, and discount coupons clogged our mailboxes, letters from relations and friends were often delivered at regular intervals. Notes from the "old country", the armed services, or alumni were always anticipated, greatly enjoyed, and circulated to interested parties. Anyone not receiving private mail was to be pitied.

V-grams were heavily censored small letters written by those in uniform around the W.W.II era. Using tiny pieces of writing paper was considered patriotic and helped the war effort conserve precious resources for the ultimate victory over our enemies. These miniature dispatches were full of pathos. Small pieces of parchment were all that bound the homefront to the war effort. Oftentimes, they traveled halfway around the world in search of loved ones. Sometimes, the correspondent had perished before the correspondence was delivered. A communiqué from the dead was devastating. The power of the pen was mighty and much respected. As a sign of reverence, letters were folded carefully, returned to their envelopes, and rarely thrown away.

Variety stores such as Woolworth's and Grant's invariably displayed local scenes on their metal postcard racks. The Youngstown area postcards featured blazing blast furnaces, glittering Idora Park, the staid Tod House Hotel, the palatial Palace Theater, and the old Central Square. Camera perspectives of Federal Street in its heyday made downtown Youngstown look like an avenue in Manhattan. Rural folks frequently bought and sent picture cards to show others what the big city was like.

Telegrams were usually dreaded by all. They tended to bring bad tidings. When a young man wearing a uniform, cap, and gloves was seen delivering a telegram, people invariably held their breadths. The announcement of the death of a soldier or sailor was particularly hard to take for the recipients. When memorabilia of the deceased was kept, the cursed telegram was reverently preserved, along with yellowed snapshots and well-read letters.

Today, it is hard to fathom a world were the written word was once king. Typewriters made languid letter writing easier and less personal. Computer keyboards made communication short, pithy, and emotionless. Both shorthand and stenography have now virtually disappeared in our midst. Laser printers now do most of the writing for us.

I still miss florid longhand from teachers, doctors, and professors. The stolid messages I once received from the vanguard of civilization made everything seem sane in an illogical world. Little notes of thanks, common courtesy, or commerce are not part of my life now.

No longer do I get messages wrapped around glass bottles from the milkman. I think we have lost more than we know.

Milestones

by Richard S. Scarsella

In the not so distant past, many classic trademarks once symbolized the Mahoning Valley. Both visitors and natives alike once marveled at the distinctive institutions that made the Youngstown area unique and memorable.

The long abandoned McKelvey's department store once towered over other Youngstown storefronts. This grand mercantile monster consisted of several buildings linked by elevators, escalators, and tunnels. Once known as "Youngstown's Greatest Store", it was the ultimate purveyor of luxury goods and basic commodities.

Up until the Cleveland based Higbee Company purchased it, McKelvey's was the trendsetter in local fashion. Its bridal salon, furrier, jewelry department, and interior design studios were first-class. Wedding consultants were available by appointment only and had exquisite, exclusive couture styles in stock for discriminating clients. The furrier once stocked the largest selection of mink stoles, wraps, and coats between Cleveland and Pittsburgh. The McKelvey label in a garment was the ultimate status symbol. Jewelry collectors once drooled over the expansive DeBeer's diamond collections McKelvey's cut and set. Many a young man, when purchasing a wedding set, had an installment plan with this trusted venerable store. Society matriarchs decorated grand urban homes, country estates, and Lake Erie cottages with eclectic McKelvey's furnishings. Making a purchase here was both a good investment and a sign of good taste.

The decline of the steel industry and the invasion of suburban malls sapped the strength of McKelvey's. The flight from the city, the decaying central city, catastrophic urban renewal, changing tastes, and the casual chic movement all doomed this flagship retailer. No longer did busloads of buyers disembark under the McKelvey's canopies on West Federal Street. The Parkade mini-mall of shops and parking garage ceased being novel. The famed McKelvey's Hall of Music became increasingly silent. The McKelvey's Grill and Bakery quit catering to crowds of hungry consumers. Refined, urbane display windows no longer had throngs of shoppers to awe. Construction of the Federal Street pedestrian mall was the death knell for McKelvey's. It was the end of an era.

When travelers cruise what is left of once vibrant downtown Youngstown, they can scarcely imagine what has been irretrievably lost. Empty lots and boarded facades all once were occupied by McKelvey's peers. The Palace, State, and Paramount theaters, Hotel Youngstown, Mural Room Restaurant, Livingston's, Lustig's, and Woolworth's, McCrory's, Murphy's, Kressege's, and Grant's variety stores all were contemporaries of McKelvey's. All have inexplicably vanished.

The imminent demolition of the McKelvey complex is yet another assault on a landmark of happier, more prosperous, and more cultivated times.

Mill Creek Metroparks' Historical Points of Interest

by Richard S. Scarsella

Mahoning County residents are blessed with one of the best urban park districts in the nation. Known as Mill Creek Metropolitan Park District, this complex of land, lakes, streams and buildings is unique in both its size and depth of offerings. The park is rich in geological, natural, and architectural history.

Lanterman's Mill Museum, also known as the Old Mill Museum, is located on Youngstown's South Side, on Rt. 62 (Canfield Rd.), next to Lanterman's Falls. Here, one will find a recently restored working gristmill, complete with an operating water wheel. Built in 1845, this living museum has four floors of displays of authentic tools, equipment and pictures, that trace the history of the once numerous mills that used the old Mill Creek for waterpower. History buffs might want to walk over to the overflow parking lot. Why? A haunting and heartbreaking view of the old Idora Park ballroom, coasters, and reputed Native American burial/ceremonial grounds awaits you. This lot is situated on former Idora land. Interestingly, Lanterman's Falls was called Idora Falls for many years.

The Ford Nature Center, located on Youngstown's South Side, at 840 Old Furnace Road, features live and stuffed animals, nature walks, hands-on exhibits, and realistic displays of the wild. This former mansion was donated by the Judge Ford family to Mill Creek Metroparks. It welcomes school students and adults year-round to attend its many educational programs. Hikers may want to hike down the hill, visit beautiful Lake Glacier, and take a ferryboat ride. This area of the park gives real meaning to the term "green cathedral".

Mill Creek Metroparks' latest addition is the William Holmes McGuffey Wildlife Preserve. Donated by the William Holmes McGuffey Historical Society, this 74 acres of flora and fauna, located on McGuffey Road, in Coitsville Township, features a National Historical Registry Landmark Monument, which honors one of the most famous American educators of all time. Here, one can see the

McGuffey family well and pond. Geology fans will enjoy the unusual glacier formations, found in the drumlin. Trails and picnic pavilion are open to the public.

For more information about these Mill Creek Metroparks facilities, phone Lanterman's Mill (330) 740-7115, Ford Nature Center (330) 740-7107 and/or McGuffey Wildlife Preserve (330) 702-3000.

Minutia

by Richard S. Scarsella

Life is made up of small details, trivial matters, and trifling circumstances. The business of living can oftentimes overwhelm the senses. However, if one takes the time to listen, almost forgotten echoes from the past can still be heard and visualized in the dim recesses of one's memory.

Even now, I can vividly recall when Youngstown's major thoroughfares—such as Mahoning and Belmont Avenues and Oak and Market Streets—were illuminated with high voltage curb lamps. The "white way" streetlights, installed in the 1950's and 1960's, were viewed as a partial remedy for vagrancy, teen gang loitering, petty thefts, and storefront defacement. These bright ribbons of light, which later intersected with the Route 680 innerbelt and Route 7-11 bypass, gave our gritty metropolis a big city ambiance. Rural folks marveled at the sight of daylight on city roads, long after the sun had set. Unfortunately, these grand civic improvements were unable to stem the invidious urban decay of the post-World War II era.

In Youngstown's heyday, bustling vintage neighborhoods and new developments required many forestations citywide, so as to insure adequate response time. Children of all ages routinely visited the local firehouse to "chew the fat", pet the department Dalmatian dogs, and to ring the fireballs. Having a tour of the firemen's living and work quarters was a much sought after privilege. Sitting in the fire truck was the epitome of adventure for children from a more innocent time of life. Before centralized forestations became the norm, the nearby safety forces were very much a part of our daily lives.

For children living within the city limits, the public playground was the place to "hang out" with friends. During the summer months, playground directors became veritable big brothers and big sisters to us all. Checker and chess tournaments, baseball clinics, jump rope contests, competitive games of jacks, and arts and craft shows all were major attractions for bored youth. Long before television and air-conditioning kept children indoors on balmy days, we encamped at the playgrounds days on end.

Well into the 1950's, spring-cleaning was a grand spectacle. Across the city, homes were vigorously emptied of furnishings and serious purgation commenced. It was not at all thought odd to see sofas, chairs, tables, and china buffets on someone's porch or front lawn. Area rugs were rolled up, hardwood floors were stripped and revarnished, and mattresses were hung over lines and left to "air out" for a day. White vinegar and hot water concoctions were used on the windows and screens, Milsek oil was applied to woodwork and case goods, and wallpaper was vacuumed or sponged down during these annual rights of purification. A spotless home was once considered a symbol of class, propriety, and hygiene.

When death descended on one of our neighbors, the whole neighborhood mourned. Women would bake up a storm, serve meals, and take turns comforting the bereaved. Men would cut the yards, take out the trash, and stoke the furnaces for the house of lamentations. Children would pick flowers for arrangements, run errands, and tend the pets for those in grief. Everyone wore black. The parade of shiny ebony funeral limousines, flower cars, priests, ministers, rabbis, and local politicos were a sight to behold. Playing host to extended family of the deceased was considered a duty and an honor. When the angel of death claimed one of our own, the chill of our own mortality was disquieting.

To this day, I still miss those all familiar faces of my old stomping grounds. It is hard to fathom that they all have long ago retreated to their graves, never to be seen again. Like faded photographs from happier days, all the echoes of the past bear mute testimony to that which once was and is no more.

Mirage

by Richard S. Scarsella

The demolition of "Youngstown's Greatest Store", the McKelvey/Higbee complex of buildings, is a true milestone in more ways than one.

First, the blatant disregard for area landmarks continues unabated with the wanton destruction of this venerable landmark. These actions speak poorly about our area's priorities and sensibilities. The fact that the Strouss-Hirschberg building lives on as the Phar-Mor center is proof to skeptics that historic buildings can be "reborn" and utilized in the modern era.

Second, one can now argue that downtown Youngstown is no longer a true downtown. Rather, it has become city blocks of parking lots surrounding isolated freestanding buildings. The remaining survivors of this so-called urban renewal seem oddly out of place now, with the context of their neighbors denied to them. A few trees do not make a forest. A few urban buildings with adjacent parking do not make a downtown. The contrast between Youngstown's central core and the downtowns' of Warren and Columbiana is stark.

Lastly, the loss of distinctive, architecturally rich structures robs future generations of their social and cultural heritage. Rome would not be Rome without its aged renowned edifices. Youngstown has loss an important part of its essential essence by destroying the McKelvey/Higbee block.

To this day, residents still speak wistfully about the long gone elegant Palace Theater. As we all know to well, a parking lot replaced this jewel and helped cut the soul out of the once bustling central business district. Central Square never regained its vigor after this fatal loss.

The McKelvey/Higbee complex was gifted to the city and the misnamed Community Improvement Corporation. This present should have been mothballed appropriately, awaiting development. Inexplicably, this was not done. The public's best interests were not served by those entrusted with the fate of this classical symbol of more prosperous times. This is a modern tragedy.

To have allowed this once sophisticated mercantile flagship store to become derelict was criminal. Sadly, we will never see the likes of this building in our midst again. Ironically, New York vultures scavenged the building for irreplaceable stone cuttings and sculptures. Like a long dead dinosaur, this monolith will not lie in peace. Its remains will become a subject of study, far from its native roots. Hopefully, the Idora Park Ballroom, the Isaly's building, the State and Paramount theaters, to name a few, will escape similar oblivion. They are true survivors in a concrete jungle.

As I cruise the Rt. 680 innerbelt highway, a contributing factor to the demise of traffic and life in the urban center, from afar, I glimpse the familiar skyline. The art deco Rockefeller Center designed Central/Metropolitan Tower is nicely complemented by the Home Savings signature clock steeple. As I approach the downtown, like a mirage, it seems to retreat further into the horizon. Once there, it is unrecognizable. Then, it occurs to me. As a famous writer once wrote, "There is no there there."

Modern Martyr

by Richard S. Scarsella

In the year 2000, the 1950's and 1960's seem remote. However, those two decades were instrumental in laying the groundwork for today's widespread prosperity. During those years, America reluctantly came to grips with gross inequalities and prejudices, which were firmly rooted in the past and oftentimes institutionalized. These chains from the past threatened the future of America.

Leading the charge for change was a black, Southern man of the cloth named Martin Luther King, Jr. Born in 1929, raised in Georgia and educated in Boston, Massachusetts, this preacher's son became the conscience of a post-World War II nation flush with victory, economic expansion, and doubts. He was called both a prophet and agitator. His likes had never been seen before in our nation.

Framing his resonant oratory in Biblical terms, he utilized Gandhi's principles of nonviolence and a curious press to spread this message of love, peace, dignity, fairness, and harmony. His civil rights marches in the 1960's forced a country to grapple with highly charged issues of race, segregation, integration, and equal opportunity. He became the lightening rod of pivotal social paradigm shift.

In King's 1963 Washington D. C. proclamation of "I have a dream...that all men are created equal," he singularly, eloquently voiced the pleas of generations of oppressed minorities that the time had come for America's Constitution to be applied to all, regardless of color, creed, or race. After this exhortation, the nation was never the same. He later was awarded the Nobel Peace Prize for his notable contributions to society.

Like other great figures of antiquity, Rev. King was a visionary. Circumstances beyond his control made him a man of destiny, to an oftentimes skeptical, disbelieving, unenlightened audiences. Along with his stoic wife, Coretta Scott King, Rev. King ushered America into a modern era, where citizens were valued as individuals and accorded full rights, unlike any enjoyed elsewhere in the world. However, his work is far from finished.

The Cold War years of Sputnik, Bay of Pigs Invasion, Cuban Missile Crisis, Camelot, Great Society, War on Poverty, moon landing, Viet Nam and Watergate all seem like dim memories now, in a nation mesmerized with cutting-edge technology and networked computers. Leaders such as Roosevelt, Churchill and Gandhi are little discussed on the World Wide Web. We all feel decidedly future-oriented, free from the shackles of prior centuries, despite lingering enclaves of intolerance and reactionaries.

Like so many legends of history, Rev. King was assassinated, along with contemporaries President John F. Kennedy and Senator Robert Kennedy. His untimely death in 1968 made him a modern martyr. In death, he became a continuing influence in our lives. His words are still echoed strongly from his grave. It's true. One cannot escape history. It is always with us. Martin Luther King's utterances and deeds are timeless.

Mortality

by Richard S. Scarsella

I was born into a "mature" family. Death was no stranger. Elder relatives periodically retreated to area graveyards for their final resting places. In our youth, we foolishly thought we were safe from the Grim Reaper.

In a rough gritty steel town, the specter of death was ever present. It was not unusual to pick up a newspaper and read an account of the latest industrial fatalities. Many laborers departed this life in the grips of a blast furnace or under the wheels of a locomotive. To die in the harness was a distinct possibility for any union members of the trades. It was a fact of life.

There was a time when it was not unusual to see long serpentine lines of cars, all outfitted with funeral flags, creeping along valley streets. Limousine funerals, complete with flower cars, were once the norm. Great expressions of grief were evidenced by wakes of several days, huge floral arrangements befitting royalty, and elaborate post-interment feasts. For some, bereavement became an art form. Widows of all ages, dressed somberly in black with matching hats and veils, reminded us that no one gets out of this world alive.

When notable personalities passed away, the nation momentarily paused out of respect and due to morbid curiosity. The national tragedy of President John F. Kennedy's assassination in 1963 literally transformed mourning from a personal family rite to one of mass audience participation. For several days, America and the world, courtesy of television, were transfixed with the commitment to the earth of the martyred president's mortal remains. His death was a warning that even young, handsome, rich, and gifted icons were easy prey for the icy hand of death.

In 1964, four lads from Liverpool, England helped us forget our sorrow. Their name was the Beatles. We later knew them intimately as Paul McCartney, John Lennon, Ringo Starr, and George Harrison.

These irreverent non-conformists led the British invasion into America's rock and roll soul armed with a "new" sound. Music was never the same again. Elvis Presley and Frank Sinatra both were pushed momentarily to the sidelines. American culture would never be free from the Beatles' influence, despite great concern by establishment powers.

In time, as America matured, the Beatles were viewed as less than counter-culture revolutionaries. Their long hair, flirtations with drugs, Far Eastern mystical theology, anti-war philosophy, and environmental concerns were all merged into the mainstream of American life. The Beatles, collectively and individually, held our attention throughout the years. We all aged together.

John Lennon's murder by a rabid fan on a New York City street was a cruel shock to baby-boomers desperately trying to hold onto youth and sanity. Surely, symbols of the 1960's youth vanguard were to be spared an early demise. Apparently not, we later found out. We all grew a little wiser by this revelation.

When the quiet Beatle, George Harrison, had his first brush with cancer, it was assumed he would recover fully. And he did. Attacked in his own home by a deranged fan, he rallied yet again. Rumors of yet another bout with cancer were paid scant attention. He was still relatively young, conventional wisdom asserted. He will prevail. He did not. In the waning days of the year 2001, he gave up the ghost. Despite George Harrison's fortune and worldwide acclaim, he did not cheat death. Death is the great leveler between kings and commoners.

Regardless of George Harrison's passing, his music will still continue. He now belongs to a pantheon of rock and roll legends immortalized by longhair or pop music. Due to the wonders of technology, his voice and arrangements will forever be available on tapes, discs, and record albums.

In a way, the band still plays on for George Harrison and his devoted followers. As my grandmother always said, "Thank God for little mercies."

Musings

by Richard S. Scarsella

The modern-day world is fast-paced, disconnected, and impersonal. People move frequently, change jobs often, and pay scant attention to relics from another age. More landmarks have been demolished or abandoned than have been preserved or rejuvenated. Robust, individualistic towns have been replaced by languid, nondescript suburbias. Only in our memories are former days conserved for future reference.

It does not seem long ago that polio was the scourge of the nation. Protective parents fretted over letting their children go out in public, lest they catch this dreaded disease. Everyone knew someone who had an acquaintance in an iron lung. When perfected, polio vaccinations were a necessary procedure all youth underwent. Smallpox was another feared disease. Vaccinations became a childhood right of passage. The resulting disfiguring round scar was a trademark of impunity. Thankfully, polio and smallpox no longer menace innocent lives. No longer do families of polio and smallpox victims make vigils at the children wards of South Side, North Side, and St. Elizabeth hospitals praying for the lives of their loved ones.

At one time, musicals captivated audiences. Broadway stars, such as Ethel Merman, were lured to Hollywood and cast in extravagant productions. The 1952 "Singing in the Rain", starring Gene Kelly and Donald O'Connor, was the epitome of seamless fusion between dance, music, and comedy. Although these spectacles lasted into the early 1960's, peaking with "The Sound of Music", musical comedies and melodramas are virtually extinct on screen now. A quintessential American art form is in danger of disappearing forever in this century. The venues of the great American musicals also are vanishing. In Youngstown, the Palace Theater is long gone and the Paramount and State theaters are almost beyond salvage.

In 1953, it came as quite a shock for smokers to be told that scientists had concluded that tars from tobacco could produce cancer in mice. For those who cared to listen, the implications were clear. Cigars, cigarettes, and pipes could kill.

Regardless, Madison Avenue advertising agencies responded with ever enticing and more sophisticated marketing. Romantic rugged images of the Marlboro Man dominated television screens and print advertisements. When legends such as Humphrey Bogart and Gary Cooper died of cancer Americans discovered that addictive products could silence even heroes.

In 1955, Americans were enthralled with the opening of Disneyland in Anaheim, California. The creators of Mickey Mouse and Donald Duck pioneered mass merchandising for and to children. The television show "The Wonderful World of Disney" expertly integrated entertainment, popular culture, and retailing for "our viewing pleasure". The later Barbie and G.I. Joe crazes all were based upon stupendously successful Disney sales strategies. The consumer mentality took firm hold of our youth and never let go. Children became savvy consumers. Hand carved wooden soldiers and porcelain china dolls were replaced by plastic toys. Childhood never quite seemed the same after this transition.

In an irony of history, our former enemies, Japan and Germany, became our most fierce world trade competitors. I recall some saying we won the war but had lost the peace. In 1952, Japan produced the first pocket-sized transistor radio, courtesy of Sony. In 1959, Sony introduced the first portable transistorized television. Germany later flooded the country with Volkswagen Beetles, a car first designed by Nazi engineers at the request of Hitler. German-made Mercedes and B.M.W.'s, along with Japanese Toyotas and Hondas, soon became familiar vehicles in our midst. Our country was becoming cosmopolitan, like our European cousins. Even more unbelievably, European and American automakers merged and formed international transportation empires. Buying an item stamped "made 100% in America" became an almost impossible task.

Disturbingly, another Nazi-inspired idea, the autobahn, gave birth to American highways. They soon dominated our lives, after ripping the hearts out of neighborhoods and downtowns when being built. They were a necessary evil, we were told, in the automobile age. Sadly, it became apparent that much beloved American motorcar symbols such as the Packard, DeSoto, and Imperial could no longer compete in the internationalized motor vehicle markets.

In 1960, the first Weight Watchers group was founded in Queens, New York. Haute couture miniskirts were premiered. The dance song "The Twist", by Chubby Checker, swept the country. President John Kennedy established the Peace Corps. as an overseas outreach program. These once innovative things became commonplace, were absorbed into our society, and later were taken for granted, despite their continuing influence in our lives.

182   Memories and Melancholy: Reflections on the Mahoning Valley and Youngstown, Ohio

So many changes occur in any given year, we scarcely notice the passage of time. Sometimes, the mind travels down memory lane to visit old familiar places. One best not dwell there too long, or one may not want to return to reality.

Neighborhood Theaters

by Richard S. Scarsella

In Youngstown's golden age, the central business district was like a few blocks of New York City. Towering office buildings, specialty shops, cozy restaurants, huge department stores and bustling traffic all gave the downtown a Manhattan veneer. Up into the 1960's, everyone faithfully went downtown for professional, legal, shopping, dining and entertainment purposes.

The former Baroque, rococo vaudeville houses along Federal Street offered the Mahoning Valley a slice of New York's 42nd. Street. Marble floors, porcelain tiled walls, imported cut-glass chandeliers, velvet draperies and gold-gilded architectural carvings made these movie palaces shimmer and glow. The Warner, State, Paramount, Palace, Hippodrome, Dome, Capital and Park Theaters were as much an experience as were the films they featured. Suburban growth in the early 1950's slowly began to sap the appeal of these grandiose showplaces. The result? Suburban theaters.

The Newport Theater on East Midlothian Blvd. straddled the upper South Side and Boardman's Newport Glen district. Built in the 1940's, its Art Deco design replicated Hollywood's aura of elegance. Soaring block glass windows, hand painted murals on the lobby ceiling and sweeping chrome accents, along with plenty of free parking, made this theater an instant success. It specialized in epic films, such as Ben Hur. Sadly, after many years of being dark, it was demolished this year for a chain restaurant.

The Belmont Theater was opened on the North Side's upper Belmont Avenue by the Wellman family. This pioneer business dynasty owned the Wellman and Mock Theaters in Girard and the Wedgewood Plaza Theater in Austintown. They foresaw the trend to suburbia. Unfortunately, their futuristic Art Moderne, state-of-the-art Belmont Cinema lasted only a few years, since it could not readily book the first-run films shown downtown by studio affiliated theaters. The Wellman family was part of a national anti-trust lawsuit to break up this film distribution monopoly that Warner Brothers, Universal, MGM, Columbia, 20th Century Fox and RKO Radio Pictures had with local theaters. The verdict dismembered the movie cartel. Suburban theaters now began to proliferate. Tragically, the Belmont Theater never realized its promise. It was converted into The Atlantic Discount Department Store. Its trademark plaster casts of tragedy and comedy still adorn the old entrance.

The Boardman Plaza, Liberty Plaza, Lincoln Knolls Plaza and Wedgewood Plaza Theaters all opened in the 1960's. They fiercely competed with both the downtown motion picture houses and older neighborhood theaters, such as the Foster, Uptown, Home, Mahoning and Schenley. Combined, these playhouses, along with drive-in theaters, all slowly drained off the decreasing throngs of moviegoers from the once premier downtown movie screens.

Television's popularity in the 1950's made movie patrons less prone to travel downtown for a movie. Neighborhood theaters survived because of their convenience. Marquee-front, no-cost parking gave these film houses the edge in the movie wars. Lower overhead allowed these theater hybrids to undercut their antique, high overhead, increasingly obsolete downtown rivals.

Walking to a neighborhood theater was a time-honored ritual in the late 1940's until the 1980's. Before air-conditioned cars and homes became commonplace, the local theater was a cool retreat from the "dog days of summer". Freshly-cooked popped corn, with real butter, Goobers, Snow Caps, Dots, Raisenettes and Good and Plenty snacks made going to a double-feature movie a real treat. Double-feature matinees, at reduced prices, made movies a bargain as well. Teenage Romeos and Juliets found the local theater an ideal meeting place. The saying "going to the movies" meant different things to different people. However, the movies were a big part of our lives, regardless of age.

Times and tastes change. In the 1990's, cable television is a major contender in the film business. VCR tape rentals and sales have now cornered a large portion of the movie viewing market. Suburban entertainment megaplexes boast ten screens under one roof. The neighborhood cinemas seem quaint now. Only the Austintown Plaza Theater, with three screens, represents some semblance of the once popular neighborhood theater traditions. Like the once dominant downtown theater dinosaurs of the not so distant past, the neighborhood cinemas have all but vanished. They were all social and cultural milestones for their eras.

Ironically, the Youngstown area has more screens than ever. However, they are located in a few relatively isolated locations, out of walking distance for most people. Memories of the grandiose downtown movie halls and their neighborhood theater offsprings live on as testaments to another much missed time.

To this day, I think there is nothing sadder than the forlorn look of a deserted theater.

New Years Observances

by Richard S. Scarsella

Every Christmas holiday season is completed by the observance of New Year's Eve practices. This last hurrah of yuletide cheer evokes many cherished memories in those of us old enough to remember distinctive local customs that have long since passed from the scene.

Area wine shops and bars once featured spirits from brewers and vineyards located in the tri-state area. Youngstowners favored liquors from our native owned and operated Renner Brewery. Its full-bodied, European type lager was a favorite of both blue collared mill workers and white collared businessmen. Mahoning Valley New Year's parties always served the once ubiquitous Renner Beer, until Prohibition and out of town competition sounded the death knell for this proud dynasty.

Long lines of families, led by widows dressed in black, dutifully decorated graves on New Year's Eve. Calvary, Oak Hill, Tod Homestead, and Belmont Park cemeteries seemed to bloom in wintertime, coming temporarily alive with fresh garlands, wreaths and flowers. Cruel memories of war, illness, and accidents were acknowledged amongst the solemn, engraved, and stoic headstones. After visits to the interred, only a New Year's party could lift the gloom in our souls.

Hosts and hostesses would stock up on ribbon candy, hard tack, colored after-dinner mints, bridge mix, candy canes, Fanny Farmer milk and dark chocolate, caramel and nut filled turtles, non-pareils, salt water taffy, chestnuts, fancy mixed nuts, and beer nuts. Vernor's and Canadian Club ginger ale, root beer, quinine water, seltzer water, tonic water, phosphates, NeHi soda, and Golden Age cherry and orange pop were all staples for entertaining. Youngsters loved to make a Shirley Temple cocktail, which was a mix of cherry pop and ginger ale garnished by a cherry.

New Year's Eve was once the opportunity to view the huge Christmas tree and manger crèche in bustling downtown Youngstown. Carloads of families and teenagers would cruise the North Side's once posh Fifth Avenue, in search of holiday light displays. The mansions ensconced around Wick Park were absolutely Dickinsonian in their architectural ambiance of old world money, prestige, and entitlement. These urban fortresses of hand-cut stone, towers, and mansard roofs were Christmas card perfect tableaus.

On New Year's Eve, high atop the old Union National Bank building, the once exclusive Youngstown Club catered to the valley's elite in classic club, formal dining, and party rooms. Here, formally dressed waiters and waitresses served cosmopolitan entrees, using bone china, imported cut glassware, and silver flatware. Patrons could dine on pure linen tablecloths, under crystal chandeliers, with the Youngtown skyline as a backdrop.

Also downtown, the mighty lodges of the Elks, Eagles, and Mason fraternal organizations all entertained members in sumptuous style, bedecking their oak paneled grille rooms and dining halls with gourmet repasts. Around the valley, church and grange social halls and V.F.W., American Legion, and Army and Navy posts offered spaghetti dinners and sauerkraut and pork sandwiches to hungry revelers.

New Year's Eve was once a night to dress up. Black tuxedoes, tight fitting cummerbunds, long flowing gowns, fur wraps, foil party hats, and shrill horns all gave this evening a surreal flavor. Clanging pots and pans on the front porch at midnight, while church bells peeled, made New Year's Eve indelibly memorable.

New Year's rituals will probably always focus on food, drink, merriment, friends, and family. However, each twelvemonth begins with recollections of the previous years still fresh in our minds. Nothing will ever replicate the grandeur of ballroom dancing, under the twinkling lights and revolving mirrored sphere, at the Idora Grand Ballroom. Guy Lombardo, who once said he would take New Year's Eve with him when he passed away, at New York's Waldorf Astoria, will never be equaled. His band, playing the haunting tune Auld Lang Syne, while the Times Square ball descended prophetically each year, is a national memory etched in our consciousness.

After all, New Year's Eve is more than a celebration of things to come. It is also a heart-felt lament for things past and much missed. In all the jubilation, one can keenly sense echoes of another time; when the valley was prosperous, when we were young, and the future seemed unlimited.

Oblivion

by Richard S. Scarsella

Idora Park's grand ballroom is no more. This glittering palace of Art Deco suspended cloud ceilings, rainbow hued flickering lights, and mirrored rotating sphere was the victim of gross neglect, vagrants, arsonists, and the endless march of time. It deserved a better fate.

Once the showplace of Youngstown, it justifiably claimed to be the social and cultural center of the metropolitan area. Receptions, balls, music festivals, concerts, dance marathons, sock hops, reunions, trade shows, convocations, and political events all made the ballroom the place to be and to be seen.

Featuring the largest dance floor between Chicago and New York City, the Idora ballroom attracted the best bands. Known nationwide as a "good gig", Idora offered a weekly schedule of music that included immortals such as Guy Lombardo, Lawrence Welk, the Dorsey Brothers, and Artie Shaw. Fans from the Cleveland, Akron, Canton, and Pittsburgh area willingly made the trek to Idora for premiere entertainment. They never left disappointed.

The ballroom was the crown jewel of the 27 acres of attractions known as Idora Park. Open year round, it touched our lives in many ways. Home shows, car events, talent contests, charity drives, bridal expositions, baby pageants, and religious revivals all were routinely held in this legendary dance hall. Situated next to Mill Creek Park, at the base of the midway and next to the Jack Rabbit coaster and Old Mill/Tunnel of Love water ride, this huge dance hall commanded a view like none other.

One found welcomed refuge under its shady porches on hot summer days at the park. Its natural "air conditioning", provided by cool breezes from Mill Creek gorge and Idora Falls, coupled with the midway aromas of vinegar drenched French fries, hot popcorn, and sweet cotton candy and the fragrances of exotic botanical gardens made the ballroom setting unforgettable. It will be sorely missed in a valley that has lost many other beloved landmarks.

Built in 1910 to replace a smaller dance pavilion, it original architecture was an exact duplicate of a Coney Island ballroom. Up into the mid-1950's, the Idora ballroom was embellished with fanciful Moorish towers, colorful cupolas, and hand carved adornments. No other building in the area had the size or ambiance of the famed Idora ballroom. It had no peer. Valley residents all hoped that the ballroom would survive, long after the 1984 and 1986 fires had shuttered the amusement park.

In the early 1990's, the Idora Park Historical Society listed all of the amusement park land and structures on the National Registry of Historic Places. Disagreements amongst club officials led to the expiration of the society's purchase agreement for the park. In 1994, a local church repurchased Idora Park, even though it had lost it to foreclosure in 1988. Unfortunately, the park and the ballroom never reopened again. This vast complex was doomed in an unnatural limbo.

The 1999 100th anniversary of the opening of Idora Park rekindled fond affection for the spacious ballroom. A lush pictorial book named "Idora Park: The Last Ride of Summer" lovingly documented the rise, heyday, and fall of this admired site.

The Idora ballroom now joins the list of other lost landmarks. The Palace Theatre, the McKelvey/Higbee department store, the Jeanette Blast Furnace, to name a few, have all vanished from our environs. Only the Jack Rabbit and Wild Cat coasters and the reputed Native American burial grounds stand as silent sentinels over the ruins of the ballroom that once was the light of our valley's life.

Idora memories live on. Youngstown's "Million Dollar Playground" and its elegant ballroom have now become urban milestones.

Ode to Bozo

by Richard S. Scarsella

In the early years of television, once known as kinescope, on-the-air personalities became well known to us. Cerebral comic Steve Allen, wholesomely acerbic talk show host Johnny Carson, and groundbreaking news anchor Walter Cronkite were like neighbors to a country entranced by a new medium. Of all the small screen characters I recall, Bozo the Clown is the one I mourn most of all.

Just recently news from the windy city named Chicago caught me unawares. Why? The last syndicated children's show titled "Bozo the Clown" was shutting down production. For the first time since the early 1950's, America would be without her favorite funnyman.

It seems that changing tastes and a proliferation of polished kid's entertainment has driven the folksy pioneer Bozo off the air into "early" retirement. The Disney Channel and Nickelodeon, to name a few cable networks, have driven Bozo from the airwaves by their professionally packaged sophisticated juvenile fare far different from what Bozo represented.

America's clown, with all due respect to iconic Red Skeleton and legendary Emmett Kelley, once entertained children and adults alike to acclaim. His secret was homespun corny jokes, classic burlesque-like routines, and vaudeville inspired skits. Filmed in front of a live audience, with children on the stage as willing participants, Bozo captured the youth market by tapping their sense of humor, honesty, and abandonment.

Unlike the hopelessly idealized or morbidly realistic children amusement productions commonplace today, Bozo's spectacles were rooted in timeless traditions of Western culture. His "peanut gallery", a term he made famous, consisting of regular kids, always rooted for the good guys and stood up for traditional values. In effect, his shows were minor morality lessons and tales fostering concepts of right and wrong, good and evil, and a sense of fair play. These seemingly simplistic offerings combined with talent contests, animal acts, pie throwing contests, and musical numbers grounded American children in the middle-class culture and mores they were expected to mimic if they were to realize the American dream. Good clean fun was the vehicle for educating impressionable minds.

The three ring circus-like atmosphere of Bozo shows, complete with water gags, cheap costumes, and magic now seems quaint. However, during its heyday, well into the 1970's, Bozo was the undisputed king with children. His image appeared on all sorts of products. Cereal companies and toy corporations vied viciously for coveted commercial spots on this invincible media darling. When Bozo did a personal endorsement of an item, America listened and bought accordingly. Bozo was viewed as a true trusted friend. Long after he began to fade slowly from the mainstream, his influence continued. The ultra-urbane Seinfield made Bozo the center of one of his television comedies in the mid-1990's. Even McDonald's clown symbol Ronald McDonald bears a striking resemblance to the indomitable Bozo.

Along with recently departed Captain Kangaroo and Mr. Rogers, Bozo was part of the vanguard that recognized children as distinctly different than the teen or adult markets. His show was considered safe for even the youngest viewer. Like family, we trusted Bozo with our innocence.

I had not thought of Bozo for a long time until I heard the unexpected news of Bozo's cancellation. Now, I surprisingly ache a little for this guilty delight of childhood. Of course, Bozo lives on in our dimmest memories and in endless reruns. Life without Bozo, Captain Kangaroo, and Mr. Rogers is inconceivable to me. They were, in a very real sense, pillars of childhood. I forgot how much I missed them.

Of Aunts, Uncles, & Others

by Richard S. Scarsella

Looking back over my life, I now realize that life is made of a lot of little things and a few memorable people. For most, families provide a rich source of characters, all of which greatly enrich our lives.

My family was a colorful collection of varied personalities. My Great Aunt Carmel Schettine was considered a feminist before her time. At the young age of eighteen, she rejected the advances of eligible beaus and left her hometown Washingtonville, Ohio for the big city. Her destiny was the metropolis on Lake Erie called Cleveland.

Much to the shock of her relatives, she started a career in the Cleveland Public City Schools as an audiovisual specialist. Her income allowed her to maintain a comfortable apartment and an independent lifestyle. This state of affairs was considered quite unusual for the year 1923, when she embarked upon her personal quest for self.

Once considered a beauty in her own time, she gradually rejected cosmetics, became a chain smoker, was not adverse to an occasional drink, and became decidedly stout in appearance. When retired, she routinely visited her Youngstown kin bearing gifts for all.

I recall her bringing small wrapped packages from Halles, May Company, and Higbee's department stores. Inside, we found hand-carved wood toy soldiers, porcelain dolls, and novelty items not easily found in the Mahoning Valley. Trips to and from the downtown bus station and passenger railroad terminals to fetch or deliver our spinster great aunt were integral parts of our childhood. When she passed away, unmarried and childless, a chapter of my life grudgingly closed forever.

My Great Uncle George Schettine was my Great Aunt Carmel's older brother. He was a decorated veteran in both world wars. His salty navy tales of the South Pacific and Atlantic merchant marine fleets were fascinating to a young boy dreaming of far-away places. His wavy silver gray hair, crowbar moustache, and elegantly slim physique made him look every bit the figure of a naval officer, though he was only a galley head chef.

Great Uncle George favored a "liquid diet" and held his alcohol well. He liked imported cigars, baseball, and fishing, in that order. When he retired to the Youngstown area he took up residence at the family's Washingtonville homestead. Whenever we visited, he would show off his organic garden, grille fresh water pond fish, and try to get up a game of gin.

He later moved to Texas to be near a favorite nephew, since he sired no children from his two failed marriages and several flirtations. Until the end of his life, he could curse a blue streak, boasted that he had buried seven family doctors, and drank "the hard stuff" with few ill effects. It was later said of him that he worked hard, played hard, and lived hard. He knew no other way. I still have a silver dollar he gave me when he returned from one of his Las Vegas trips. A good luck charm he called it.

Our family was very proud to have one of our own called to God's service. My mother's second cousin, Sister Miriam Schettine, a Holy Humility of Mary nun, resided at the Villa Maria Motherhouse outside of Youngstown. We oftentimes went to visit on Sundays. Watching the "blue sisters" work, pray, and congregate was thought provoking and soothing to laymen. These devoted women of the cloth appeared to me to be ambassadors from another world and dimension. They seemingly lived in a blessed enclave removed from the gritty profane world, which surrounded their paradise. Little did I know that there was much doubt and unhappiness between the hallowed walls of the convent.

Even now I occasionally drive through the countryside and stop to walk the scenic grounds of the Villa Maria cloister. When I stroll amongst the faded tombstones I pay reverence to my late ancestors. The graves of the dead are haunting reminders to those that survive.

Sister Miriam and all of my other relatives still are very much a part of my life. In memories, they live on and on.

Old Friends

by Richard S. Scarsella

It is hard to fathom the passage of time. The years just drop away with little thought given to days past. Thinking back, I oftentimes ponder the loss of once familiar friends.

The recent passing of teen heartthrob Troy Donahue seems strangely incongruent. Can America's archetypal beach boy really be gone from our lives? Donahue enshrined the easy-going sophistication of California's lifestyle. His blond locks, pearly white shores, waxed surfboards, bikini-clad girls, and beautifully tanned bodies Troy Donahue movies popularized took America by surprise in the staid late 1950's and early 1960's. His boy-next-door chiseled looks, smoldering sensuality, and contemporary views about "young love", rebellion, and personal expression hit a cord with a nation long repressed by stifling conformity, double standards, and establishment values. "A Summer Place", his tour-de-force of passion and scandal immortalized him in our culture. Along with his dew-kissed co-star Sandra Dee, Donahue made "A Summer Place" a cultural milestone. Somehow, summer was never the same after this film premiered.

In television land, another beloved legend has been silenced. His name? Mr. Rogers. This pioneer children's entertainer literally raised American youth on old-fashioned standards. Kindness, being a good neighbor, mutual respect, and the virtue of honesty—all once taken for granted in our country—were themes Mr. Rogers wove seamlessly into his variety shows. The friendly postman, the make believe castle and train, and lessons about "life" made Mr. Rogers' productions palatable, engaging, and timeless for child and adult alike. Along with equally famous Captain Kangaroo, another dinosaur of the entertainment industry, Mr. Rogers can be seen in perpetual reruns around the world. Television without either of these two symbols of fantasy is unthinkable.

Even now I can still vividly recall unmistakable faces from yesteryear. Although I forget their names, they still seem very real to me. The same sales clerks at the downtown Woolworth's five and dime variety store dutifully manned their counters for years on end. They watched us grow up and become adults. These loyal salespeople could always be counted upon to fit us properly for slippers, to advise us on gifts suitable for Mothers' and Fathers' Day, and to assist us in selecting a Halloween costume. These merchants of yore, outfitted in drab smocks and "sensible shoes", patiently counted our allowance money, consisting of small change, when they "rung up" our purchases on manual cash registers. They nobly treated us as their own kin and we trusted them as family. At one time, Woolworth's was as American as apple pie. Sadly, the store and its once accustomed expert staff are all gone now. They have been inexplicably swallowed into the annals of local history.

One cannot look back too long or too often, for it seduces one into a time that no longer exists in the here and now. However, shadows and ghosts of history abound and are very much a part of our daily lives. Yesterday still lingers strongly in our subconscious and subtly influences the present. The "good old days", yesteryear, and auld lang syne are poignant reminders of what once was and is no more.

A wise man once said, "You cannot hold back the dawn." Likewise, memories will not be denied. They have an enduring life of their own and offer needed comfort and respite in an oftentimes-uncaring world.

Omnibus Nostalgia

by Richard S. Scarsella

There was a time, until the early 1970's, when many Mahoning Valley residents regularly used public transit to "do business" in downtown Youngstown. Before the malls opened in the 1970's, the central business district was the hub of retail, professional, and government services. When electric streetcars disappeared in the 1940's, combustion engine buses became the conveyance of choice and necessity for at least one member of most area residences.

In the 1940's, 1950's, and 1960's, two car homes were rare. Housewives, students, the elderly, newlyweds, and lower income populations all depended on public transit to get them to stores, school, doctors, employment, and recreation spots. Tall, iron vertical poles, with orange stripes painted on them, were silent sentinels every few blocks on major thoroughfares, advertising bus routes. They guarded small spaces of common ground for those awaiting transference to another spot in town. Wood benches sometimes were placed next to the poles, as an added convenience.

Long, tall, hulking diesel engine, smoke belching packaderm-like motor coaches would glide up to these markers with screeching airbrakes numbing eardrums. Twin doors would open brusquely to allow entry. Once on board, one was greeted by a uniformed driver, wearing a bell cap, sitting royally behind a huge steering wheel and next to a change collector/sorter, which brimmed with silver coins. Dollar bills were not accepted. Die-hard travelers had monthly passes or transit tokens. If a rider was short on fare, oftentimes, kindly drivers would kick in the difference.

These modern-day jitneys were marvels of wide expanses of shiny glass, glittering chrome handrails, and glove leather seats. Pressing one's nose against the slightly tinted glass, one could swiftly see Youngstown's bustling avenues slip effortlessly before one's eyes from a vantage point only truck drivers enjoyed. Riding the bus was very thrilling.

Bus schedules were free for the taking and were none too easy reading. A would be rider had to judiciously pick which bus line to take on a system that was serpentine in nature. The city map, indexed by time and route numbers, was truly fascinating, especially when choosing where and when to transfer to another route.

Heavily traveled lines included Market, Mahoning, Midlothian and Idora. All lines used Central Square and adjoining East and Federal Streets as final destination points. Throngs of passengers would exit packed buses every half-hour under the protective canopies of Strouss', McKelvey's, Woolworth's, and Livingston's. Under the shadow of the Home Savings signature clock, Central Tower and the Mahoning County Courthouse, downtown denizens fanned out from bus stops to go about their tasks, ever mindful of the time the last bus would leave on the return route.

When in town, nickel transfers could whisk riders up to another part of town in no time. The trendy Uptown area, culturally elite Wick Park, the Isaly Dairy West End ice cream parlor, and the famous McGuffey Plaza Bowling Lanes all were accessible for those without cars. The most frequented stops included St. Elizabeth, Northside and Southside hospitals, local cemeteries, Idora Park, the Elms Ballroom, Youngstown College, Y.M.C.A., Y.W.C.A., Ursuline, and Mooney High Schools. Of course, on Saturdays, downtown lured thousands to the mighty Palace, Warner, State, Paramount, Park, and Regent theaters' matinees.

The Wilson Avenue line was mesmerizing as it snaked amongst the industrial smoke stacks of fiery blast furnaces. The Glenwood line was fragrant as it skirted the boundaries of bucolic Mill Creek Park. The Idora line delivered whole families to the wonderment of "Youngstown's Million Dollar Playground". The Mahoning line was breathtaking at its summit, at Belle Vista Avenue. Below, the Youngstown skyline, highlighted by skyscrapers ringed in mist and smog, evoked a major metropolitan aura.

Today's children will never know the experience of riding on the Midlothian Blvd. line in its heyday. Going west, one would see the giant red apple sign of the long gone Point Market. One would smell the cake-like Schwebel bread well before one could see the giant slice of bread, high atop the bakery. Destination? The magic of the cathedral-like Boardman Rollercade. Here, buses would unload crowds of teens and preteens, with skate boxes in hand. Once inside, skaters would be met with the twinkling lights and a revolving mirrored sphere, reflected by the polished wood floor. The organist in the glass booth would play haunting romantic tunes of life, love, and times past. This was just one of the many varied destinations which buses could deliver passengers to, far away from the ordinariness of home neighborhoods.

A lot of people speak wistfully of the reign of the buses. They are much missed by many. They were important components of our own personal histories.

On the Riverfront

by Richard S. Scarsella

Civilizations all have one thing in common. Countries, cities, towns, villages, and farms need water available to sustain life and insure continued existence.

In the Mahoning Valley, the Native Americans of many tribes settled along the lush banks of the languid Mahoning River. This winding ribbon of freshwater was a life source for plants, animals, and humans.

When John Young ventured forth into the Ohio Territories from Connecticut with his land grant in hand, he also homesteaded near the ancient Mahoning River. He and his compatriots used this waterway as a supplier of drinking water, fish, and transportation.

Thick forests once lined the shores of this oversized stream called Mahoning by the indigenous people. Many trees were cut and floated downstream as logs, enabling Young's town (Youngstown) to build housing for a burgeoning population.

The once pristine shallow Mahoning tributary provided recreation for pioneers as well. Swimming and boating were favorite pastimes. During winter months, figure skating, ice fishing, and sledding were popular activities indulged in on the surface of the frozen watercourse.

As the metropolitan area grew, the meandering channel was hemmed in by bustling gritty foundries, mills, and factories. The iron and steel industries used the water of the Mahoning River as a coolant in the manufacturing of alloys and metal plates.

Industrial refuse and raw sewage began to pollute the Mahoning River heavily by the early 1900's. The once pure pearl of a river turned a poisonous brown. No longer would local inhabitants use its water for drinking, cooking, bathing, or farming. The ice houses, which once cut blocks of ice out of the frozen river's surface during wintertime to be used in ice chests and ice boxes during the warmer months, now looked elsewhere for "fresh ice".

Native Americans, pioneers, run-a-way slaves, curious youth, hoboes, tramps, and gypsies all had a fondness for the diminutive river. It provided sustenance, safety, pleasure, and adventure. Riverfront factories, warehouses, concrete embankments, water retention systems, filtration stations, and a series of dams all conspired to make this fountain of life inaccessible. It was tamed and exploited mercilessly.

Urban encroachment upon the primordial watershed resulted in devastating floods. Downtown Youngstown, iron and steel facilities, and low-lying neighborhoods began to dread the spring thaw and the accompanying rainy season. The indomitable Mahoning River regularly overflowed its banks and wreaked havoc on a community, which had taken nature for granted. Reservoirs were erected to tame and hold back the once lively river, which was still the lifeblood of more than a dozen municipalities.

When the canal craze swept America, the Mahoning River was made part of a route which once connected the Great Lakes region to the Ohio River panhandle. There was talk for many years about the construction of the Lake-to-River Canal, which would have accommodated large barges and ships from Lake Erie via the Mahoning River into Pittsburgh. Railroad interests killed this natural transportation grid. Ironically, tracks were laid close to the river to take advantage of the flat topography. Although trains were also intermittently stalled by river surges, they managed to thrive in a valley, which once was totally dependent upon a glacial channel.

Modern folks scarcely recognize the existence or importance of the haggard Mahoning River. Greater Youngstown is now in a post-industrial sunset. Highways ship raw materials, goods, and services now. Water transportation is viewed as slow, inefficient, and as quaint as a Mark Twain tale. Although major rivers, such as the Ohio and Mississippi, continue to be major economic factors in commerce, small rivers like the Mahoning are of little importance today vis--vis days gone by.

River reclamation projects hope to dredge and rehabilitate the Mahoning River. Some few venture into its muddy currents in canoes and on rafts. Enclaves of hardy fish and migratory fowl are sometimes sighted. Varied flora and fauna survive along the marshes, swamps, and inlets to the surprise of aquatic explorers.

Some urban architects tout riverfront development, replete with parks, marinas, walkways, and amphitheaters as a means to give rebirth to rivers long ignored and senselessly abused. Today, several generations view the Mahoning River as a novelty and not a requisite for survival.

In central Youngstown, a new convention center is being erected next to the long-suffering and once noble Mahoning River. These grand civic projects are viewed as the major catalyst and last hope for the reincarnation of a dying metropolis. The controversial riverside location is considered aesthetically pleasing. Ironically, the renaissance of Youngstown is rooted in the historic Mahoning River.

History does repeat itself.

Only Yesterday

by Richard S. Scarsella

Persons, places, and things that were once so much a part of our lives imperceptibly disappear. We are so busy, we scarcely notice their absence until one day we feel the void their departures leave behind.

It seems like only yesterday when every child on my block knew the bus schedule into town. In days when parents were not private taxis for children's activities and the streets were safe to walk, it was not uncommon for hordes of youth to catch the transit to get around. Favorite day destinations included the Y.M.C.A., Y.W.C.A., and Pemberton Pool. Oftentimes, we would need a transfer to #8 Market or #9 Mahoning to complete our treks. Of course, we were always home in time for dinner.

It seems like only yesterday when downtown Youngstown buzzed with excitement. Well-dressed crowds filled the wide sidewalks, which led to fine specialty shops, grand department stores, and ornate theaters. Livingston's show windows were tableaus of New York, Parisian, and Italian fashion scenes. White fox furs, rhinestone jewelry, alligator handbags, and beaded couture garments all beckoned us into this luxurious women's emporium. Boys would blush when forced to accompany their mothers' into this female bastion.

It seems like only yesterday when a trip to the main library, located on Wick Avenue, was a necessary part of a student's academic preparation. In the days before computer research and spacious branch libraries, this classical fortress of higher learning daily attracted throngs of valley residents. The once revolutionary microfilm projectors catalogued world, national, and local history alike, all free for the asking. Hours literally flew by in the marble floored, cathedral ceiling reading rooms and dark, musty stacks.

It seems like only yesterday when we would pick up loved ones at the seemingly romantic B & O, New York Central, Pennsylvania, and Erie Lackawanna railroad terminals. These passenger and cargo depots transversed our lives. Seasoned conductors and well-tailored porters readily shared tales of the rails with adventure hungry juveniles. Casey Jones was a story well known to all that frequented these once important stations.

It seems like only yesterday when long, low, curvaceous, chrome ladened automobiles made by DeSoto, Packard, Studebaker, Imperial, Nash, Hudson, and Edsel cruised area streets. Naturally, Wick Avenue was a mecca for car lovers. Barrett Cadillac, Kroehle Lincoln Mercury, and Strausbaugh Dodge were legendary auto showrooms that serviced generations of families as their own. Family owned and operated, they were leaders in civic affairs.

It seems like only yesterday when eating lunch at the Italian Restaurant or the Tod House Hotel Coffee Shop before attending a matinee at the Palace, State, Paramount, or Warner theaters was a common practice. These opulent movie palaces made Clark Gable, Tyrone Power, Gary Cooper, Bette Davis, Joan Crawford, and Mae West American royalty. Hollywood magic made life in a steel town bearable.

It seems like only yesterday when Idora Park was the entertainment center of the metropolitan area. Trolley cars, electrified buses, and station wagons all daily filled this historic amusement park with thousands of patrons. The aromas of freshly made popcorn, cotton candy, and roasted peanuts still linger on the palette. Screams from the Wild Cat and the Jack Rabbit wooden coasters still seem to echo through the long abandoned midways. This hapless landmark of more prosperous, gentile times still haunts our collective psyches.

It seems like only yesterday when we would partake in huge front porch reunions at my maternal grandparents' urban homestead. Glass pitchers of sour pink lemonade, stirred with sugar cubes and shaved ice, seemed bottomless. Elderberry pie, peach chiffon cake, and sweet cream custard all were staples of these repasts. No one worried about dieting. If we overate, Alka Seltzer and Bromo Seltzer were readily available for relief.

It's hard to believe that once familiar persons, places, and things now belong to history. As I remind myself of this harsh truth, I sometimes hear an inner voice. It's always the same message. The words? "It seems like only yesterday when…."

Parochial School Days

by Richard S. Scarsella

In years past, up into the 1960's, going back to school for some children meant attending a fortress of God. Where? The local Roman Catholic, Byzantine Catholic, or Greek Orthodox schools, referred to as parochial schools.

At these church-supported institutions of virtue, a fourth "R" had been added to the curriculum. Its name? Religion. A student would be instructed, some said indoctrinated, in literature, handwriting, arithmetic, as well as a particular Christian doctrine.

In these academies, like in the days of Plato, Aristotle, and Socrates, spiritual growth was fostered alongside intellectual development. The lofty aim was to mold mind, spirit, character and patriotism. Impressionable children were in awe of solemn crucifixes, life-like statues, soaring lit tapers, perched on gold candelabras, and Gregorian chants, oftentimes sung in Latin or another non-English vernacular. Soldiers of Christ, called nuns, priests, brothers, or monks were the bulk of the faculty. Their long robed garbs, starched collars, bat winged sleeves, shadowy hoods, and wooden rosary beads gave them an otherworldly aura of authority that few children dared to test. Seemingly, the hallowed halls of these lyceums had the imprimatur of God ever-present.

Parochial students, some of who were of Protestant, Jewish, or of other faiths, went to morning Mass weekly, with their classmates and teachers. Both the homilies and catechism instruction reiterated passages from the Holy Bible, guaranteed to keep children on the right road to salvation, lest they tempt the scourges of purgatory or the damnation of hell. The dedicated clergy took seriously their mission to save their young wards from the temptations of an increasingly secular world.

Scholars at these schools needed to memorize prayers, sing liturgies, and have their missals (prayer books) on hand for devotions. Splashing holy water, laughing during silent prayer time, or not genuflecting or kneeling at appropriate moments brought swift, oftentimes physical reprisals, from ever-watchful instructors of the faith. Good habits were seen as integral for redemption and shields to temptations.

Public school children were always fascinated by parochial students. Not eating meat on Friday was of constant interest to non-Catholics. Holy cards, religious medals, Saints' Days, Holy Days, indulgences, palms, Confession (now called Reconciliation), May crownings of the statue of Mary, stations of the cross, relics, incense, and scapulas all were part of the parochial school environment. Today, these practices are rarities.

Few clergy are available now to serve in parochial schools. Modern religious men and women, for the most part, no longer dress like their medieval predecessors. They have become more of this world, like the laity they serve. Students still wear uniforms in the parochial schools, but they no longer reek of bleached cotton or scratchy wool. Lay teachers try to set examples for their charges, but lack the regal, anointed, austere, celibate presence of the now vanished legions of priests, sisters, brothers, and monks of the not so distant past.

Whenever I hear a pipe organ in a church, see girls and boys in Communion or Confirmation clothes, experience an Easter vigil, or attend a sober High Mass, my mind takes me back to my former parochial school days. All the many ethnic Roman Catholic, Byzantine Catholic, and Greek Orthodox parish schools in the valley bear testimony to the importance of a certain Christian heritage, that parochial schools sought to preserve and nourish. Despite their warts, these schools enriched America by instilling the lessons of the Ten Commandments. The founding fathers knew that a country without a sense of God would not endure or prosper for long. Obviously, children had to be morally cultivated, so that they could protect their immortal souls and their country from dark forces. Parochial schools were and are entrusted with this weighty task.

Hopefully, the millennium will not be the requiem for more parochial schools. Finances, not faith alone, make or break these tenuous strands to a rich pedagogic tradition. These schools are and have been bastions of morality in a very immoral world. Along with Protestant schools and Jewish academies, these denominational school enclaves have been oasises in a country that seems intent on isolating faith from mainstream America. A nation founded by a belief in the freedom of religious expression, has almost forbidden religious expression anywhere in public life, including public schools, regardless of the consequences. Ironically, Congress still begins its sessions with a non-denominational prayer. Public schools may not do the same. Let's pray that religious affiliated schools continue to check the moral relativism that has gripped our country. Amen.

Patron of the Arts

by Richard S. Scarsella

The Mahoning Valley has long been portrayed as little more than an industrial corridor between our sister cities Pittsburgh and Cleveland. When one thinks of Youngstown, steel and iron are the first associations one usually forms. The rich local histories of famed educator William Holmes McGuffey and the pioneer movie family called Warner Brothers have dimmed over time. One man has escaped oblivion due to his own foresight. His name? Joseph G. Butler, Junior.

Known for the Butler Institute of Art, which Butler endowed, few now know that he wrote an autobiography titled "Recollections of Men and Events", published in 1927 by G. P. Putnam & Sons, New York, New, York. This fascinating book is a literal travelogue throughout his hometown and extending around the world.

Butler was a noted collector of American art. His museum was the first gallery dedicated to domestic painting. However, he fully appreciated European fine arts. Therefore, he traveled widely on the continent to expose himself to the "masters".

When not spearheading efforts to build the National William McKinley Birthplace Memorial in Niles, Ohio, Butler embarked upon a series of intercontinental travels. The tragic assassination of the martyred president weighed heavily upon him, since he was a boyhood friend of this beloved leader. His friendship with President Taft and Pittsburgh industrialist H.C. Frick allowed his vision of the McKinley monument to become reality.

His first love was collecting fine art. He did so with great relish. Butler's taste was nurtured by an intellectual curiosity and fed by worldwide exposure to ancient civilizations. In Europe, he found inspiration to later build an elegant edifice to house his personal art collection.

In 1908, Butler and his family sailed across the Atlantic Ocean passage in search of culture and illumination. In Germany, he toured the famed Sans Souci Palace, which housed the royal holdings of several generations of German rulers.

The solidity and practicality of German architecture most impressed this man of taste and discernment.

While in London, Butler and his entourage lodged at the Grand Hotel. From there, he rediscovered English history and lore in the bowels of legendary Westminster Abbey. Within its hallowed halls, Butler was surrounded by the graves of prominent English men and women from over a thousand years. He later remarked that this visit was "A journey back through the centuries." In Europe, he found a respect for civilization not so readily accepted in his own land.

When Butler toured George Washington's ancestral home, named Sulgrave Manor, he proposed formation of an association to properly preserve it for future generations. His idea was realized in England and he considered this to be a crowning, if little known, achievement of his life.

During a later sojourn to France, Butler traversed through Limoges, a fabled porcelain-manufacturing center, and through Aubusson, the renowned tapestry region. He made purchases that later graced his home and museum. Butler appreciated the fact that many great American painters and sculptors received their initial education in France. Butler later helped arrange the sale of French art to America to fuel the French wartime effort. The grim scenes of battle preparation touched him. He pointedly remarked, "What does civilization mean if it fails to include justice and consideration for others?"

Butler was oftentimes asked what motivated his philanthropy. His answer was stated, "He had a wish to do some act of kindness, which, while giving him pleasure, would pass on, giving others benefit and added pleasure." The grand edifice named the Butler Institute of Art carries on his timely wisdom.

Personages

by Richard S. Scarsella

Life is full of faces, voices, and tableaus. Once experienced, they leave indelible marks on our psyches. Perhaps unknown to us, we are ever on the lookout for the familiar in this strange new world we inhabit. Intonations from the past do not quickly fade.

Several generations grew during the years of the Huntley & Brinkley News Show. Dominating the airwaves in the 1950's and 1960's, gravel voiced Chet Huntley and suave David Brinkley somberly reported every nuance of the Cold War and every heartbreaking detail of the horrific Kennedy assassinations. These affable dinnertime "talking heads", known to us in shadowy black and white staged television reposes, were very much a part of our daily routines. Even now, when I hear a haunting refrain from the classical score, which introduced this nightly program, I still hesitate. Echoes of "Good night David" and "Good night Chet" still swirl in my head.

The telegenic John F. Kennedy set a new standard for media imagery. His dark theatrical good looks, upper crust Bostonian accent, and all-American mannerisms endeared him to an electorate tired of the bland Dwight D. Eisenhower years. Memorable speeches, a glamorous Jackie Kennedy as a dutiful wife, and two adorable children made "Jack" a living icon. When ruthlessly gunned down in Dallas, with cameras rolling, Camelot screeched to a halt and the Viet Nam War ignited. Kennedy's immortal phrase "Ask not what your country can do for you, but what you can do for your country" still resounds in the year 2002, as we come to grips with international terrorism and cultural degeneration.

Richard M. Nixon rose to power after Lyndon B. Johnson impaled himself in our Southeast Asian "police action." Although Nixon was considered a "hawk", he ardently sought "peace with honor". When this rabid anti-Communist aficionado sought rapprochement with "Red China", some thought the world was entering a new period of stability. Unfortunately, "Tricky Dick" was soon embroiled in the insipid Watergate scandals. Ironically, this master politician is probably best remembered by his pathetic proclamation, "I am not a crook."

When Nixon unceremoniously resigned, in a vain effort to avoid national condemnation, his rambling exit remarks were haunting. His bittersweet "v" for victory sign, flashed before he disappeared into the bowels of an army helicopter and was whisked out of Washington D.C., revealed a complex conflicted fallen titan of our times. We knew his likes would never be seen again.

Garbo, Gable, Dietrich, and Gary Cooper all were larger than life in their heydays. When a washed-up B movie contract player, Ronald Reagan, made a bid for the presidency, even Hollywood was in disbelief. After Reagan won the election, the marriage of stardom and politics was inarguable.

"Ronnie" exuded a John Wayne Yankee confidence, bravado, and rugged independence. An archconservative, swept into the White House by landslides in a liberal country, Reagan confounded critics by enormous acclaim. Although not an academic genius or a geopolitical strategist, he gave voice to a prophetic phrase. Namely, he called the Soviet Union "An evil empire." His intent was clear. He would use "star wars" technology to checkmate and vanquish Russia and her satellite captive neighbors. Reagan's bold proclamation helped de-stabilize the corrupt Lenin-inspired kingdom. When the USSR inexplicably dissolved, Reagan's detractors were silenced. Like Winston Churchill, Great Britain's indefatigable wartime leader, Reagan uttered the thoughts and feelings of the democratic ideal.

I still miss these dignitaries of old. Perhaps, Queen Elizabeth's continued popularity can partially be attributed to the masses wanting an easily identifiable symbol in a troubled era. When the queen's royal gold gilded coach seemingly floats over the narrow cobblestone streets of London, I realize she knew Kennedy, Nixon, Reagan, and a pantheon of greats. Like other notable personages, she also appeared many times on the venerable Huntley & Brinkley broadcasts. In a true sense, her royal majesty epitomizes living history. She is a surviving dinosaur in the celluloid age. Long may she live.

Pianoforte

by *Richard S. Scarsella*

In the years before television, computers, tape-recorders, and video players dominated our lives, most every household had a radio for "family entertainment." After dinner had been served and the dishes were done, households would take to the easy chairs and turn on the radio dial to their favorite stations and shows.

Through the magic of the airways, stage and screen stars entertained us for free. Milton Berle, Bing Crosby, Bob Hope, Burns & Allen, Judy Garland, Peggy Lee, and Ethel Merman, to name but a few, flooded our living rooms with classics from vaudeville, Broadway, Hollywood, and night clubs. Drama, comedy, burlesques, and musical repertoire riveted our attention well through the early 1950's.

Many might not recall that even during the heyday of radio, pianos were integral parts of our lives. Most every middle-class home had one. So did many poor homes. A child's education was not considered complete without piano lessons. The legendary downtown Youngstown department stores made owning or renting an instrument affordable, convenient, and accessible for those that sought to acquire culture. Strouss' and McKelvey's music halls furnished instruments, sheet music, and instructors for several generations.

In my neighborhood, music teachers could be seen daily walking to homes with musical scores in hand. Most were old maids, widows, eccentrics, or aspiring concert performers moonlighting from the Dana School of Music. From three o'clock until eight o'clock, dutiful students practiced scales, rondos, sonatas, and rhapsodies in sync with key wound metronomes. Non-serious students could expect a slap on the wrists with a ruler, shrill oral reprimands, or icy glares from frustrated trainers.

Our family took instructions for years from the same piano instructors. It was not uncommon for several children in a home to study the same musical selections from the same master until age eighteen. In many cases, these ambassadors of the muses and of harmony became close family friends. Their presence at dinners or for tea was considered a privilege. Driving or walking them to the bus line was good manners. For the small fees they charged, their knowledge and artistry were both a luxury and a bargain.

When our musical taskmasters were not present, practice was oftentimes a bore or a punishment. Throughout any given weekday evening and all day Saturday or Sunday, Youngstown neighborhoods were filled with amateur pianists pounding out tunes on the eighty-eight. During this era, the din of television and stereos did not hold sway. No, this time belonged to uprights, spinets, and baby grand pianos.

During the reign of forte-pianos, a sign of success and accomplishment was when one traded or sold an old piano for a newer, larger, and more expensive model. Old-timers favored the Chickering brand. This company was known for a saloon/jazz/populist sound, like the famous player pianos of the turn of the century. Wurlitzer catered to those that liked a "theatrical" tone, similar to the vaudeville organs and pianos found in depression era movie palaces. Baldwin and Kimball dominated the family clientele. Their genuine African ivory and ebony keys, handsome solid cherry, mahogany, and walnut cases, and matching benches and stools nicely complimented American interior décor. A home was not considered well furnished unless it had a piano in the parlor.

A symbol of refined expertise and investment was the Steinway. Hand-made in Long Island City, New York, the Steinway grand pianos were and are considered unrivalled for a quality of sound and responsiveness of touch. The voice of this internationally renowned instrument was discernible to even an untrained ear. Going to a Steinway sponsored recital was considered to be an important social event.

In our youthful ignorance, little did we know that exposure at an early age to our musical heritage would stick with us throughout our lives. Whether I am in church, at a concert hall, watching vintage Lawrence Welk reruns, or listening to the radio, a piano movement can still stir long dormant recognition to a spectrum of sound and a palette of tonal color almost forgotten.

When my parents sold the family homestead and moved into a retirement community, our prized family heirloom became an orphan. No one wanted it. I had already purchased a baby grand piano for my daughter—who reluctantly takes lessons—and had not need for another pianette. However, I relented. Now residing in a basement recreation room, I sometimes hear the familiar cords I once grew up on. Occasionally, in the dark of the moon, our cat trods gingerly over the well-worn keyboard. I can almost feel the music.

Planting Time

by Richard S. Scarsella

In years past, Youngstown area residents spent many hours in and around their yards. Before two-income families, air conditioning, cable television, and yard-care maintenance services changed our lifestyles, families expended a great deal of time and effort in their yards. Having friends or families compliment you on your flowerbeds or healthy weed free grass was a status symbol.

McKelvey's and Strouss' once both had premium lawn and garden centers. The latest innovations were debuted at these venerable retailers. Self-pulling mowers, battery-operated edgers, and electric shears all were made popular and affordable at these mercantile landmarks to throngs of curious and avowed gardeners. Many households would take advantage of lay-a-way and ninety days same as cash plans to finance their purchases. Other homeowners would be persuaded to use a charge card for the first time, so that they could acquire riding mower tractors.

It was not uncommon at one time to see many shoppers heading to and from downtown, by bus or car, with all matter of lawn equipment in hand. Having McKelvey's or Strouss' technicians sharpen, tune-up, or repair trusted lawn and garden implements was a much-honored tradition in our valley that disappeared with the closing of these legendary stores.

Dixie's Garden Emporium, on West Midlothian Blvd., was a family-owned institution devoted to horticulture. This combination nursery and greenhouse earnestly counseled one with Old World arboricultural husbandry techniques and state-of-the-art technology. Dixie Tocco, owner, dispersed seeds, wisdom, and humor with equal aplomb. With his retirement, the area lost yet another retail fixture whose void has never been filled.

Before huge discount and do it yourself mega-stores opened in our communities, the original Country Gardens of Austintown was a veritable mecca for gardeners and cultivators. This huge expanse of flowering plats, mounds of fertilizers and manure, and burlap wrapped saplings seemed endless. Petunias, dahlias, tulip bulbs, climbing roses, and tomato vines all were displayed in wide rows. This allowed one to pull one's own wagon, cart, or wheelbarrow with ease. Even wheelchair bound shoppers could be seen navigating these Garden of Eden aisles searching for plantings to make their homesteads welcoming and cozy for summer entertaining.

In the 1960's, 1970's, and 1980's, Consolidated, Bargain Port, and Hill's department stores all catered to consumers who were pressed for time and looking for less expensive household greenery. Burpee seed packets, plastic gardening tools made in China, and pre-measured and bagged lime all could be checked out alongside other purchases. The days of making a pilgrimage to a favorite landscape center were soon eclipsed by new shopping trends. Today, catalog and Internet sales allow one to purchase flora and fauna without ever leaving one's home.

Whenever April showers give way to May flowers, my thoughts always go back to the days when my grandparent would endlessly discuss what to plant each season. The days of cherry, apple, pear, plum, and peach orchards in a family's backyard seem remote now. Did I ever pick fresh rhubarb in a neighbor's yard and have a pie made of it by dinnertime? Did I imagine picking mint leaves in the backyard and chewing on them to freshen my breath? I shake my head and wonder.

I do vividly recall, however, the wrought iron birdbaths, grape arbors, forsythia covered trellises, plaster caste fountains, lucky stone rock gardens, life-like deer and rabbit lawn figures, marble angels, St. Francis of Assissi statues, and Mary shrines which were all once common sights in area yards.

There was an era when the lawns and garden-beds around our porches and patios were literally windows into our souls.

Plaza Appeal

by Richard S. Scarsella

Older valley residents clearly remember a time when the phrase "going to town" meant more than shopping. Up into the 1940's, the central district of downtown Youngstown serviced our needs for merchandise, entertainment, dining, and professional care. Huge anchor department stores, named McKelvey's and Strouss', first-run movie palaces, named Warner, State, Paramount and the Palace, fine dining halls, named The Mural Room and the Youngstown Club, and skyscraper office buildings, full of doctors, attorneys, and physicians, all acted as magnets to lure people downtown. Patrons from the tri-county area braved congested, narrow streets, inclement weather, parking meters, and parking decks to do their business.

After World War II, visionary developers began to clear land on the outskirts of town. The local DeBartolo and Cafaro families led the way nationwide in the building of strip plazas, in what would later be called suburbia. With the opening of the Mahoning, Liberty, and Boardman Plazas in the 1950's, we no longer had to go downtown to shop. Youngstown would never be the same again.

These new, long, flat, air-conditioned, modern market places featured free, well-lit storefront parking, wide covered sidewalks, evening hours and one-stop shopping. We could buy a prescription, fill a grocery order, peruse a variety store, eat lunch, select a new wardrobe, and have the car serviced, all in a single location. Baby-boom parents and their children, hordes of teen-agers and Depression era elders all instantly adopted these new temples of commerce.

Consumers were enthralled with these contemporary piazzas. Gray Drugs featured the latest cosmetics, huge candy displays, fast pharmacy service, and chrome-plated lunch counters. Homemakers could easily walk to the A & P, Kroger, Loblaw, or Century food stores, while they clipped coupons and collected savings stamps. Western Auto offered drive-in service departments, complemented by state-of-the-art appliance, radio, television, and stereo departments. Penney's offered two-floors of mainstream family fashions and its famous catalog departments. Murphy's, Grant's, Woolworth's, and Kressege's displayed a cornucopia of sundry items, including rows of toys, house wares, and hardware. These plazas were indeed convenience centers, located near the new neighborhoods of the burgeoning valley. As their popularity grew, downtown lost its grip and preeminence in our lives.

Later shopping centers built included the McGuffey, Lincoln Knolls, Austintown and Wedgewood Plazas. Gradually, plazas began to grow larger and more diverse in time. Theaters, bowling alleys, post-offices, arcades, discount stores, chain restaurants, health clubs, and adjoining professional parks turned these complexes into community centers. In the 1960's, we now used the phrase "going to the plaza". They had become our new town squares.

Ironically, the malls of the 1970's began to sap the vitality of the plazas. The plazas had done the same to the downtown. Eerily reminiscent of the now derelict downtown, all area plazas now have vacant storerooms for rent. Customers have changed their preferences again. They now favor indoor shopping complexes—the ultimate cathedrals of consumption. Plazas no longer reign supreme. They have been eclipsed. Malls are the new downtown. History does repeat itself.

Post-Holiday Melancholy

by Richard S. Scarsella

Every year, area families rediscover the unwritten rule of holidays. Its name? Holiday blues.

When the heady excitement and anticipation of Christmas and New Year's passes, the somber realities of the everyday world we inhabit reassert their unyielding dominance. We find solace in the warm recollections of the past holiday seasons to give us strength to soldier on.

The huge after-Christmas sales and clearances are a very unsentimental exercise in last minute purchases, exchanges, and due bills. The old Strouss' and McKelvey's department stores once drew thousands of shoppers downtown with their legendary markdown inventory sales. For shoppers, armed with gift certificates, this was the last hurrah of consumerist frenzy. Once gaily decorated emporiums of Santa's workshops soon became stripped of their festive magic. They were literally picked clean by bargain hunters, hell-bent looking for good deals. The commercial aspect of the holidays became apparent to those caught in this mad rush.

Oddly, gifts that to many seemed so appropriate were now viewed callously as impractical and kitsch. Disassembled store displays seemed to rob merchandise of that special holiday magic that surrounds the buying and receiving of presents. Bills, statements, and IRS notices received in the mail, which all too soon replaced greeting cards, seemed to be particularly anti-climatic for such a joyous season.

As the winter freeze begins to take hold, post-holiday revelers are confronted with many tasks. Every year, decorations must be taken down, packed, and stored for the next occasion. Half burned Christmas candles, stale punch, cookie crumbs, ribbon candy bits, and rejected fruitcakes all must be dealt with, so the environment can return to normalcy again.

Evergreen trees, with strands of tinsel still attached, litter sidewalks. Some are ignobly interred in plastic trash bags, awaiting final disposition. All are silent sentinels to what has now passed. By this time, everyone is tired of leftover food.

Turkey potpies and warmed-over wedding soup exit our menus. They are replaced by less exotic fare.

New Year's resolutions begin to haunt us, as it becomes apparent that old practices are not easily changed or disposed of. The hopes and aspirations we have for the beginning of the year oftentimes are challenged by lingering hangovers, weight gain, post-holiday stress, and remorse for things that are, were, and never will be.

Fresh calendars are proudly displayed after New Year's. Unmarked by disappointment, illness, or death, these timepieces become journals of our lives. Diary keepers begin anew as well, as they set aside their previous entries, with not a little regret for times now gone.

Probably most heart rendering of all after-holiday rituals is the removal of commemorative decorations from area graveyards. Loving wreaths, many made of black ribbon, garlands, and votive candles are all taken away by devoted family and friends, in keeping with cemetery regulations. To the survivors, the message that the holidays are over is deafening, as one drives away with memorials from the eternally departed.

Some individuals seemed to have a remedy to ward off the post-holiday melancholy. My grandmother seemed very deft at preserving holiday cheer and hope, in a very unflashy manner. Every year, alongside the family Bible and faded albums, she faithfully saved colorful ribbons, elegant bows and inspiring Christmas cards in her old oak cedar chest. Throughout the year, she would unwrap her treasures from layers of yellowed tissue paper and wax paper and let her grandchildren view them. We were always thrilled by her keepsakes, many of which were more than double our age. Each item had a parable associated with it.

In her own way, our grandmother had discovered and fostered the true essence of the holidays, by holding onto the priceless, irreplaceable memories of seasons past, which all had roots in the miracle at Bethlehem. Hopefully, all area families are blessed with the same sage wisdom.

The Power of Fashion

by Richard S. Scarsella

Up into the early 1960's, good fashion sense was a must for anyone wanting to be accepted socially in business, church or community circles. In this much-stratified time, well-dressed maids and matrons wore hats, gloves, and demure dresses. Gentlemen donned conservative suits, white kerchiefs, and top hats. The youth revolt of the 1960's ushered in the era of hippies, yippies, and free spirits. Social mores crumbled. Style became more individualistic and treacherous.

Magazines, such as Vanity Fair, Vogue, McCall's, Esquire, and Gentlemen's Quarterly, dutifully documented the evolution and devolution of fashion. When runway fashion shows premiered what Americans would be wearing, one magazine empire took to the footlights with its own extravaganza. It continues to this day. Its name? The Ebony Fashion Fair.

This pioneer celebration of haute couture and casual elegance showcases both minority models and designers, as well as internationally known design houses. Names such as Givenchy, Oscar de la Renta, Dior, Pierre Cardin, and Hugo Boss come alive in the traveling Ebony trunk show. Over a half-million dollars worth of originals dazzle audiences, with beads, leathers, furs, fabrics, colors, textures, and drape, not normally found in the Mid-West. It is considered the best in the country. The Youngstown Club of National Association of Negro Business and Professional Women's Clubs, Inc. bring this spectacle to town annually as a benefit.

In this day of care-free, wrinkle-free, perma-press, no-iron, low maintenance, wash and wear, drip-dry egalitarian clothing, the Ebony productions spotlight a more sophisticated, discerning, refined, genteel, cosmopolitan chic, that old Hollywood movies immortalized. Americans are still captivated by style, as witnessed by the national obsession with Jackie Kennedy, Marilyn Monroe, Audrey Hepburn, Princess Diana, Cary Grant, and John F. Kennedy, Jr. Their names still evoke indelible pictures in our minds of a certain ambiance or national mood.

In these turbulent, disconnected, disemboweled, impersonal, computerized, and homogenized times, Americans view the world of fashion as a window to another time, real or imagined. Retro styles of years past, are reborn for succeeding generations, in almost predictable cycles. The radical bell-bottoms of thirty years ago are now back in style, ironically, in a "politically correct" time. Classics and fads, from the Roaring Twenties, the Big Bands of the 1930's, Hollywood and Vine in the 1940's, 1950's Donna Reed, the Beatles' 1960's mod scene, the 1970's disco days, and the 1980's Ronald Reagan years of excess, all give expression and meaning to our contemporary lives. Our clothes have become declarations of what we believe, value, and discount.

Although newly minted millionaires are usurping cafe society, average Americans still seek a fashion standard to emulate or flaunt. Those that seek to be seen, heard, or acknowledged can do so by what they wear. Ebony Magazine and other such publications act as guides for would be men and women of the world. The search for savoir-faire is endless. Designer shows inspire infinite interpretations of what modern urbanites and suburbanites might wear in the future. Clothing is seen as signals of lifestyles, attitudes and quality of life.

The Ebony Fashion Fair is a beacon in this quest for self-expression and affirmation. Making a fashion statement is, after all, part of one's actualization and empowerment. The kings and queens of yore knew this to be true and adorned themselves accordingly. Hollywood royalty utilized the potency of image, on and off the screen, and defined Americana in the process. Fashion still rules today.

Preachers, Sisters, and Brothers

by Richard S. Scarsella

In a time not so distant, the clergy were integral parts of our daily lives. We regularly saw them and knew them outside the confines of sacred places. Like Christ, they were of the communities they served and not separated by clerical boundaries.

Well into the late 1960's, in the Youngstown area it was not uncommon to have breakfast at an Isaly's coffee counter with the local pastor. Savvy preachers—priests and ministers alike—knew the pulses of parishioners were easily and painlessly discerned in casual places of congregation. More than once, boy parishioners were caught unawares during their furtive purchases of comic books in corner dairy stores and at corner newsstands by world wise religious leaders. Vicars, dressed all in black or in civilian garb, exuded moral authority well outside the church halls and sanctuaries.

When a calling for a vocation was considered a blessed event and a badge of family honor, sub-deacons, deacons, seminarians, and clerics of all ranks were aggressively courted by "respectable" families. Having an ecclesiastic to dinner or tea was considered a social coup. Ancestral china, silverware, and table settings all were used to make a "good impression". A personal relationship with the vicarage was considered a must for households of good lineage. Astute clergymen cultivated these fraternal bonds, realizing a happy flock could be counted upon for support.

Roman Catholics, Byzantine Rite, Orthodox, and Anglican nuns were more elusive figures in our contemporary lives. When not going about their business in parish schools, orphanages, and in hospitals, these "brides of Christ" rarely ventured from their cloisters. Their long dark wool habits, white starched veils, and austere leather corrective shoes symbolized their separateness from daily communion with the laity they served in humility and in poverty.

Taking music lessons in the convent social hall, buying a memorial Mass card for a funeral at the visitors desk, or paying respects for a deceased sister in the nunnery chapel all were voyages into a serene mystical oasis amidst a secularized world. These ambassadors of God were subjects of much discussion amongst curious and ignorant youth. As much as we knew them, they were intrinsically unknowable to us. In a real sense, they were yet another mystery of church life.

A trip to the motherhouse of one of the religious orders was a surreal experience. When the public was invited into these blessed compounds, the laymen were in the minority. The avowed seemed to possess a sincerity, wisdom, and spirituality we could only guess about. When a novice became a consecrated member of an order and took final vows, these women of the cloth became earthly symbols of Mary's likeness, we were told. My grandmother always warned, "To cross a sister is to gamble one's soul."

When I went away to college, I attended a Benedictine priory academy. St. Leo's College in Florida was also an abbey. Built by the profits made from orange groves, this Old World monastery seemed oddly out of place in the tourist infested sunshine state. The brothers' and sisters' ministries to Native Americans descendents, migrant Hispanic crop pickers, and Cajun transients were a revelation to my mid-western point of reference.

These men and women of the Order—as the rules of St. Benedict are known—led purposeful lives. They exemplified unselfishness, the love of stewardship, and dedication to a higher good. One could not help but feel venal in their presence. However, our classes, social gatherings, and worship ceremonies brought fellowship—if only briefly. The hallowed seemed to hold the profane at bay.

The colorful missionaries, "born again" evangelists, and iconoclastic ascetics all were signposts in a world that once respected the invaluable roles the religious held in a now skeptical society. Although then, as now, some pledged to the religious life were known to be less than perfect, we still held clergymen and clergywomen in the highest of esteem.

I oftentimes have fleeting images of these personages of faith. Now, more than ever, they call out to us to stop, consider, pray, and reflect. An old world-weary abbot I once knew gently chided "Rid your mind of all the perfumed garbage and take the time to hear the one hand clapping."

I'm still listening.

Random Thoughts

by Richard S. Scarsella

For many of us, the Mahoning Valley has always been "home", regardless of where we traveled, went to college, or relocated. Memories include visions of a crowded downtown, prosperous steel mills, and vibrant neighborhoods. Though many of us now live in suburbia, our hearts remain in the once thriving city affectionately nicknamed Y-town.

I still recall bumper-to-bumper traffic on Youngstown's major thoroughfares named Oak Street, Market Street, Belmont Avenue, Mahoning Avenue, and South Avenue. The sight of huge steel hauling flatbed trucks, black and white checkered taxicabs, elephantine transit buses, and chrome-laden automobiles "stuck in traffic" was once a common occurrence. Now, eerie silence on these roads is surreal. Where did everyone go?

I can clearly recollect frequenting the Tod House, Pick Ohio, Voyager, and Youngstown hotels. These landmark hostelries once housed throngs of well-dressed traveling salesmen, blushing newlyweds, and vacationing families. Their luncheonettes, barbershops, beauty salons, and ballrooms were a slice of Manhattan in our midst. Not having a "grand hotel" downtown seems unthinkable to me and wholly unnatural.

I well remember the merciless bulldozers going about their insidious business as they leveled entire neighborhoods for the "superhighways" of the President Dwight Eisenhower administration. No one knew then that this wanton destruction of native architecture and culture was the beginning of the end for a way of life we took for granted. When we could avoid the central city via freeway, we unwittingly sapped its vitality and led to its eventual demise. Now, only the still imposing skyline remains as mute testimony to another more prosperous age in local history.

I am often reminded that "going to the movies" no longer means attending a double bill or a matinee at one of our elegant movie palaces. Seeing a Hollywood film at the State, Warner, Paramount, or Palace theatres was a real thrill. Marble staircases, tiled restrooms, crystal chandeliers, heavy velvet draperies, hand-carved wood paneling, and plaster bas-reliefs of European motifs gave these inimitable motion picture houses a grandeur now unimaginable. As the lights dimmed and went out for the last time on their once familiar marquees, it seemed that we knew that we were losing something irreplaceably valuable in our lives.

It does not seem that long ago that the prestige address in our area was the North Side's Fifth Avenue. This sophisticated boulevard once was home to industrial barons, leading financiers, cosmopolitan patrons of the arts, shrewd politicians, and mafia dons. Watching archetypal mansions become low-income housing, offices, and group homes desecrates the memories of those who built them to last the generations.

The disappearance of gleaming stainless steel passenger trains, flocks of pigeons on Central Square, scruffy hoboes, circus caravans, traveling gypsy clans, door-to-door salesmen, boxy home-delivery milk trucks, Esther Hamilton's Christmas Show, and beloved Idora Park all leave me aching for things long gone.

The future is uncertain, the present is commonplace, and the foregone seems provocatively alive if elusive in my consciousness. As they say, the past is always with us.

Remembrances

by Richard S. Scarsella

It is odd, with so much modernization, we still cast our eyes to the past. Obviously, memories are selective. We tend to filter out the hard times and dwell on the good times of yesteryear. In fleeting moments, I oftentimes conjure images of the shadowy past.

Not long ago, no lady would dare be seen in public without wearing gloves, hat, and silk or nylon stockings. Even the 1950's groundbreaking television series "I Love Lucy" portrayed ditzy Lucille Ricardo and faithful sidekick Ethel Mertz dressed in the conformist styles of the era.

Men also had fashion expectations thrust upon them. Gentlemen always wore ties, a dress shirt, and pressed pants. Ward Cleaver of "Leave It To Beaver" fame epitomized the idealized middle-class male role model. In America, clothing defined and stratified individuals into certain classes, like it or not. To flaunt convention invited ostracism.

In Youngstown, grocery shopping was conducted primarily in cozy neighborhood stores well into the 1950's. Family owned groceries, such as Anzevino & Sons and Rulli Brothers, were forerunners of sterile chain supermarkets that now dominate the food trade. It was once not unusual to phone ahead an order to a merchant, pick it up in a box, and pay the bill at the end of the month. In the days before credit cards, an "account" at the local market was considered a real convenience.

There was a time when it was typical for boys and girls to be members of a Boy Scouts, Girl Scouts, or Camp Fire troop. Uniformed youth once dominated public and private schools, churches, buses, libraries, and playgrounds as they went about their affairs in their quest for merit badges. Community service projects allowed impressionable minors to make constructive contributions to a society they would someday lead. These cadres of morality, patriotism, and wholesomeness made adults rest easy that all was well with America.

Tent revivals held by itinerant preachers once attracted throngs of sinners seeking salvation. City dwellers willingly traveled to the outskirts of town to be saved from evil and born again. Before television ministries became popular, Youngstown's divergent immigrant populations were regularly evangelized to by a wide assortment of traveling clergymen in search of a flock. Both white and black seekers of God looked forward to the sermons and services held under the stars.

As a child, I still vividly recall the screeching air raid horns mounted atop schools and other public buildings. Schoolchildren routinely and dutifully would hide under their desks and wait for the "all clear" sign before resuming their seats. The fact that these drills of the 1950's Cold War were considered normal now strikes me as strange.

UFO sightings in the Mahoning Valley and across the nation were once popular topics of spirited conversation amongst adults, teens, and young children. Orson Wells' famous Halloween radio hoax of invading Martians still lingered in our psyches into the 1960's. Hysterics over the Russian Sputnik satellites seemed to validate the theories of doom awaiting an innocent populace. Watching the precedent-making film "The Day the Earth Stood Still" shocked and confounded Americans. Regardless of nationwide sightings of unexplained phenomena, the military steadfastly claimed there was nothing to fear. Too many the post-World War II years seemed more menacing than the war years. Old-timers could be heard to lament that at least in the old days we knew whom the enemies were. Many a night passed by as we warily focused our gazes into space.

It is hard to believe that going to a movie downtown, buying a Strouss' malt, or having a picnic at Idora Park are no longer part of our lives. Those many unmemorable days of yore now seem without rival. Who would have thought that things once considered commonplace would be elevated to a stature of things greatly missed?

Renaissance

by Richard S. Scarsella

Youngstown, Cleveland, and Pittsburgh once shared a common heritage. All three cities were built on the backs of men toiling at iron and steel mills. Blast furnaces, full of fire, and oxygen furnaces were once trademarks of these communities. Names such as United States Steel, Republic, Carnegie, and Sheet and Tube once reigned supreme in this gritty corridor of immigrant laborers. No more. Times have changed. Heavy industry has been eclipsed by the fast growing technological and service sectors of our economy.

Cleveland and Pittsburgh made the transition to the "new world economy" and preserved much of their indigenous architecture and culture. Downtown Cleveland boasts of the magnificent Playhouse Square district and has won national acclaim for its preservation. This complex of historic ornate theaters has become a symbol of Cleveland's rebirth and vitality.

Downtown Pittsburgh aggressively developed its riverfront properties in order to attract residents and tourists alike. Venerable Station Square, a former railroad depot, replete with stained glass windows, boutiques, cafes, and nightclubs, has become a huge success. This gentrified structure is second to none in Boston, San Francisco, or New York.

Both Cleveland and Pittsburgh reached back into their pasts to find attractions for modern affluent consumers. This strategy has been the key to the survival of their central city cores. By transforming what they had inherited from their glory days, they insured bright futures.

The Mahoning Valley is steeped in tradition as well. Area residents speak wistfully of such vanished landmarks as the Palace Theater, Tod House Hotel, Elms Ballroom, Mural Room Restaurant, Hotel Youngstown, Livingston's, and Eagle's Club. These buildings once represented the "steel valley spirit".

Concerned citizens agonize over other much-threatened symbols of our environs. Idora Park, the Isaly Building, the State and Paramount Theaters, McKelvey's, Wick Park, and the entire Uptown strip are in dire condition. All of these places are unique to Youngstown and are visible testimonies of what we were and are now. They are still integral parts of a post-industrial community and are links to our much cherished past.

Collectively, the historic neighborhoods and structures of the valley are signatures writ in stone, brick, and mortar. They make us different from other cities and bear witness to our prosperity, innovativeness, artistic expression, and customs.

Just as the Home Savings tower clock anchors the downtown, our industrial, commercial, and residential edifices give roots to our region. This continuity nourishes the spirit and builds pride in our ancestry. We know we belong by the monuments left behind to remind us of this fact.

The long-awaited movement to recycle the abandoned State Theater as a Youngstown Playhouse facility is a good omen. Our valley has demolished too many irreplaceable jewels. This one must be saved. The arts oftentimes lead the way to the future, even if the present is full of skeptics.

Hopefully, Youngstown will take a cue from its sister cities of Cleveland and Pittsburgh. We must preserve if we are to endure. We are running out of time. Ironically, our future is in the past. As a wise man once said, "You may be done with history, but it is not done with you."

Riparian Rites

by Richard S. Scarsella

In the Mahoning Valley, after the winter thaw and April showers, residents began to prepare in earnest for summer fun. Local variety stores named Murphy's, McCrory's, Woolworth's, Grant's, Kressege's, and Ben Franklin's would all feature huge displays of Coppertone Sun Tan Lotion, Golden Age, NeHi, and Holly pop, Indian patterned beach blankets, Hawaiian straw hats, and Italian made leather sandals. Colorful plastic toy buckets, shovels, and rakes would be "on sale" in sets right next to water goggles, scuba gear, and inner tubes.

Mother's Day kicked off the unofficial opening of the summer season. Longer days and warming temperatures lured sun worshippers outdoors. Mill Creek Park would reopen trails. Idora Park would open the gates on weekends for special bookings. Like clockwork, valley residents were drawn to the local water holes for recreation and meditation.

Urban families found refuge from their concrete environs in the bowels of Mill Creek Park. This jewel of a metropolitan greenway featured three man-made lakes. Generations of inhabitants once lulled around the shores of Cohassett, Glacier, and Newport lakes. Fishermen, boaters, and swimmers all enjoyed these freshwater havens, until pollution and runoff fouled their once pristine watersheds. Sailing on the Lake Newport ferryboat, paddlewheeling on Lake Glacier, or catching frogs from atop lily pads at Lake Cohasset all were cherished springtime rituals enjoyed by all ages. These watery retreats were once very important parts of our lives.

Lake Milton, once owned by Youngstown, beckoned city dwellers to the lakeside resort of Craig Beach. Cottages, docks, beaches, nightclubs, and a small-scaled amusement park all hugged the shores of this reservoir. Toasted marshmallows, grilled wieners, diesel gas vapors, and carnival smells of vinegar soaked French fries, cotton candy, and freshly made buttered popcorn all flooded our senses. These scents and the cool breezes from this tranquil body of water made the drive to this countryside haven worthwhile and memorable. Dropping stones off the causeway and making ripples on the lake's surface were childhood rites of passage.

For the more adventurous, the coast of Lake Erie was only an hour away. This Great Lake's waterway once was full of unique blue perch, now extinct, and native trout species. White caps gave this lake an oceanic aura. Long convoys of picturesque ore boats could be seen on the lake's horizon, bellowing dark smoke from their stacks, as they languidly ferried Canadian minerals to awaiting American railcars.

The historic port town of Ashtabula was the gateway to tourist mecca Geneva-On-The-Lake. This Atlantic City styled strip of bingo parlors, fudge and donut shops, souvenir novelty stands, cabins, and dance clubs was the summer home to many Youngstowners. Here, miniature golf reigned supreme, day and night. State of the art mercury lamps and insect repellants allowed visitors to stroll the boardwalk at will, despite menacing clouds of Canadian soldier mosquitoes.

Lakeview Amusement Park, like nearby Idora Park, was frozen in time. Coney Island Moorish art deco concession stands, festival attractions, a funhouse, train, ferris wheel, kids' coaster, and lakefront ballroom all mesmerized youngsters. As wide eyed children rode the kiddieland attractions, world weary parents and grandparents would sip a phosphate, under shade trees, and tap their toes to the carrousel's calliope beat. The fog and mist offshore would oftentimes envelop the park and give it a dreamlike, timeless quality.

When the panoramic Lake Erie sunset began, scores of tourists would watch in awe. The smells of burning charcoal bonfires, dead fish, wet seaweed, and humid lake water all intermingled with the aromas of Eddie's Grille's steak burgers, salt-water taffy, and fresh roasted peanuts. This huge inland sea, formed by melted glaciers, was the area's ultimate getaway for city denizens.

Today, whenever I hear and see large flocks of seagulls begging for food at area suburban fast food parking lots, my mind travels back to fond recollections of riparian ways on the shores of area lakes. In fact, these memories are never far from my mind.

Roller-Skating Days

by Richard S. Scarsella

Since the turn of the century, valley residents have loved roller-skating. In its heyday, Idora Park had both an outdoor rink and indoor ballroom skating as well. The old Rayenwood Auditorium, on Youngstown's Rayen Avenue, billed roller-skating in between other arena events. Reed's Arena, under the B&O R.R. Bridge in downtown Youngstown, featured rhythm and blues and soul music for its urban crowds.

However, up until the 1980's, the roller-skating rink that predominated over all others was the legendary Boardman Rollercade. Situated on West Midlothian Blvd., on the Youngstown boundary with Boardman, the Kalasky family owned and operated the facility until it was sold to Schewebel's Bakery. Why does its memory live on?

Skating aficionados still argue that the Rollercade oak floor—several layers of hardwood atop each other—was the key to its fame. Professional skaters speak knowingly of the "grip" and "give" of this surface, to which amateurs paid scant attention.

Novice skaters grew fond of the Rollercade because they usually were introduced to the sport by way of school or church skating parties. Many generations recall renting well-worn skates and attempting to skate the "Hokey Pokey" and "Mexican Hat Dance".

Many youth had their first kiss or romance at the Rollercade, while holding hands under the twinkling lights and the revolving, mirrored, ballroom sphere. The rink nurtured young love, with classical and contemporary love songs in constant play during the couples' skate.

The Rollercade was an ideal winter sport destination. Its skating was indoors, it was well heated and it offered lessons as well as team competition. Although roller-skating did not have the cache of its Olympic cousin, ice skating, its appeal was wide, especially to restless youth looking for an affordable activity. Hearing the latest Top 40 radio music on the Rollercade sound system was well worth the admission price.

Families were attracted to the Rollercade. Seniors could be seen skating the waltz, in between sessions of energetic youth skating the flea hop. Youngsters would "wipe up the floor" in the center of the rink, under the watchful eyes of skate guards. Roller-skating was as wholesome as apple pie. Girls dressed in long poodle skirts and boys in cardigan sweaters epitomized the zenith of this pastime.

On any given night, the Rollercade was a microcosm of the valley. Suburbanites, farmers and city dwellers all mingled around its snack stand. Fresh made popcorn, limeade and sticky cotton candy gave the Rollercade a festival-like quality.

Every year, the Rollercade welcomed, entertained, and bade goodnight to thousands of local patrons. To this day, I can still see and hear the organist, in the glass booth over the rink, play a haunting tune. His last words? "All skate!"

Ruminations About Life

by Richard S. Scarsella

Life is lived in the present. It is anchored in the past. On any given day, we are reminded of things, places, people, and happenings from our previous foregone lives.

The Mahoning Valley is full of such ghosts. A ride along the murky Mahoning River still conjures images of once bustling monolithic steel and iron mills belching soot, fire, and acrid smoke throughout the cityscape and countryside. The now somnolent riverbed gives little hint of the importance it once had for area industry.

Abandoned salt, coal, and ore mines dot the county. Many farms and homes now reside upon the skeletons of these vanishing pits. Even now, an occasional sinkhole will unexpectedly reveal the graves of these subterranean caves.

Apple, pear, and cherry orchards gone to seed once were the scene of careful cultivation. Before "fresh" fruit was shipped in overnight by bus, train, or airplane, local groves fulfilled our needs. Anyone who has tasted wild regional varieties of apples, pears, and cherries will tell you that they had a distinctive delicious tartness not found in commercially grown fruit. A homemade pie, tort, or preserves containing native fruit species still remain unrivalled for flavor.

Youngstown area vintners and "moonshiners" were both famous and infamous for their products. Before, during, and after Prohibition, locally fermented liquor flowed cheaply and freely. Old World grapevine cuttings and Appalachian "recipes" provided those prone to imbibe a wide selection of spirits. Store bought brands just never seemed to have the "kick' or lingering aftertaste homebrews possessed.

Well into the 1950's, ladies and gentlemen frequented dressmakers, milliners, tailors, and haberdasheries in order to look their best. European clothiers brought their artistry and craftsmanship to our gritty town and made it all affordable for those seeking to be "respectable". I recall well the tradition of burying the deceased in their finest garb. To be interred wearing factory-made garments was a fate to be avoided at all costs.

Church guilds were once commonplace. Devoted and dutiful men and women belonged to these clubs as a way of expressing thanks to God and to demonstrate their union with their congregations. Trimming the church grounds, cleaning the sanctuary, and painting the social hall all were signs of good stewardship and a vibrant flock of believers. For a parish to hire "outsiders" to render services was considered a luxury and a sign of weakness.

Gardenbeds once captivated our daily lives. Old World War II "victory gardens", ripe with hearty Yankee vegetables—squash, rhubarb, and rutabagas—were carefully tilled. A bountiful harvest was considered a status symbol and a sign of thriftiness. We pitied folks eating grocery store produce.

In the days when flying kites, catching crawfish, and climbing trees were considered ordinary activities, their was great excitement when the Goodyear blimps—headquartered in Akron, Ohio—were sighted overhead. These graceful air yachts were hopelessly romantic and languid. Once these small dirigibles were seen, we all secretly and guiltily wondered if one would catch fire and crash a-la the legendary Zeppelin. In the pre-Sputnik age, these magnificent bulbous airships filled us with adventure, amazement, and dread.

At night, one no longer hears the shrill sirens of the local foundries and factories announcing the change of shifts. However, if one listens very carefully, one can hear the faint mournful railroad locomotive whistles. When heard, they invariably stir up long dormant memories of times gone by. Whether we realize it or not, the past is always with us.

Sanctuary

by Richard S. Scarsella

Throughout our lives, we need to take refuge from the harsh realities of the world. War, depression, civil strife, corruption, strikes, and all the rest wear you down. Without relief, your spirit can crack and succumb.

In the Youngstown area, hardship was no stranger in our lives. Industrial accidents, economic downturns, organized crime activities, and international conflicts all affected our lives. Extended families provided safe harbor for their own. Aunts, uncles, grandparents, and a multitude of cousins without fail gave solace and aid in times of sorrow, misfortune, trouble, or uncertainty. Food was the salve. Huge breakfasts, dinners, and suppers, featuring many courses, seemed to nourish both the body and soul. These grand multi-generational repasts still kindle warm memories today.

Places of worship once were opened all day for those seeking deliverance from their woes or thoughts. Darkened churches and temples, aglow with lit candelabras, provided a dramatic change of mood for the weary. The release from temporal concerns helped alleviate distress, anxiety, and doubt. Temples of the almighty were truly oasis-like for those drowning in secularism and materialism.

Entertainment provided temporary asylum for those in need of it. Downtown motion picture palaces featured vaudeville, burlesque, minstrel shows, and both A and B movies at reasonable rates. Box seats were also available, on a limited basis. Balcony seats were favored by youngsters and couples. Majestic organ music, emanating from hand-carved consoles and banks of pipes, created an escape from the gritty Mahoning Valley conditions. "Going to the movies" seemed to lighten your heart and improve your demeanor. Before television dominated our lives, opulent theaters showing the best Hollywood and European films anchored our lives.

Working-class families found ready deliverance in social clubs and corner taverns. It was once not unusual for family members to be active in activities such as horseshoes, knitting, gardening, and neighborhood improvement. Many belonged to the Elks, Eagles, Odd Fellows, Moose, Mason, or Knights of Columbus lodges. These fraternal organizations offered all manner of services to their members. Aid was but a phone call away.

Neighborhood saloons, lounges, cocktail bars, and nightclubs all provided fraternity as well. Like English pubs, these watering holes had a class structure, rituals, and unwritten rules. Outsiders were suspect. You were considered like family if you were a regular patron. Bartenders acted as counselors and the older clientele advised the younger crowd.

Nature-lovers found safe haven in the "green cathedral" named Mill Creek Park. This urban wonderland featured streams, caves, lakes, gardens, and golf courses. Traveling to the park for some "fresh air" was a time-honored tradition for those seeking immunity from the travails of life. The primordial cool park breezes seemed to calm us.

Carnivals, festivals, circuses, and fairs all provided brief respite from the daily grind. Budget entertainment offered temporary reprieve from anything trying or distressing. Sad clowns, performing animal acts, games of chance, novelty acts, freak shows, and midway delicacies, such as cotton candy and corndogs, all were welcomed diversions for those hard-pressed.

Children believe in and hold onto magic longer than adults. The Disney empire is built upon this premise. Locally, Idora Park was our enchanted kingdom. To this day, elderly residents can wistfully recall jarring rides on the Wild Cat wooden roller-coaster, gentle turns on the lethargic Ferris Wheel, and romantic waltzes in the starlit grand ballroom.

The cheap chic of "Youngstown's Million Dollar Playground" attracted denizens of all ages. Idora Park appealed both consciously and subconsciously to our need for renewal. No matter how many times we attended its well-known attractions, we always felt rejuvenated, refreshed, and replenished. Idora Park provided an affordable sanctuary during the summertime. Without it, I feel a little lost. Old friends are not easily replaced.

As disillusioned Ashley Wilkes told a distraught Scarlett O'Hara in the epic book "Gone With the Wind"—a morality tale of crumbling civilizations and lost worlds—"I mind very much losing the world I once knew." Now, more than ever, we need sanctuary. The question is where do we find it?

School Haze

by Richard S. Scarsella

In the back of my mind, school days linger in obscurity. A period of my life that was fraught with anxiety, energy, possibilities, accomplishments, disappointments, and warm feelings only occasionally crowds my adult thoughts.

As we count the days to Labor Day, the traditional end of summer, I cannot but help revisit the back-to-school regimen all of us have known well. Today, getting ready for school begins in earnest after the Fourth of July.

There was a time when many pupils had to wear uniforms to class. The outfits were usually vaguely inspired English prep academy styles. Invariably, they consisted of scratchy wool cloth, button-down shirts and blouses, and "sensible shoes". Both private and public school students were expected to act and look like "serious" scholars.

When fast foods were rarely indulged on by families, cafeteria fare was considered a treat for the school age population. Baked macaroni, lasagna, French fries, hot dogs, and hamburgers were gladly consumed by kids raised in homes where balanced meals were the norm. We pitied those that brought a bag or box lunch to eat. Home-prepared lunches consisted of meatloaf, sardines, grilled peppers, and Spam.

When newspapers and news magazines were kings and most residences subscribed to publications, "current events" assignments were the bane of those pursuing a diploma. Finding "suitable" articles, which could be discussed in class without causing discomfort or derision, was not always an easy task. Obviously, topics such as civil rights, strikes, class struggle, or women's equality were off limits in schools of middle America, for fear of the wrath of citizens, parents, and other vested interests.

There was also a time, I clearly remember now, when membership in the debate society, FTA (Future Teachers of America), or student council was considered chic and an indicator of sure future success. Clubs dedicated to science, chess, citizenship, and morals were also once in vogue in schools. Of course,

Camp Fire, Girl Scouts, and Boy Scouts troops were considered pure unadulterated Americana.

For years, "respectable homes" vied with each other to host faculty, administrators, and school board members for social events. The best linens, china, stemware, flatware, and refreshments were utilized to create a good impression. These formal niceties cemented families to schools and humanized all those involved. When teachers were commonly old maids or bachelors, invitations to homes were the highlight of their otherwise dull calendars.

Athletics always were an invisible glue in communities and neighborhoods. Cross-town rivalries once held schools and families enthralled. South High, East High, and North High, to name a few schools, all were once fierce competitors attracting throngs of fans. Sadly, these schools cease to exist. However, alumni and followers of these closed legendary institutions still mourn their passing. Whenever the first crisp fall air settles upon the valley, thoughts turn to former football seasons. The result? Echoes of the past rush clearly into view, if only for a short time.

Memories have a way of inviting themselves into our present-day lives. We never really leave our school days behind. They have taken up permanent residency in our collective consciousness.

To this day, whenever I hear a school bell ring, I am transported to days gone by.

Seems Like Old Times

by Richard S. Scarsella

Like clockwork, every year the holidays come around. They make us stop our hurried lives and take stock in what we have done and where we have been. Inevitably, we find ourselves thinking back to former days.

Old-timers wisely caution that things do not change much. Regardless, people are born, live, and die. Once a year we gather with friends and family for Thanksgiving, Christmas, and Easter. We give thanks, renew old relationships, and feast on special foods. Religious observances also are part of the holidays for most of us.

Thinking back, holidays are made up of seemingly unimportant traditions. Buying freshly dressed Barth Farms turkeys at Century, Loblaw, Kroger, and A&P food stores was a long held custom by area families. These pioneer supermarkets made shopping convenient with plenty of storefront parking, wide aisles, and trading stamps. These modern grocery stores employed our neighbors. We felt comfortable shopping amongst friends. Going "to the market" was an enjoyable activity. Many times I have witnessed patrons swap recipes, give household hints, and exchange baking secrets at these now vanished grocers. Even now, when I go shopping during the holidays, I half expect to patronize one of these legendary markets.

For years, families would purchase fine chocolates from Fanny Farmer Candies and Fron's Confections. Fanny Farmer had its main store in the downtown Paramount Theater building, right next to the box office. These Chicago made delicacies were displayed in immaculately clean beveled glass showcases. Sales clerks, dressed in white uniforms, gingerly hand packed family assortment boxes of dark, milk, and white chocolates. Figaros, buckeyes, and chocolate covered cherries were area favorites. At Fron's in Boardman, both city folks and suburbanites indulged in hand-dipped chocolates, high butterfat ice cream, and rainbow sherbet. Unbelievably, both of these familiar confectionaries are gone. Their absences are heartfelt during festive seasons when we try earnestly to salvage family rituals.

In the past we always stocked up on ice for entertaining purposes. Throughout the valley, icehouses were kept busy delivering huge blocks of ice and bags of ice cubes. Getting your ice order in early was a must, for no one had freezers, icemakers, or shaved ice at home. When these unique vendors slowly disappeared from our midst, some of the holiday magic evaporated as well.

Up into the 1950's, chimney sweeps and the coalman were very much part of our holiday preparations. The grand fireplaces of stately urban homes required the annual cleaning of a chimney sweep. When this service was rendered, one knew the holidays were not long in arriving. The first delivery of coal was equally portentous. Children delighted in the spectacle of a huge truck in the drive shoveling a half-ton of coal onto a chute into one's cellar. Burning coal furnaces were a sure sign that the holidays were upon us. Chimney smoke engulfed the neighborhoods in a dream-like fog, making the holidays even more enchanting.

Beloved radio personalities once conducted holiday broadcasts that entire families could enjoy together. Jack Benny, Burns and Allen, and Arthur Godfrey would set the holiday mood with old vaudeville skits, vintage Broadway tunes, and sanitized burlesque comedy routines. Many families sang along with their radio hosts until sign-off time. The tubes of crystal sets and radio consoles worked overtime during the celebrations of Thanksgiving, Christmas, and Easter.

Television in the 1950's promoted holiday themes endlessly. Bob Hope, Perry Como, Bing Crosby and Lawrence Welk yearly produced extravagant holiday "specials". Live performances by Nat King Cole, Frank Sinatra, Judy Garland, and Peggy Lee graced the airways with holiday melodies that still endure. Many of these shows gave birth to classics, such as "White Christmas" and "Frosty the Snowman". Even now Lawrence Welk's "champagne music" continues in perpetual reruns on cable television, making the holidays a little more familiar in the strange days we now inhabit.

Whenever I see a televised Macy's parade, hear sleigh bells, touch angel hair, smell fresh-baked minced meat pie, or drink fresh eggnog, my mind momentarily drifts back to earlier times. Memories warm the soul for what lies ahead.

Shades of the Seventies

by Richard S. Scarsella

The recent surge in energy prices reminds one of the fuel crises in the 1970's. Then, as now, consumers began to experience electric "brownouts", long gasoline lines, and astronomical heating bills. However, the gray 1970's of polyester conjure more than these bleak images.

Kent State University riveted our attention on May 4, 1970 when news broke that four unarmed students were shot to death by the National Guard. Governor Jim Rhodes, who just passed away at a ripe old age, defended his decision to squash the bitter anti-Viet Nam War protesters. Many warned that this debacle was an omen of the eventual decline of the American colossus. The hit movie M.A.S.H., of the same year, was a graphic reminder that this modern war, like the Korean War, was very unlike the patriotic World War II crusade of another generation.

Jumbo jets began transatlantic service that year, effectively drawing the era of grand ocean liners to an end. The "jet set" of European and Arab royalty, Andy Warhol-like pop figures, and rock and roll mega-stars cared little for the somnolent pace that floating hotels offered on the North Atlantic passage.

Disney World debuted in 1970 in central Florida, built upon hundreds of acres of swampland bought by visionary Walt Disney. This city-within-a-city, complete with its own subterranean garbage disposal system and power grid, packaged Disney "magic" like never before. The fact that plastic Mickey Mouse ears were manufactured in Asia—at the cost of American jobs—mattered little to Fantasyland addicts intent upon having a dream vacation. This magical kingdom quickly became a corporate symbol of how to capitalize on children's tastes. America was losing the last vestiges of innocence in a world where geopolitics and return on investments outweighed old-fashioned ethics and traditions.

President Richard Nixon, a vintage 19950's survivor, met his nadir in the conspiracy driven 1970's. The bungled 1972 Watergate break-in led to his ignoble resignation from public office. This stellar international negotiator, who opened diplomatic relations with Communist "Red" China and signed S.A.L.T. accords limiting nuclear missiles with the Cold War adversary Soviet Union, was crucified by a relentless press intent on getting a story. Middle America was disillusioned, numbed, and set adrift by Nixon's untimely departure during the tumultuous 1970's. Prosperity seemingly brought discord, cynicism, and mistrust.

Bar codes introduced in 1973, warnings of ozone layer depletion in 1974, and the 1975 reign of disco all seemed strangely alien in a land yearning for the 1950's complacency and normality that typified the President Dwight Eisenhower presidential years. The 1976 emergence of punk rock music coincided with the celebration of the Bicentennial and the founding of the Apple Computer Company. These events seemed out of sync for a society weaned on legendary Frank Sinatra tunes and sock hops.

Crooner Bing Crosby's obituary in 1977 was not unexpected. The shocking death of Elvis Presley at age 42 in that same year demoralized the baby-boomers, who worshipped youth and believed they were immortal. When the "king" died, Americans knew beyond a doubt that time catches up with us all.

AIDS reared its ugly specter in 1977. Moralists proclaimed this scourge as punishment for wrong living. This "gay plague" soon was discovered in heterosexual circles and became America's new disease to be targeted for research. Hypnotic Elizabeth Taylor's pleas for money to combat HIV startled a populace content with being entertained by Hollywood idols.

Mother Theresa's Nobel Peace Prize for her work with the Calcutta, India outcasts in 1979 represented the best in humanity. This contemporary saint acted as a conscience for a world lost in consumerism and relativity.

A 1979 accident at a nuclear plant at Three Mile Island, Pennsylvania alarmed all of us that technology had limits and could destroy those it supposedly served. Many wondered if the promise of science had seduced a trusting public into dependency. Old-timers warned that Americans had gone soft and urged a return to the "good old days." The idea that the Depression scarred 1930's and World War II years of the 1940's could be nostalgic for anyone seemed pathetically ironic to younger people who only knew a high standard of living.

I must confess that when our latest oil shortage began to lay siege to our suburban lives of gas-guzzling S.U.V.'s and electric air-conditioned homes, I felt a twinge of déjà vu for times gone by.

Who would have conjectured that denizens of the computer crazed year 2001 would be held hostage by fossil fuel? Shades of the 1970's have come back to haunt us. After all, there is no escaping history.

Shadows of Time

by Richard S. Scarsella

Time slips away silently, incrementally, and irrevocably. I sometimes wonder where the years, months, and days have gone. A wise man once said all we ever really own is time, if only for a little while.

Vestiges of other eras remain as mute testimonies to eras that have long disappeared. To those that care to look and ponder, cultural symbols are all around us, regrettably overlooked amidst the modern-day hustle and bustle.

In the shadows, you can find hulking abandoned steel mill hugging the banks of the acrid Mahoning River. These once roaring bastions of iron and steel sit forlornly, partially hidden by weeds, debris, and new construction. Within their wombs, thousands of men smelted ores and grew old.

In the shadows, boarded up corner dairy stores languish as former anchors to once thriving urban neighborhoods. Going to an Isaly's or Lawson's family owned grocery for a loaf of sliced bread was a time-honored tradition. Buying a baker's dozen of Poulakos' donuts at these establishments was a typical Sunday practice. The penny candy on display was a children's paradise.

In the shadows, blank marquees mark once glittering movie houses. The colorful blinking bulbs and oversized poster letters of these theaters used to dominate boulevard vistas for blocks around. When the shimmering lights were dimmed for the last time, these once glamorous motion picture palaces all but disappeared from the streetscapes. They now find uneasy refuge in their new-found anonymity.

In the shadows, rusting Plymouths', DeSotos', Packards', Ramblers', Studebackers', and Imperials' lay in state at obscure sites named scrap-yards. These once sleek chrome encrusted cruisers of the highways bespeak a much-missed time when fuel economy was shunned and style glorified. Junkyard dogs jealously protect these artifacts of America's motorcar golden age.

In the shadows, once popular consumer item castoffs from the 1940's, 1950's, and 1960's live on, despite planned obsolescence. Grandparents still utilize vintage art deco Toastmaster toasters. Others wear retro black James Dean styled

#501 Levi jeans. Former flower children nurse lava lamps and original Volkswagen Beetle automobiles. Many mass-produced goods still toil on, against all odds, and quietly epitomize the decades they once dominated.

In the shadows, now full cemeteries welcome fewer visitors per year. The former grave tenders have now joined their loved ones in the afterlife. The result? Massive repositories of human remains are perpetual caretakers of generations that have spent their seed. Tombstone inscriptions bear cryptic witness for those who are with us in memory only.

In the shadows, broken spirits find precious solace in the places of worship of their choice. The harsh realities of life are greatly alleviated in the protective darkness of churches, temples, and mosques.

In the shadows of our minds, our conscious and unconscious wrestle for dominance and peace. Our life baggage plays itself out in our black and white dreams. During our waking hours, especially at dusk, our eyes anxiously scan the horizon for familiar landmarks of time.

Without them, we lose a little of ourselves.

Somewhere in Time

by Richard S. Scarsella

Time unfolds quietly and gradually. Days turn into months. Months turn into years. Years turn into decades. Why look backwards? A wise person once stated, "The contours of the future are in the observations of the past."

Mahoning Valley heritage is a rich tapestry of rugged settlements, prolonged growth, and unrelenting evolution. Early settlers, notwithstanding Native Americans' protestations, tamed mineral laden rolling hills and verdant pastures nature had blessed with abundance. Immigrants from across Europe made this land their own, embodied democratic values and the "American dream", and transfigured a wilderness into a modern metropolis.

Once established, the greater Youngstown area literally boomed with prosperity and promise, except during the cataclysmic Depression years. Iron and steel became the implacable backbone of this industrial beehive, situated amongst fertile farmsteads. Ingots, pipes, sheeting, plates, and related items were routinely shipped across the nation and over oceans to satisfy a demand for metal products.

Although heavy industry is rapidly disappearing in our midst, its legacy continues. Villages, towns, and urban townships are inhabited by the sons and daughters of the hardy pioneers we scarcely remember. Though most have deserted the central city, its influence remains strong.

Few in suburbia realize that their isolated subdivisions, carved out of old growth forests and generational farms, were made possible by comprehensive expansion of "city services". Youngstown extended water lines and sewage lines into inner ring suburbs, allowing a transmigration of families and businesses from the urban corridor. Local demography would have been dramatically altered had Youngstown withheld the tools requisite for development.

Ironically, middle class and affluent enclaves are duplicating the mistakes of yesteryear that doomed once-mighty Youngstown, the county seat. Uncontrolled building, exploitation and decimation of indigenous habitats, spiraling taxes, deficit municipal budgets, indifferent and compromised politicians, and apathetic nonvoting citizenry are allowing history to repeat itself in new seemingly impregnable locales.

Insidious urban blight, unaddressed social ills, and virtual total disregard for historic preservation are dire warnings of what is yet to come. Mistakes and lessons concerning the rise, fall, stagnation, and eclipse of once gilded Youngstown seem little referenced today. Are we to relive the ignoble past? Have we learned nothing from olden times? B. H. Fairchild said it best when exhorting that "We are what we forget."

Somewhere in time it will be noted that we lost things needed for our well-being. Regardless, we will be recalled in spite of ourselves.

Summer Icons

by Richard S. Scarsella

When schools close for the summer break, older area youth indulge in an intense social calendar involving pool parties, bonfires at the shore, dates at the movies, and cruising the streets. At age sixteen, with a driver's license in hand, male and female teens "hit the bricks" in search of thrills.

Today, malls, fast-food restaurants, video shops, gourmet coffee cafes, and electronic stores are all favorite haunts of the cable television watching, computer networked millennium adolescents. Especially made summer blockbuster films, catering to both adults and young audiences, no longer fill cavernous "chilled air" movie palaces. Movies are now made and targeted to niche markets, categorized by age and demographics.

In the 1950's, two Hollywood teen idols captivated America with riveting portrayals of young lovers. Their names? Sandra Dee and Troy Donahue.

During the twilight of the movie industry's reign, Americans were both shocked and made curious by the personae of these two stars. Apparently, "baby boom" youth were not satisfied with material things. They sought more freedom and self-expression than their prudish elders did. Sandra Dee and Troy Donahue personified the troubles of "growing up", the chains of crushing middle-class conventions, and the toll of youthful romance in a 1959 melodrama titled "A Summer Place".

Released by Warner Brothers during the same year the first copier was made, the first portable transistorized television was perfected, and the death of rock and roll pioneer Buddy Holly, "A Summer Place" epitomized the cultural and generation gap, which was splitting and deepening in the post World War II affluent United States. Sandra Dee and Troy Donahue were devastating in their indictment of society's callous disregard for feelings and truthfulness, all for appearance's sake.

The natural, all-American innocent summer dalliance was given an unforgiving edge in this frank movie set in coastal Maine. Even adults, portrayed by demure Dorothy McGuire and hunky Richard Egan, could not escape the fate summer sweethearts oftentimes endured.

Sandra Dee, who was sweet, perky, possessed of platinum hair, full billowing skirts and slips, and pumps, was both tempted by and the temptress for equally confused Troy Donahue. This handsome archetypal golden haired youth was sired by an old blue blood, alcoholic father. He was torn between duty and his heart. He both courted and resisted the feminine mystique. Both characters discovered the high price one pays for carnal bliss and fulfillment.

Unbelievably, "A Summer Place", in grand Technicolor soap-operatic style, dared to have a happy ending, despite two divorces, several affairs, and an out-of-wedlock pregnancy! This classic of the cinema was an accurate portent of things to come. The introduction of the pill, the wide usage of drugs, the counter-cultural revolution, anti-war, free-love 1960's made the scandal of this summer release seem quaint. America grew up in the 1960's.

We did not know that Sandra Dee was abused as a child and suffered eating and emotional problems. Few knew then or now that Troy Donahue had a career-ending alcoholic dependency. They are forever frozen in time as symbols of what was, could be, and never was.

Typically, people prefer to remember history selectively. Every Memorial Day, when families head to Lake Erie beaches, open up their cottages, and absorb the sun's rays, my mind goes back to "A Summer Place". I wonder, will love find a way?

Summer Solstice

by Richard S. Scarsella

Twice a year the sun is at the furthest distance from the celestial equator. On about June 21 and December 22 these turning points happen with few taking any notice. Ancient societies marked the summer solstice and winter solstice with great fanfare.

Our mortal lives also reach culminating points, as do civilizations. In the Mahoning Valley, locals still look back wistfully to so-called "better times". Those days of yore included a vibrant regional economy, growing population base, and confident faith in the future.

Obviously, the death of the steel corridor, which has been blamed on cheap imports, deregulation, corporate merger madness, lust for quarterly profits, escalating union demands, and pre-W.W. II infrastructures, was the beginning of the metropolitan eclipse. For many, the hankering for return of former days has become a yearning to leave the graveyards of their lives.

Those that care to reflect on the embellished "golden days" reference the airtight ethnic ties that held the once grand urban neighborhoods together. Slavic, Italian, Greek, Irish, German, and other nationalities made greater Youngstown a cosmopolitan enclave amidst farm country. Specialty foods, soulful music, colorful religious services, and old world wisdom enriched American culture immeasurably. Although the rugged communities hugging the murky Mahoning River were gritty and hard-bitten, they oozed camaraderie and friendliness. In these places, neighbors were like family.

Old-timers still fondly speak about how a high school graduate could readily find employment at steel and iron mills and foundries and go on to become a supervisor or an executive. The "American dream" was within reach to those willing to "pay their dues".

There was a time when retailers were from local families. Leading merchants came from the Strouss, McKelvey, Hartzell, and Lustig households. These pioneer businesspeople were also stewards of area civic groups, foundations, cultural societies, community improvement associations, and religious establishments. In these halcyon decades before the Viet Nam War, prosperity was not flaunted but shared with the less fortunate. Up into the 1960's, one could argue that we inhabited a more civilized era.

In by-gone days, simple pastimes were the norm. A day at Lake Erie was a typical diversion. Going to the shore was a welcomed relief from the smog enveloping the valley. The less adventurous would visit Lake Milton. Craig Beach was a favorite haunt. Everyone visited primordial Mill Creek Park, which was located in the heart of the city. Boating on Lake Glacier, fishing at Lake Newport, or walking the trails were common recreations for generations. It was rare for folks to travel beyond Pittsburgh or Cleveland. You were considered well traveled if you had been to Chicago, St. Louis, or New York City.

Naturally, the change of seasons always brings thoughts of yesteryears. Holidays, back-to-school preparations, and planting time all evoke remembrances of people, places, and customs no longer present. Whether the days shorten or lengthen, the cycle of life hums forward for the inhabitants of this part of the Connecticut Western Reserve territory.

Some few look to the skies with melancholy as we head reluctantly towards the winter solstice. Briefer days and longer nights can spark an aching in the heart. Loss of light brings the shadow of time uncomfortably close. It has been said that time is meaningless. Yet, in a very real sense, it is all we truly ever have, if only for a moment.

Summertide Holiday

by Richard S. Scarsella

Independence Day means many things to many people. For some, July 4th is the ultimate day of patriotism. Grand parades once were held in bustling downtown Youngstown. Powerful politicians, leading businessmen, and civic leaders observed this national holiday with great solemnity and fanfare. Central Square, East and West Federal Streets, and adjoining downtown streets all were festooned with red, white, and blue flags, ribbons, and bows. Marching bands, flag lines, and majorettes all stepped in line to rousing John Phillip Sousa marching medleys. Images of venerable paternalistic Uncle Sam could be seen on posters, hanging proudly in show windows, or on corner bus-stop poles. The marquees of the Palace, State, Paramount, Warner, and Regent theaters all featured nationalistic slogans such as "God bless America". Churches held special services to give thanks for freedom. Stores closed for the day. Family reunions were held. This workingman's holiday was much appreciated in the gritty Steel Valley.

Typically, urban dwellers would pack picnic baskets and head outdoors to get some "sun and fresh air". Mill Creek Park was a favorite destination. Families would arrive early at park pavilions and save picnic tables for extended families. By noon, station wagons would empty throngs of chattering children, awkward adolescents, dutiful parents, and elderly grandparents into the park environs. Many visitors brought jugs and would store fresh well water from one of the many spring fed park fountains. Alcohol consumption was strictly forbidden.

Frisbee was a popular pastime, as were horseshoes and croquet. Badminton birdies sailed through the stately trees, some never to be seen again. Young girls played jacks. Young boys played marbles. Teen-agers would try to tune into the old WHOT AM station, featuring radio announcers Boots Bell, Dick Thompson, and Johnny Kay, on their portable battery operated transistor radios. Adults sat vigilantly and gossiped the day away. Talks centered upon union issues, strikes, and possible layoffs in local plants. Grandparents would fondly reminisce about "the olden days" and tell tales of their youth. With sunset, lanterns, candles, sparklers, and firecrackers would fill the summer's eve. Fireflies would come alight, twinkling in the moonlight. Picnic baskets would be repacked for the journey home.

As darkness took hold, Youngstown's skyline stood in deep contrast to the horizon. Towering "skyscrapers" gave the city a cosmopolitan feel. Nearby, billowing smokestacks and fiery open-hearth furnaces reminded one that heavy industry was the lifeblood of the community. The many cemeteries in the area all were decorated lovingly with tributes for fallen war heroes and loved ones. Wreaths, laurels, crosses, and medallions marked the final resting places for legions of the dead. Tiny American flags and lit votive candles were poignant markers in these vast graveyards of generations.

No July 4th was complete without the spectacular fireworks display over beloved Idora Park. From throughout the surrounding neighborhoods, lavish displays of pyrotechnics illuminated the darkened sky. "Youngstown's Million Dollar Playground" put on a show like none other. When Idora Park closed its gates for good, Independence Day was never the same again.

Today, downtown Youngstown is vacant. Many once elegant urban neighborhoods have been abandoned. The steel mills stand empty. Idora Park is slowly disappearing. And there are no longer magnificent parades in the central city.

Invariably, when July 4th is celebrated, I close my eyes and think back to the not so long ago days of the past. I smile a little, in spite of myself, and watch the lightening bugs.

Summertime Hospitality

by Richard S. Scarsella

In years past, Mahoning Valley residents had well ingrained routines in the spring. Before yard services, cleaning companies, and interior/exterior repair businesses relieved homeowners of maintenance chores, families all pitched in to do spring-cleaning.

Old-timers would put their furnishings on their front porches and back yards to "air" them out. Area rugs and oriental carpets would be hung up on clotheslines. Children delighted in hitting them with straw brooms to get the dust out of them. Thrifty consumers would wash and dry windows with home-mixed vinegar and water concoctions and old newsprint. Cotton summer curtains would be hung and chintz slipcovers would be taken out in anticipation of summertime entertaining.

Up into the late 1960's, even the best of homes rarely had central air conditioning. Many homes had Casablanca styled overhead fans for "the dog days of summer". In the 1950's, Westinghouse, of nearby Erie, Pennsylvania, made cast iron "portable fans" for both home and businesses. Although they made more noise than breezes, they had a cooling psychological effect.

Decorating one's front porch was a high priority in urban neighborhoods. Wood floors were scraped, sanded, primed, given two coats of paint and sealed. Battleship gray was the favored color. Some say this custom took its roots in the World War I and World War II eras, since this color was the only one readily available or affordable during wartime.

Stambaugh Thompson's and Wilkens & Leonard hardware stores were beehives of activity. Turpentine, linseed oil, Milsek furniture polish, Fels Napta soap, "angel hair", and lime were all bought in huge quantities. Cherished bamboo and rattan deck chairs were brought to these emporiums to be repaired. Replacement cushions and covers were meticulously chosen to match original materials.

Most porches were considered extensions of the parlor room. They were outfitted with lush hanging and potted plants, colorful fragrant flowers, canopies, valances, screens, and outdoor carpets. It was not unusual, on a summer evening, to see the glow of a radio console or television set on the verandas. Pungent citronella votive candles held mosquitoes at bay. As the evening wore on and temperatures cooled, homes became more habitable for sleeping. Before turning in, the last one to bed religiously covered the porch furnishings with waterproof throws.

Throughout the Youngstown metropolitan area, these informal vestibules were integral parts of our lives. Men of all professions held card games on their porches, since women would not allow cigars, pipes, or cigarettes to be smoked in their living rooms. Spittoons and ashtray holders would be brought out for these games of chance and skill. Homemakers and career women found their decks to be ideal settings for novel get togethers. Luncheons, teas, and showers all were held outdoors, with Chinese lanterns, summer place settings, and lemonade pitchers. Children adopted these environs as extended playrooms. Rocking horses, blocks, toy boxes, and miniature kitchen sets all were standard outdoors gear for the youngsters. Romantic couples would while away the hours, seated closely on swings, as part of much honored courting rituals.

There was something indescribably comforting to see and experience the front porch culture once so prevalent in our midst. Neighbors were able to visit each other regularly and make small talk. Conversation, laughter, music, and summer food and charcoal smells wafted through the neighborhoods and over one's banisters. It all made us feel connected and at peace with our fellowman. Baby gates and handrails could not keep out the spirit of comradeship that existed in most neighborhoods. In a real sense, our homes lengthened beyond our front thresholds.

Nodding to old friends from a rocker or easy chair, high above the yard and sidewalk, made one feel like one belonged. It was all very familiar, cordial, and welcoming. Porches beckoned neighbors up for a chat or the latest gossip. They were a big part of one's social life.

When I look back to the "good old, bad old days" of years past, I can't help but ache a little with regret about the passing of this one part of civilization, which has all but vanished, from our lives. I still miss the old front porch of my family's homestead. Luckily, memories keep it and all it represented alive.

Sunday Drives

by Richard S. Scarsella

Looking back at the years long gone, I have fleeting images of things once familiar now vanished from our midst. When I sometimes revisit these glimpses of yesteryear, I can't help but pause. These unforgettable tableaus are etched indelibly into my memory banks.

I recall Sundays with clarity not reserved for the other days of the week. The Sabbath did not change much, month after month or year after year. A large breakfast, worship services, visiting relatives, going to a movie, and taking a ride all were routine practices.

A hearty morning meal—one to put meat on your bones—consisted of Sealtest milk, fresh from a glass bottle, Barth Farm eggs, grown locally, and Wonder Bread, baked at the Mahoning Avenue bakery. Jams, preserves, and currants were from fruits grown and canned from our own backyards or area orchards. Some fresh fruit was bought from the Amish peddlers or at the legendary Pyatt Street Market.

Church services dictated dressy attire for adults. Ties, suspenders, hats, and gloves were worn by grownups and children alike. Of course, youngsters wore their "Sunday best" complete with patent leather shoes. Not to dress up for devotions was considered scandalous. Church ushers were known to escort those not properly groomed to the back pews or out the doors.

Visiting relatives was a time-honored tradition in Youngstown. On the day of rest, it was not unusual to see several generations of a clan sitting on an elder's roomy front porch or encamped under a shade tree "chewing the fat." Homemade pink lemonade and darkly brewed ice tea were favorite refreshments for those that traveled to see their kinfolk. Large dinners and suppers oftentimes were served. These informal get-togethers became memorable for there spontaneity and fraternity.

Attending a film was a real Sunday treat. A trip to the becalmed downtown Youngstown, enroute to the motion picture palaces now abandoned, was thrilling. Parking on Federal Street, without putting coins into the meters, was a real novelty. Walking city blocks, passing darkened display windows, brimming with fashionable goods, was a riveting experience. Entering the ornate marble inlaid lobbies of the Palace, State, Warner, and Paramount theaters into a shadowy world of entertainment and escapism to this day is an unmatched encounter with the glamour and glitter of Hollywood.

One custom stood out amongst all others. What was it? A Sunday drive. For a child, to "take a drive" could mean a trip anywhere for any length of time. It was fraught with possibilities.

A tour through the countryside was a favorite. Many folks do not realize Mahoning County was once dotted with scenic farms. Austintown, Boardman, Liberty, or Coitsville Township were frequent destinations for area families going out for the day. Heading out of the city limits was a real adventure. These once undeveloped locales were brimming with fertile pastures, well-stocked fruit stands, fields of wild flowers and berries, and horse farms. City folks, ensconced in their chrome-laden sedans, cruised these relatively solitary crossroads in search of nature and fresh air.

Journeys up and down Market Street, via the Uptown district, were always interesting. Elegant specialty shops, trendy boutiques, new car showrooms, and furniture store show windows featured an array of consumer items most could only dream about ever owning.

Touring Mill Creek Park entailed stops at the Lily Pond, Lanterman's Falls, Lake Glacier, and Lake Newport. Feeding the gold fish and migratory ducks were favorite pastimes. The natural spring water fed drinking fountains were always visited as well. This "green cathedral" oozed primordial appeal for those in search of peace, beauty, or wilderness.

Before historic Idora Park fenced in its midways and attractions, we could freely park our automobile, walk in, and buy a custard or vinegar drenched French fries without paying an admission. The roar of the wooden coasters, the melancholy melodies of the hand painted carrousel, and the haunting strains of Big Band music emanating from the grand ballroom made these visits outstanding, without fail.

I guess without memories we forget who we are. Ironically, memories make victims out of the survivors. And every week I still remember those Sunday drives.

Thanksgiving Traditions

by Richard S. Scarsella

The Mahoning Valley is a colorful quilt of distinctive ethnic heritages. American customs merged with imported practices and created a hybrid American culture.

In the Youngstown area, the very American holiday of Thanksgiving fostered a number of traditions. Many places of business catered to our once prosperous region, as it celebrated national commemorations of gratitude to both God and our forefathers.

Barth Farms, in the New Middletown area, once dominated the markets with its freshly dressed hen and tom turkeys. Many housewives would drive to the country and select their entree in person. Other homemakers would shop at such local grocers as the Lazar Brothers or Schiavones. These family owned and operated markets knew their customers by name and made every effort to provide first-class groceries at affordable prices. Ethnic foods, not stocked at chain supermarkets, could always be found in the aisles of these stores.

Pyatt Street Market, still open off of Market Street, in the Uptown district, dazzled consumers with farm fresh fruits, vegetables and meats. Buying from farm families, many of Amish or Mennonite descent, was a real experience for city kids. Haggling was the norm and was very entertaining to witness.

More affluent families ordered pastries from the once famous Strouss' and McKelvey's bakeries. These grand department stores had chefs featuring exotic French desserts and all-American favorites that were picture perfect. Minced meat, raisin and pumpkin pies, along with chiffon cakes, were specialties of these fabled establishments.

Children were more than willing to go to Lawson or Isaly Dairy stores and buy ice-cream for the Thanksgiving feast. Up into the 1960's, you could buy a quart of vanilla ice-cream or sherbet for a quarter at one of these neighborhood dairies. Other favorite flavors included Whitehouse, banana and spumoni.

Fanny Farmer Candies once had shoppes all over town. This Chicago confection retailer made fine milk chocolate both accessible and popular. Youngsters especially liked solid chocolate cigarettes, cigars and foil-wrapped turkeys.

On Thanksgiving Day, legendary theaters, such as the Palace, Warner, State, Paramount, Newport and Uptown, debuted Christmas blockbuster movies. Reservations were made in advance. Lines of dressed-up moviegoers would be snaked around city blocks, waiting for entry.

The erection of an enormous, locally grown evergreen tree on Youngstown's Central Square, marked the official beginning of the holiday season. A festive Santa Claus parade drew thousands of families to the once vibrant downtown. The countdown to New Year's began as well.

Area high school football teams once competed fiercely on Thanksgiving. The bleachers of South and Rayen Stadiums once throbbed with the excitement of fans cheering on the teams of East, North, South and Rayen high schools. Only The Rayen School survives today. Both stadiums have long ago closed.

Of all the above mentioned observances, only Pyatt Street Market and the downtown Christmas tree ceremony remain. However, the fond memories live on and on.

The 1940's

by Richard S. Scarsella

Few decades in recent history match the 1940's for drama, bloodshed, or rebirth. In these years European nations continued their feudal wars, America came of age, and the world lurched into the atomic era.

In 1940, Great Britain stood alone against Hitler in what was dubbed World War II. The German "mad dog" brilliantly and ruthlessly pursued his vision of empire. With the unbelievable collapse of France, the United Kingdom boldly defied common logic. It refused to buckle under superior Nazi strength and found refuge in its oceanic retreat. Hitler aligned himself with socialistic Russia, aristocratic Italy, and imperial Japan and bullied his way across the unprepared continent. American stood anxiously on the sidelines, clinging to futile neutrality in a mad world, which pitted supposedly civilized countries against each other in savage warfare.

In Hollywood, Disney's studios premiered Fantasia, a spectacular cartoon tour de force, complete with stereophonic sound and living color. This classical music-filled full-length feature film was an eclectic blend of fairy tales, nursery rhymes, mythology, Mickey Mouse sentimentality, and orchestra masterpieces. Not surprisingly, a world transfixed with war ignored this cinematic milestone.

In 1941, Germany invaded its friend Russia, the Japanese bombed Pearl Harbor, and the United States declared war against the axis powers. The Yankees were called upon again to fight for freedom "over there". Ironically, the devastating Great Depression began to recede as the nation converted into a wartime economy. Germany's much vaunted technological prowess and penchant for efficiency pressed the Americans to meet and exceed high standards set by the Aryans.

The Russian winter defeated near-invincible German panzer divisions. In 1942, Italians dismissed Mussolini and called upon King Victor Emmanuel to form a new government. In 1943, both Russia and Italy became American allies against the once impregnable Third Reich. The fortunes of war seemed to be changing from might to right.

In 1944, Franklin D. Roosevelt won an unprecedented fourth term as United States president. British Prime Minister Winston Churchill, Free French General Charles DeGaulle, and Russian Communist Party Chairman Joseph Stalin made an uneasy partnership under the leadership of the American military colossus.

In April of 1945, Hitler committed suicide. In August of the same year, two atomic bombs were dropped on the Japanese cities of Hiroshima and Nagasaki. Sadly, F.D.R. never lived to see the end of this last "Great War", dying April 12, 1945. Under Harry Truman, the Marshall Plan rebuilt Europe, Germany and Japan became American allies, the Russians became the new menace of the world, and the United Nations was born.

German atrocities against Jews, gypsies, and gays shocked an already war-weary world. The 1946 debut of ENIAC, dubbed the "grandfather of all computers", elicited both hope and dread. The 1947 "new look", ushered in by fashion designer Christian Dior, was an attempt to reclaim some of the style, grace, and gentility, which was lost during the brutal war years. Americans particularly wanted to move on into the future and leave the weight of the past behind them.

In 1948, the first McDonald's restaurant was opened. Edwin Land developed a film system, which developed pictures in about one minute inside of a camera. Scrabble, the board game, was launched to huge applause. In 1949, George Orwell published his archetypal novel Nineteen Eighty-Four. Arthur Miller won the Pulitzer Prize for his poignant play Death of a Salesman. Music magazine Billboard started a country and western chart and used the phrase rhythm and blues. The era of Kate Smith and Bing Crosby was over. The 1950's promised to be a contemporary interlude in a world preoccupied with the baggage of history.

Looking back, the 1940's seem impossibly challenging to modern day inhabitants. War food rations, p.c. coupons, and massive conscriptions all seem alien to a land long at peace and in prosperity. We now think of the 1940's as the "golden age" of Hollywood, where legendary figurer such as Bette Davis, Joan Crawford, Clark Gable, and Humphrey Bogart reigned supreme. Only Veterans' Day parades and new Holocaust obscenities act as grim reminders of these deadly years.

Few take the time to ponder how close the world came to the brink of destruction. Had the German army not been stopped outside the gates of Moscow, the outcome of the war most assuredly would have been different. Had the Japanese not bombed Pearl Harbor, the Americans may have hesitated too long entering the fracas and forfeited the ability to turn things around in favor of democracy. Had the Germans perfected their futuristic U-2 rockets or atomic weapons systems sooner, England may have well folded under the onslaught. The result? European nations would probably still be under the Nazi yoke.

For Americans who lived during the 1940's, these years were the "good old bad old days". Families were intact, prayer was still in public schools, and citizens believed in their country right or wrong. Selective memories and creative historic revisionism glosses over the social, racial, economic, and religious inequities of those years. Nostalgia tends to sugarcoat harsh realities.

However, survivors of these tumultuous years almost uniformly exclaim, "Those were the days!"

The 1950's

by Richard S. Scarsella

Many baby-boomers, born after the World War II epoch, think fondly about the 1950's. Thoughts of huge cars, with lots of chrome and exaggerated tail fins, and hip wiggling rock and roll music symbolize these times. In the years of Elvis Presley's heyday, the decline of the Hollywood movie industry, and peacetime prosperity, the 1950's seemed modern compared to the 1940's.

The Big Bands were already on the wane. Television was becoming a national past time. Europe, with the exception of Russia, formerly known as the Soviet Union, was no longer a threat to national security during the mid-century decade. The future seemed bright.

People and nations have very selective memories. The Senator Joseph McCarthy Communist Party witch-hunts grimly held America in awe. The Congressional hearings were televised live, in black and white. What unfolded made average Americans fearful and cynical about political, governmental, and media manipulations of the "truth". The search for "pinko spies" throughout the nation left a lasting scar on the American psyche.

In October of 1950, North Korea's armed forces invaded South Korea and seized the capital city of Seoul. Americans were shocked that World War II had not made the world safe for democracy. The specter of an ever-widening conflict hung over the lives of a war-weary country. Unbelievably, American troops, ships, and planes headed to an obscure Asian peninsula to "preserve the peace" in a country few had ever heard of before. The eventual United Nations counterattack on North Korea, the dismissal by President Truman of iconic, aggressive, arrogant General MacArthur, and the establishment of an uneasy cease-fire—which lasts to this day—all signaled to Americans that the United States had by default become the "policeman of the world".

The atomic and hydrogen bombs, ironically, were too fearsome to be used in "armed conflicts", lest the superpowers of Russia and America were willing to go eyeball to eyeball and risk an Armageddon confrontation. In response to this reality, citizens began to build bomb shelters in their homes, stockpiled food and water, and conducted air raid drills in the schools. The threat of "total war", along with iron lung machines and polio scares, made the 1950's unnerving, despite the trappings of affluence enjoyed by an expanding middle class.

Sputnik, a Soviet satellite, launched 500 miles above the earth, sent chills through the American government and schools in 1957. The victorious W.W. II Americans seemed to have a rival in Russia for both military and scientific leadership. Washington responded with a flood of soothing patriotic rhetoric and posturing, lavish funding for increased science and math studies and research, and an increased emphasis on rocket related programs. The space race was on. It was not at all clear if America would win. Incredibly, former German Nazi scientists led our nation's charge into the unknown. They guided the Soviet efforts as well.

In 1958, the beatnik movement gained popularity, the hula-hoop craze swept the nation, and DuPont marketed Lycra, artificial elastic. Clothing styles would be forever changed by "miracle fabrics" and loosening social conventions. Technological advancements commanded our attention. Ultrasound scanning techniques to examine unborn babies, the first bifocal contact lenses, and the atomic submarine USS Nautilus' voyage under the North Pole all seemed futuristic and portents of things to come.

In 1959, Castro became dictator of Cuba, Hawaii became the 50th state of the Union, and rock and roll singer Buddy Holly died in an airplane crash. The scandalously frank film of love and desire titled "A Summer Place epitomized the changing taste, mood, and morality of an increasingly liberal culture. The aged President Eisenhower administration was winding down. Youthful President Elect Kennedy stood in the wings awaiting destiny.

No one knew, late in 1959, that the Kennedy Camelot mystique, so sorely needed by a fatigued nation, would only last until 1963. An assassin's "magic bullet" jolted our republic to its very core. As we speechlessly watched the heartbreaking funeral procession of beloved President J.F.K., replete with statuesque stoic wife, saluting J.F.K., Jr., and princess-like Caroline, we knew we had entered a new, more troubling era. The voice and vision of a brave new generation had been senselessly silenced.

To this day, Americans of these times still ponder what might have been.

The 1960's

by Richard S. Scarsella

The 1960's were a troublesome decade in American history. During this span of time, America's best and worst traits were held up to close scrutiny. Surprisingly, there was much reason for hope and alarm as these years waned.

In 1960, the American U-2 aircraft was shot down over Russian airspace by Soviet Union missiles. The United States military vehemently denied and later reluctantly admitted that the state-of-the-art plane was on a "surveillance" flight. The Cold War heated up over this incident and fueled fear of the Communist "red menace". Meanwhile, in Cuba, America's one time friend, Fidel Castro, nationalized all Yankee owned property, in retaliation for alleged United States economic imperialism and aggression. The world that America fought to keep free in World War II and Korea seemed strangely forbidding and dangerous. Despair began to take hold of the North American colossus. Did we fight the wars to lose the peace? Would a nuclear holocaust be triggered over Third World confrontations?

As if by magic, a young, telegenic, and sophisticated senator, named John F. Kennedy, took the helm of the presidency. The nation had high hopes that this "new breed" of a leader could break ranks with the failed politics of old and lead the country into the New Frontier. Jack and Jackie Kennedy, his wife, epitomized the style, elegance, wit, intelligence, and accomplishment of American society at its best.

The 1960's were a not so subtle transition into a supposedly modern era. Bible Fundamentalist film "Ben Hur" won ten Oscars, even though the ranks of the "unchurched" began to swell. Young people began to question stifling 1950's mores and increasingly turned to secular philosophies or to eastern mysticism for spiritual nourishment. Mainline Protestant churches watched in dismay as their membership declined. Roman Catholics were both enamored with and disheartened by sweeping changes ushered in by the Vatican Council. Nothing seemed sacred in this rapidly automated and impersonal world.

In Hollywood, the old star system slowly disappeared. Skyrocketing production costs and million dollar "mega-star" salaries helped dismantle this venerable industry. Movie studios were divested of their theater chain outlets, by decree of monopoly-busting federal bureaucrats. The subsequent loss of revenues dictated that fewer films were put into development. Low budget, independent, cult films became the rage. Both rugged matinee idol Clark Gable and ultimate sex symbol Marilyn Monroe died in the early 1960's. Their last film? "The Misfits". They had become living anachronisms, despite fame. Realistic, gritty movies became popular, despite the successes of "Hello Dolly" and "The Sound of Music". Veteran moviegoers gradually abandoned the weekly movie-viewing habit for network television. Young movie fans began to dominate ticket sales. They identified with films such as "Easy Rider" and "The Graduate". Legendary screen stars no longer commanded our attention.

At home, mature audiences watched "The Lawrence Welk Show", "The Ed Sullivan Show", and "Gunsmoke". Family entertainment began to falter as onlookers were targeted by advertisers and producers according to age, income, and gender. America's cohesion, once nurtured by Hollywood's imagery, romanticism, and nationalism, now was being undermined by anti-establishment movies, irreverent television, and hard rock records, which advocated "free love", drug use, peace, pacifism, and nonconformity. Young people embraced various elements of the counter-culture and "dropped out" of many mainstream middle-class institutions or practices. The "generation gap" was born. The suburban "good life" was no guarantee for happiness.

The Viet Nam conflict, which Congress never declared a war, slowly divided the country. Hawks were itching for "total war". Doves pleaded for nonviolence and a "honorable truce". Anti-war demonstrations rocked college campuses. Draft evaders became cause celebres. Compulsory military service took mostly poor boys off to a war nobody wanted, to a land no one had heard of, and for reasons not entirely believable. Watching the war unfold nightly on television newsbroadcasts was a sobering lesson.

The assassinations of John F. Kennedy and his brother, Senator Robert F. Kennedy, buried any chances for rapid disengagement. Lyndon B. Johnson, a legendary Texan New Dealer congressman, was slowly humbled and engulfed by anti-war sentiment, high combat casualties, and pervasive cynicism. President Johnson's Great Society, which began a crusade against poverty and other social ills, was overshadowed by an unwinnable, undeclared, guerilla war. Not wanting to be known as the first president to lose a war, he enlarged the conflagration, hoping to see light at the end of the tunnel. He found quicksand, instead.

The martyrdom of civil rights leader Martin Luther King, Jr., marked the end of peaceful equality movements. Oppressed minorities became impatient, sometimes violent, and turned to rioting and increased court proceedings seeking redress. The "land of the free" now had to make good on its promises, much to the chagrin of institutionalized bigotry. Women were also seeking parity with men and began to evolve radically from the Donna Reed archetype. Long held roles and stereotypes were being challenged, redefined, and discarded throughout the land.

Richard M. Nixon's ascent to the White House was the last gasp of 1950's conservative politics. Americans yearned for the "good old days" of President Dwight D. Eisenhower. Nixon, Ike's former vice-president, attempted to defuse raging 1960's inflation, neutralize "radicals", and make the "silent majority" agenda dominant. Unfortunately, the intelligent "new" Richard Nixon was really the old "Tricky Dickey" repackaged for a nation that had seemingly lost its moorings. Nixon's neurosis mirrored the sickness of the times. Much to his horror, his 1960's nemesis, John F. Kennedy, was now referred to as a figure befitting a long lost American Camelot.

Ironically, in 1969, Nixon benefited from the Kennedy legacy by talking to the first man on the moon. Apollo 11 astronauts symbolized Yankee ingenuity, technological prowess, and determined tenacity in the wake of obstacles. J.F.K's challenge to conquer space seemed fulfilled, despite the nation's war-torn state and self-doubts. America had won the space race. However, had the nation lost its spirit?

In the 1960's, anti-establishment music by the Beatles, the Rolling Stones, and Bob Dylan pushed aside 1950's icons such as Frank Sinatra, Elvis Presley, and Kate Smith. A cultural shift had transpired during this period of economic prosperity and gut wrenching soul-searching. Perversely, older Americans pined for the 1940's of the Depression and World War II. Why? They apologized that in those years, right was right, wrong was wrong, one knew who the good guys were and they eventually won. Not surprisingly, the world-weary 1969 ballad by Peggy Lee "Is That All There Is?" was a big hit. America finally grew up in the 1960's and emerged stronger and healthier than ever. And the rest, as they say, is history.

The Forgotten Giant

by Richard S. Scarsella

Our Mahoning Valley is rich in history. The iron and steel heritage, the influence of President William McKinley, the foresight of John Butler's museum, and the Warner Brothers' pioneering in the film industry all were major contributions to the nation. Ironically, one man, who once walked in our midst, continues to be ignored both locally and nationally, despite his rightful stature as one of the greats of American civilization. His name? William Holmes McGuffey.

Born in 1800 in nearby Washington, Pennsylvania and raised on Youngstown's East Side, in Coitsville Township, McGuffey developed a philosophy of life, which he later shared with a burgeoning nation. His homespun tales of citizenship, character, conservation, and literacy were all firmly rooted in our valley's verdant soil and molten industry. He was a modern hybrid, both of the land and of the hearth. His no nonsense wisdom, earthiness, and Yankee values all made him a Pied Piper of sorts for hordes of immigrants, downtrodden laborers, and agrarian families. He embodied the "can do" American spirit of self-reliance and progress through enlightenment.

With his brother Alexander's assistance, the McGuffey Eclectic Readers, first published in 1836, became the texts that literally taught the western expanding America how to read. Outside the East Coast, most homes had well worn copies of the Bible, an almanac, and leather-bound McGuffey Readers. Unbelievably, the Readers have never gone out of print. Next to Webster's Dictionaries and the Bible, the Readers have been printed and read by more Americans than any other books in American history. As a result of this achievement, McGuffey was once known as the "Schoolmaster of the Nation."

McGuffey's anthology series offered tantalizing selections from Shakespeare, the Bible, and Walt Whitman. His use of artwork facilitated wholesome themes. Questions and instructions for both students and teachers alike made the Readers challenging and engaging. McGuffey's novel use of children focus groups, to determine the readability and interest level of materials, still is widely used today by marketers. McGuffey alone championed respect for the environment, compassion for Native Americans, and the belief that children need parables about death, to better deal with its aftermath. Sadly, McGuffey's strong reliance on faith based instruction proved to be his undoing. Being both a teacher and a preacher made him vulnerable to critics, despite his huge popularity with the masses.

As Americans became more prosperous and modern in the 1900's, McGuffey's heavy uses of patriotic and moralistic subject matter seemed quaint and suspect. The Readers peaked in popularity in the 1920's and slowly fell out of favor by the 1950's. The once ubiquitous tomes found refuge in church-run academies, Sunday schools, rural school districts, and libraries. Perversely, McGuffey and his Readers are footnotes in history.

Locally, McGuffey has a plaza, mall, and community center named after him. The path his father made, through Native American country, so he could get his "learnin", from the Coitsville Township homestead to a Wick Avenue parsonage school, is known as McGuffey Road. His tutor's name, Reverend Wick, far out shadows his own once renown.

However, in the Youngstown area, no statue, museum, or public building bears our native son's name or likeness. Efforts to have a McGuffey stamp issued have been rebuffed by the United States Postal Service. In national education circles, McGuffey is similarly overlooked. His lack of Eastern credentials and upbringing still dulls his illustrious contributions to literacy. The fact that his publisher was in Cincinnati and not located on the East Coast branded him as a non-elite academic. Only recently was the McGuffey seventy-four acre farm, a national historic landmark, accepted into the Mill Creek Metroparks. Gifted to the part district by the William Holmes McGuffey Historical Society and renamed the McGuffey Wildlife Preserve, one can visit the family well, pond, fields, trails, and lookout, located atop a drumlin, that the pioneer McGuffey clan once used.

Fittingly, the new Mill Creek Metroparks Visitors and Education Center, now under construction, will house a McGuffey exhibit in both the library and museum. This McGuffey Archives, on loan to the facility by the historical society, is all that remains locally of the proud McGuffey legacy. Interestingly, industrialist Henry Ford has two McGuffey buildings, full of McGuffey related artifacts, at the Deerfield Village Museum in Michigan. Ford referred to the Readers as his alma mater, in tribute to the Readers' potency in his rags to riches life.

In one of the many twists of history, McGuffey's Readers are making a modest comeback. Always used by Amish, Mennonite, and mission schools, the Readers are increasingly being utilized as historical secondary or supplemental texts. Now viewed as cultural curiosities and period pieces, representative of a certain era, the Readers' down to earth value-based, character centered, populist inspired stories and essays are having a rebirth. Today's homogenized, generic, politically correct, bland school texts pale in comparison to the seven venerable McGuffey Readers, which encompass the best literature of Western civilization. His texts have stood the test of time. McGuffey would be pleased.

The Long Goodbye

by Richard S. Scarsella

The recent demolition of Idora Park's Wild Cat and Jack Rabbit roller coasters is yet another sad chapter in local history. Despite being listed on the United States Department of Interior National Historic Registry, these venerable landmarks were unceremoniously bulldozed to the ground. Although these classic rides spanned several generations, little is commonly known about them.

When opened in 1899, Idora Park was first named Terminal Park. It literally was the terminus of a trolley line. Owned by a streetcar company and designed to lure urban dwellers into the country, Idora's attractions were improved and replaced to insure patronage. Lush lagoons, exotic botanical gardens, wild animals, and carnival acts all made Idora Park popular. However, it was the coasters that caught the public's attentions.

In 1924, Idora's old Dip-the-Dips coaster was deemed obsolete. The T. M. Harton Company, considered to be America's premier coaster builder, reconfigured and remodeled the Dip-the-Dips by adding a sixty-three foot drop and a series of short hills called hops. The result was a first-class out-and-back coaster named the Jack Rabbit.

This gentle new coaster offered a dramatic scenic and sometimes languid view of Idora Park and Mill Creek Park. The Jack Rabbit cradled a minor league ball field, stretched out to the Olympic Pool, later replaced by Kiddieland, and towered over the botanical gardens and picnic grounds. With an entrance near the Grand Ballroom and rear parking lot, it seemingly anchored the southern part of the twenty-seven acres comprising the amusement complex. Children had to master this "junior coaster" before families allowed them to attempt riding the ferocious Wild Cat.

The Firefly coaster was built in 1920. By 1930, it was replaced by the legendary Wild Cat coaster. Built by the Philadelphia Toboggan Company, it was considered state-of-the-art when opened. It featured tunnels, banked curves, descending curves, and an "aeroplane curve" to give it an unmatched feel. Bountiful screams from the Wild Cat attested to its "thrill factor." Crowds, too timid to attempt a ride, found great pleasure by watching more daring folk streak by in featherweight cars high atop the Wild Cat skeletal frame.

Fire in 1984 destroyed a quarter of the Wild Cat. Insurance did not cover rebuilding costs. Although Idora's owners reversed the Jack Rabbit cars and renamed the coaster the Back Wabbit, the park closed and never reopened again.

For seventeen long solitary years, the Jack Rabbit and Wild Cat stood abandoned. Idora's crown jewels were left to rot. They watched the midway succumb to a devastating fire in 1986, which leveled the Fun House, the Bumper Cars, and Heidelberg Gardens. As the Arcade, Carrousel, and Kiddieland buildings were dismantled, the coasters stood as silent monuments of a more prosperous time. The fadeout of Idora Park into oblivion did not seem real as long as the coasters stood their ground.

When arson destroyed the Grand Ballroom in the spring of 2001, the Jack Rabbit and Wild Cat coasters tenaciously survived against all odds. They had become evocative architectural symbols of a once gracious era in our valley. Now needlessly reduced to rubble, they have become poignant haunting memories in a metropolitan area that has callously ignored its once rich indigenous culture.

Summertime without Idora Park's Jack Rabbit and Wild Cat coasters is summertime no more.

The World I Once Knew

by Richard S. Scarsella

It is hard to believe that things come and go without any chance of reprieve. The only thing one can really count on is change, like it or not. The world I once knew has slowly receded into the pages of local history books.

No longer can one find traffic cops on cement islands in the middle of Central Square directing throngs of commuters to the far sides of town. These dignified handsomely uniformed men in blue, dressed in medals, starched shirts, crisply pressed pants, and white gloves once were common fixtures in our lives. I can still hear their shrill whistles and see their military-like hand signals. The automatic synchronized stoplights we now use at busy intersections are poor substitutes for these urban legends.

No longer can one shake off the small town blues in royal motion picture halls fit for a king. Our marble inlaid movie palaces in downtown Youngstown, save one, have been unceremoniously demolished, abandoned, or altered beyond recognition. The days of catching an afternoon film at the Palace, State, Paramount, or Warner theaters are regrettably long gone. These grand movie houses were cathedrals of entertainment and our connection to the glamorous world of Hollywood. When local girl Elizabeth Hartman set tinseltown on fire with her sizzling debut in "A Patch of Blue", we had proof positive that any girl or boy from the heartland could "hit the big time" with talent, guts, and sweat. The untimely demise of the star system and huge movie studios sealed the fates of our native downtown theaters. They are still much missed today.

No longer can one see great flocks of pigeons alight from downtown's Central Square. These once familiar feathered friends added color, character, and romance to our central city. Feeding pigeons downtown, out of bags of popcorn bought at five-and-dime stores, was a time-honored tradition enjoyed by countless generations. Our modern disdain for earthy past-times has vanquished these gentle urban dwellers to oblivion. Their absences make the eerily silent downtown all the more desolate and surreal.

No longer can one hear deep throaty railroad whistles echo throughout the valley every couple of minutes. These plaintive sounds were a constant companion in our hurried lives. Falling asleep with these old friends made one feel safe and secure that all was well with the world. Today, when I happen to hear a muffled train sound in the distance, I stop. Old voices are like music to my ears. They resound with memories of former days when the valley was prosperous, proud, and had a clear sense of purpose and identity.

No longer are monarch butterflies, potato bugs, and bats common sights. These once familiar creatures of my youth are now more easily found in the pages of National Geographic Magazines. Where did they go, I sometimes wonder? The great outdoors seem strangely denuded by the loss of these old friends. Luckily, fireflies endure, though not as numerous as in days past. They act as subtle beacons of our once youthful attachment to all things wild.

No longer do boys and girls seek out bears amongst the dens of Mill Creek Park. These caves have long ago been sealed off from children and adventurous imaginations, for safety's sake we are told. Modern video action games are pathetic substitutes for real-life adventures Tom Sawyer was immortalized for pursuing.

No longer do serpentine caravans of funeral hearses, flower limousines, and mourning cars clog our once busy urban thoroughfares. These opulent spectacles of grief seem out of date now, but once held great morbid curiosity for all. The chiming of church bells in tribute to the dead no longer toll in our midst. When they did ring, your heart would skip a beat. They sounded like the voice of God.

No longer are summers begun and ended at famed Idora Park. This pioneer amusement park, one of the first in the country to open and one of the last in the country to close, personified magic, music, entertainment, and romance. The lush botanical gardens were a welcomed oasis in a dirty factory town. Elegant Idora Ballroom was the epitome of style, taste, and culture. The hand carved Idora Carrousel captured our hearts as youths and warmed our memories in old age. When merciless fires swept this old landmark, our world was never the same again. When Idora died we lost a little of our precious selves. These losses and many more, both great and small, have made us strangers in our own land.

The Y and I

by Richard S. Scarsella

When I was a child, going to the Y.M.C.A. or the Y.W.C.A. was a regular part of growing up. Health clubs, spas, and aerobic centers were unheard of by any of us locals. Long before Youngstown College, later redubbed Youngstown State University, built its own physical education complex, the Y's were the only place to go if one wanted to build both body and spirit.

On any given Saturday morning, well into the early 1970's, the Youngstown area public transit buses were crowded with youth heading downtown for a "workout" or fellowship. Getting to the Y's was half the fun. When Market Street, Oak Street, Belmont Avenue, and Mahoning Avenue were in their heydays, taking a bus was quite a visual tour of a gritty, vibrant, populous, and industrious metropolis.

Elegant North Side period mansions, the West Side art deco Isaly's dairy plant, the trendy South Side Uptown district, and the East Side old world ambiance all were on the way to the Y's. Farmers with poultry, college students with books, sales clerks in neat smocks, and housewives attired in cotton dresses, matching hats, and gloves, all descended on Youngstown's Central Square to go about their affairs. We headed to the Y's.

Traversing the downtown business district was hazardous. Lines of diesel-burning buses, impatient taxicabs, flatbed trucks carrying steel coils, and flocks of pigeons made travel to the Y's challenging. One had to hold tightly one's duffel bag, equipment, lunch, and thermos. No one wanted to waste time getting to our destinations.

The Champion Street Y.M.C.A., in the shadows of the Palace Theater, throbbed with excitement and testosterone. This was a sweaty male domain. Stainless steel weight machines, iron barbells, an Olympic-sized pool, and squash courts were major attractions. Club basketball teams, skills clinics, and Golden Glove competitions all made the Y.M.C.A engaging and inviting.

At the Y.M.C.A., a cross-section of the Mahoning Valley commingled. A sense of civility pervaded the institution. One was expected to act and be a consummate gentleman and sportsman. To be asked to leave the premises was considered a stigma. For wide-eyed boys intent on acquiring the basics of manhood, the Y.M.C.A. was an incubator of citizenship and self-actualization. Losing a game graciously, being a humble winner, and giving the team credit for success all were priceless lessons learned at this downtown landmark. Generations of men had their characters tempered and formed for life in these legendary environs.

The Y.W.C.A. was up the street from the Y.M.C.A. on Rayen Avenue. It had a similar mission statement for women and girls. Good health practices, domestic programs, physical fitness classes, and cultural offerings all welcomed members and guests. In contrast to the Y.M.C.A., the Y.W.C.A. was a more formal establishment. Women and girls were oftentimes dressed in street wear and partook in teas, socials, and cultural activities. Only when they went to the gym or into the pool did females don casual garb. One was expected to be a "lady" at all times. Flaunting tradition could have its consequences. Being a member was akin to being a sorority sister. Pillars of local society guided the Y.W.C.A. wards into the rights of womanhood.

Although the Y's survive, their prominence in our lives has waned. Suburban attractions and wellness centers now compete with the Y's of my youth. Home gyms, complete with treadmills and exercise bikes, have made membership in a Y less likely now. Young men and women are more apt to be a participant in a suburban sports league than a Y league. Busy lives, lack of accessible public transportation, and the world of technology have all taken their toll on the Y culture.

Yet, the Y's endure. They have changed. Their famous cafeterias, once known for baked macaroni and cheese and cream pies, have become delis. Today's Y's allow both sexes and young children to attend. The Y.M.C.A. no longer rents rooms to travelers and the Y.W.C.A. has opened a day care center and a battered women's shelter. The Y.M.C.A. is building a new facility in Boardman and the Y.W.C.A. has closed its pool so as to concentrate on other offerings.

Even now, after many years have passed, weekends seem to be incomplete without a trip to the Y. Rubber bathing caps, the Neptune swim teams, and the resplendent Christmas parties still linger in my memory. And believe it or not, enthusiasts still go to the becalmed downtown to the Y's, as in days of old.

Somehow, I find comfort in this.

Theaters of the Past

by Richard S. Scarsella

The Mahoning Valley was once a thriving, growing, and increasingly wealthy community. Discretionary income was oftentimes spent on leisure activities. Going to the movies was an American past-time shared by all. The result? Youngstown once boasted many first-class, first-run movie houses, which featured the best of Hollywood.

Downtown Youngstown was once a slice of New York's 42nd. Street. At night, the many bright theater marquees lit up Federal Street, announcing films of every genre. Neighboring restaurants, bistros, and cafes welcomed the pre and after theater crowds until midnight. The Mural Room, Brass Rail, and Wick Avenue Diner all catered to the movie clientele. People dressed up and went "on the town".

Youngstown's theaters all had a niche in the marketplace. The Warner Theater—named after the local, pioneering Warner Studio family—specialized in action films. This showcase was truly a palace of gilt, gold, velvet, rare woods, and art. Fittingly, its last film was "Bonnie and Clyde". Now known as the Power's Auditorium, it barely escaped the wrecking ball. Its brass plated ticket booth, stage organ, and velvet ticket rope were sold before its timely reprieve.

The Palace Theater, on Central Square, was a former Keith-Albee vaudeville circuit theater. Complete with marble staircases and fireplaces, box seats and imported cut-glass chandeliers, it was the area's premier live stage house. Acts such as Frank Sinatra and Jimmy Durante graced the footlights, before being pushed aside by film presentations. Felled by the wrecking ball, it is now a parking lot.

The State Theater was the bastion of epic films, such as The Bible and The Sound of Music. Known for its unusual circular, tiered lobby with balconies, the State had an ascending "grand hall" that bridged a back alley into the auditorium. Long dark, it is a ghostly reminder of a more gracious age.

The Paramount Theater was a 1920's styled wood floored hall, with wrought iron rails. Converted into Cinerama—a sweeping, curved, wide-screened, sound enhanced presentation format—it catered to filmgoers that wanted the ultimate film experience. Now derelict, it has been the victim of incompleted restoration projects.

The Regent Theater was a small, East Federal Street "nickelodeon" that featured low budget, twin billed westerns and "race" films. Demolished for urban renewal, no local theater continued such offerings. Television now serviced this market.

Gone, but not forgotten, is the infamous Park Theater. A burlesque house, full of Borsht Belt comics, acts of illusion, and exotic dancers—and later, "adult" films—the Park was a virtual right of passage for most young men of the area. It was also leveled for urban renewal. With its demise, Youngstown lost another link in the grand theater tradition.

Children today think of movies in terms of suburban multiplexes. Void of escapist architecture, these box-like auditoriums, filled with lobbies of video games, are almost sterile in appearance and ambiance. Long gone are the days of attending the cinema in true concert halls that evoke the spirits of Gloria Swanson, Greta Garbo, and Clark Gable. The sound of pipe organs, the sight of 3-D, and the smell of real buttered popcorn are all fading memories now. Memories that are as priceless as they are elusive.

Things I Miss

by Richard S. Scarsella

It's hard to believe that time passes so quickly and unequivocally. We have all become increasingly urbane, modern, and cosmopolitan. People, places, and things we once considered ordinary, in retrospect, are irreplaceable.

I still miss the friendly egg man, bread man, milkman, and laundryman. They knew your name, shared harmless gossip, and always had time to chat with youngsters and the elderly.

I still miss the mysterious gypsies who periodically visited the valley. Their oral tradition made them a wealth of knowledge for those seeking herbal cures, psychic healing, or romantic advice.

I still miss the traveling circus, which came to town in giant railroad boxcars. Watching this spectacle unload at the terminal and trek to the old Meridian Road circus grounds was as entertaining as the circus acts.

I still miss the Canfield Fair freak shows. Watching and talking to the bearded lady, snake girl, and turtle boy was both unsettling and fascinating.

I still miss Arthur Godfrey on the radio. His calm melodic voice combined with vaudeville prattle and ukulele music all were part of now vanishing Americana.

I still miss black and white television. Before Walt Disney introduced the Wonderful World of Color programs, one could freely imagine what colors should be seen on the screen.

I still miss the brightly-lit blinking marquees of the Palace, State, Paramount, Warner, Regent, Newport, Schenley, Belmont, Wedgewood, and Uptown theaters. These grand movie houses once premiered Hollywood's best films for "our viewing enjoyment". Escaping to one of these motion picture palaces was a real thrill and a welcomed relief from the realities of life.

I still miss downtown Strouss' mezzanine. Standing next to the rail, overlooking throngs of shoppers on the main sales floor, was a novel experience.

I still miss the once constantly heard railroad whistles, which echoed throughout the area. These soulful sounds made one feel very connected with the outside world, especially in the gloom of the night.

I still miss the medley of pulsating chiming bells, which once filled the air on Sunday mornings announcing the Lord's Day. At one time, the many downtown church bellowers seemed to be in spirited competition. A non-church goer could not help feeling guilty for not attending one of the amply announced services.

I still miss Golden Age, Nehi, and Holly pops. These locally produced beverages had a distinct taste of their own unequaled by existing brands. Kids loved to mix their many flavors and make cocktails.

I still miss Parker's custard, Dairy Isle soft-serve, and Fron's sherbet. Only Isaly's frozen confections rivaled them. Unfortunately, Isaly's famous rainbow, banana, and Whitehouse ice creams are a thing of the past.

I still miss venerable Idora Park. This grand matron of an amusement park seduced generations with gentle wholesome fun and attractions. The Wild Cat, Baby Wild Cat, and Jack Rabbit coasters, Kiddieland, carrousel, Ferris wheel, fun house, Old Mill water ride, picnic grounds, botanical gardens, and minor league ball field still are vivid in my mind. The shocking abandonment of the grand ballroom makes the heart ache.

I still miss my maternal grandparents. Grandmother's vegetable garden soup and Grandfather's black walnut pies simply delighted the palette. Their unwritten recipes are now unknown.

I still miss yesterday in my search for personal history.

Things I'll Never Do Again

by Richard S. Scarsella

Time passes quietly and quickly. Our lives are literally changed by the passage of days turned into years. Looking back, I note things once considered commonplace that cease to exist for me.

I'll never again sit on my grandmother's expansive front-porch and crack open black walnuts for homemade pies.

I'll never again take a bus downtown to view a first-run film premiere at one of Youngstown's grand movie palaces.

I'll never eat an Isaly's freshly made ice-cream skyscraper cone again. These indescribable frozen confections, laden with high butterfat content, still linger on my palette.

I'll never again buy laces, potions, or jewelry from traveling bands of gypsies. These colorful and much maligned transients made life a little richer in our gritty steel valley.

I'll never attend another South High vs. East High football game. These two legendary teams once fielded ferocious teams and packed the old South Field House and adjoining stadium with rabid fans.

I'll never shop downtown Strouss or Higbee's department stores again. Long shuttered or demolished, these once prosperous anchor stores set fashion trends in our area for decades.

I'll never hear the throaty steel mill whistles in the distance again. They were once constant and comforting companions in our lives.

I'll never ride in an Imperial, Plymouth, Packard, Desoto, Rambler, or Studabaker automobile again. These chrome-encrusted cruisers are no longer commonly found on the roadways, although their names live on in our psyches.

I'll never catch a train to Cleveland or Pittsburgh from a Youngstown railroad depot again. These trips to our sister cities once were ordinary jaunts for most metropolitan families.

I'll never enjoy an evening meal at the old Antoine's, Mansion, Colonial House, or Mural Room restaurants again. These famous eateries once were the toasts of Youngstown's elites, but regrettably have passed from the local scene.

I'll never again go to a meeting or a social engagement at the once fashionable Pick Ohio, Todd House, or Voyager hotels. These venerable landmarks once hosted famous personages and local society events in their elegant suites and ballrooms.

I'll never purchase groceries at Lamar's, Century, Kroger, Lob law, or A&P supermarkets again.

I'll never worship at a Latin Mass or High Mass again, although those chants still live on in my memory.

I'll never have home-delivered milk, cream, eggs, or bread again for early-morning breakfast repasts.

I'll never read a chatty Esther Hamilton or literary Jim Bishop article in a local newspaper again.

I'll never buy Fron's candy or Parker's custard in a local storefront again.

I'll never have an acquaintance with itinerant knife sharpeners, Fuller Brush salesmen, or hoboes again. These fascinating vendors were rich repositories of all kinds of arcane knowledge and advice.

I'll never ride the classic wooden Idora Park roller coasters named the Jack Rabbit and the Wild Cat again. Once a rite of passage in our youth, they died ignoble deaths.

One must not dwell on the past too long or melancholy sets in. Brief visits to yesteryear steel the soul and quicken the heart when all seems grim. And for this, I am thankful.

Things My Child Will Never Know

by Richard S. Scarsella

As I look back on my life, I can not help but muse upon on how things have changed. My daughter takes for granted things prior generations never dreamed or thought possible. Computers, VCR's, microwave ovens, cable television, and fax machines were not even part of previous generations' language. As modern and prosperous as times are now, I still reflect wistfully of times past.

My child will never know the thrill of catching a bus to a thriving downtown pulsating with crowds, bustling shops, elegant department stores, and cozy grilles.

My child will never know the excitement of attending a classic Hollywood film in a grand old theater such as the Palace, Warner, State, Paramount, or Newport. Watching huge billowing draperies unveil the wide screen from a second or third tier balcony is an almost indescribable experience.

My child will never know the challenge of tuning into radio programs with Arthur Godfrey as host. His vaudeville-based entertainment was both soothing and informative. The ukulele was made famous by this pioneer of the airwaves.

My child will never know the familiarity we once had with such all-American television serials as Ozzie & Harriet, Donna Reed, Father Knows Best, and My Three Sons. These shows personified the idealized American family and became part of our own families. Having a good antennae was a must during the heyday of network television.

My child will never know the intoxication of purchasing Christmas gifts at bazaar-like variety stores named Grant's, Kressege's, Murphy's, McCrory's, or Woolworth's. Five dollars used to go a long way in these archetypal American institutions.

My child will never know the peace and solemnity Sundays once typified. The "blue laws" of old once closed all business establishments on the Sabbath, except pharmacies, dairy stores, bowling lanes, and theaters. The break from everyday routine was much welcomed then and is greatly missed now.

Things My Child Will Never Know

My child will never know the panoramic sunsets along the Mahoning River Valley, once full of colorful red, orange, and black acrid, gritty steel smoke.

My child will never know the taste of Sealtest's glass bottled milk, Isaly's banana ice cream skyscraper cones, Parker's fresh egg custard, Strouss' malteds, Gray Drugs' phosphates, or Fanny Farmer's figaro candies.

My child will never know the magic of Youngstown's "Million Dollar Playground", the fabled Idora Park. The melancholy carrousel calliope, shrieks from the legendary Wild Cat and Jack Rabbit wooden coasters, and Grand Ballroom big band and polka melodies only exist in my memory now.

Much of once we knew intimately in our everyday lives has disappeared, not ever to return again. Natalie Scarsella will never know what was lost before her time. Why? Words and pictures can not begin to convey the essence of a culture that has slipped irrevocably into the annals of history.

Things You Don't See Anymore

by Richard S. Scarsella

You don't see rows of taxis stopped in long, snakelike lines anymore. At one time, taxi stands were positioned conveniently all over downtown to expedite travel to the once vibrant urban neighborhoods. Black and white Independent and Yellow cabs all were once common features of city life.

You don't see elderly women dressed in black suits and wearing veils walking the streets anymore. These stoic widows were once honored figures in our communities. Some stayed in mourning the rest of their lives. Like Queen Victoria, their lives stopped when their husbands departed.

You don't see giant train boxcars of fresh fruit and vegetables at rail side warehouses anymore. Perishables are now transported from the West Coast and the South via interstate trucks. Watching tons of fresh produce be unloaded at area depots was exciting for bored youths. Why? Oftentimes, huge banana spiders or colorful exotic insects would disembark with the cargo, much to the consternation of the porters.

You don't see Fuller Brush salesmen canvassing town anymore. These slightly threadbare door-to-door vendors were amazingly patient with inquisitive children, cranky senior citizens, and demanding housewives. To this day, their genuine whalebone combs, handmade by Eskimos, remain unrivaled in simplistic quality and longevity.

You don't see custard stands on corners anymore. Parkers' Custard, on Glenwood Avenue in the Osterville district, drew patrons from miles around. Little did we know then that this delicious frozen confection was made from raw eggs!

You don't see women and men wear hats to church anymore. At one time, your Sunday best included a covering for your head. No lady or gentleman would be caught without one. Millinery shops and haberdasheries all did a brisk trade on Saturdays. Children loved the empty hatboxes. They were used to safe keep toys, crayons, or hobbies. Cub Scouts would turn them into drums.

You don't see Greyhound buses dropping off out-of-town visitors or veterans at intersections anymore. These "scenic cruisers" of the open road, complete with tinted windows, air conditioning, and bathrooms, seemed to be hopelessly romantic. Everyone knew someone who had eloped on these luxurious coaches. Receiving a Greyhound bus toy was a real treat for boys and girls.

You don't see salt-water taffy sold in many stores anymore. Atlantic City and Lake Erie saltwater taffy were once considered delicacies and were routinely eaten by children and adults as a desert. No one worried about his or her fillings coming out when this candy was served.

You don't see drive-in theaters on the outskirts of town anymore. They have all closed. Most have been developed into housing tracts and strip plazas. Well into fall, we would catch a twin bill of the summer blockbuster films for a carload fee. Disney movies named "Son of Flubber" and "The Love Bug" delighted the whole family. When the local drive-ins shut down for the season, this was a sure sign of approaching winter.

You don't see fleets of trucks with names such as Strouss', McKelvey's, Livingston's, A&P, Kroger, Loblaw, or Century foods painted on their side panels. These once trusted retailers have long ago passed from the scene.

You don't see a smoggy haze hug the downtown skyline anymore. Old-timers knew this specter to be a sign of prosperity, generated by nearby open-hearth and Bessemer steel furnaces. Youngstown, known to some as the "Ruhr Valley of Ohio, once relished its gritty roots.

You don't see grand fireworks displays over long abandoned Idora Park anymore. The grand ballroom has been strangely silent. This much beloved neglected landmark touched the hearts of generations for one hundred years. Now in ruins, it still haunts us. And like so many things, proof to the contrary, it lives on, if only in our memories.

Thinking Back

by Richard S. Scarsella

Thinking back to days long ago, I oftentimes find myself revisiting scenes of my childhood. On any given day, images of the past bubble to the level of consciousness. Modern day life momentarily takes a backseat to long gone vignettes, when my mind goes wandering down well-traveled lanes of now vanished places and things.

I fondly recall visiting the once prosperous Vienna Airport. Now renamed the Youngstown Warren Regional Airport, this link to major cities and glamorous international flights was sometimes a destination point for those touched with the travel bug. Visiting the observation deck high atop the passenger terminal was a real thrill. The wind generated by giant propeller airplanes and jet engines cooled one even on the hottest of summer days. Drinking a Boston Cooler or a phosphate float at the chrome counter of the concourse restaurant, with panoramic views of the runways, was an experience city kids relished. Yes, taking a drive out to the country to the municipal airport was a fine way to pass the time of day.

At one time, bowling was a popular sport. Mill workers and professionals alike belonged to leagues and played their hearts out several times a week. Both men and women participated in highly competitive tournaments and packed area bowling lanes with bowlers and fans for championship events. North Side and McGuffey Lanes, now both closed, once were hosts to regional and national bowling exhibitions and professional playoffs. Today, bowling has gone cosmic and is dominated by the under age eighteen crowd. No longer is bowling the "working man's" sport of choice. Like so many once commonplace activities, it has been eclipsed.

I remember well the pool halls that could be found in area neighborhoods. These storefront billiard parlors reeked of stale smoke, cheap beer, and salty perspiration. Young boys rarely were admitted. Preachers and priests railed against this "vice" and gave this past time a bad name. Many locals dreamed of becoming the next Minnesota Fats and hoped to polish their skills to make it big in nearby

Pittsburgh and Cleveland. Betting on games was normal and small fortunes could be made for possessing pool acumen others lacked. When billiard tables became affordable to average homeowners, the once easily found poolrooms in the Youngstown area gradually disappeared. Some few remain, usually in bowling complexes or near tattoo shops.

There are many other memories that sometimes make their presences known for no apparent reasons. Who among us could ever forget the taste of freshly made buttered popcorn at the magnificent Palace Theater? Does anyone still hear the old Strouss' buzzers that used to shrill loudly in code to summon clerks and managers? Can you still see the outlines of fiery blast furnaces lining the languid Mahoning River and lighting up the evening sky? Do you still feel the orange leather seats once used on counter stools at all area Isaly's Dairy Stores? Does the aroma of fresh lilac conjure images of Easter mornings? When you hear the words "Idora Park", do you at once become melancholy about this lost wonderland?

We are the sum of our experiences. They leave permanent marks on our lives. In a very real sense, we are our living past. Like it or not, yesterday is always with us. And I for one would not have it any other way.

This and That

by Richard S. Scarsella

Modern day living almost crowds out the not so distant past. Yesteryear in the once pulsating Mahoning Valley bears little resemblance to what remains in the metropolitan area.

Deep throaty train whistles used to be our steady companions. Diesel engines pulling serpentine trains laden with ore, coal, and slag were common sights in the "Ruhr Valley of the Midwest". Deafening silence has now replaced these workhorses and all they represented.

We now pride ourselves on being technologically sophisticated. I remember well the vintage black Bell pedestal telephones, complete with rotating dials, which were connected to party lines. Sharing a telephone line with neighbors was both fun and exasperating. Rabid gossips relished the easy access to others' business. Unfortunately, waiting for a turn to "ring someone" was an exercise in patience. How long ago this all seems now.

Older relatives always had great disdain for "store bought" meat and produce. Well into the 1950's, butchers and grocery peddlers roamed city streets offering freshly dressed cuts of meat and homegrown fruits and vegetables. Amish honey cured smoked hams and Lake Erie concord grapes made Sunday dinners memorable to this day.

I can still recall the great excitement generated by the visit of local clergymen to neighborhoods. It was once not unusual for preachers and priests to make house calls. Of course, they were always invited to stay for lunch and supper. For men of the cloth to dine with your family was considered a great honor. Cloth napkins, linen tablecloths, and beeswax tapers were brought out along with silver and bone china place settings. Only the best would do for men of God. These impromptu celebrations endeared us to church and the almighty.

Throughout the years in the gloaming, folks from these parts went berry picking, mushroom gathering, and hunting for small game. Before suburbia swallowed up pristine forests and pictorial pastureland, natural environs rimmed Youngstown. Blackberries and elderberries once were easily found and baked into mouth-watering pastries. Homemade mushroom soup, cooked with local dairy cream, was both a delicacy and a staple of our diets. Carving open-range turkey, quail, or pheasant for Sunday repast was a time-honored ritual in a land once blessed with abundance. These traditions still linger in my memory with acute clarity.

Of all the things missed, nothing saddens me more than the untimely demise of venerable Idora Park. How such a treasure could be callously abandoned and left to die a long ignoble death is beyond comprehension. Visions of the elegant grand ballroom dance floor, the somnolent carrousel, the menacing roller coasters, and the magical kiddieland still are fresh in my mind. I still wonder, where did it all go?

When I was but a youth, phrases now uncommonly used were plentiful. When one was at a lost for words, archaic phrases were spoken to express our thoughts or feelings. One might ask, "What are you doing?" The reply could very well be, "Oh nothing, just this and that."

And I still mourn "this and that" as I navigate the uncertain future, still being deeply rooted in the past.

Trading Stamp Days

by Richard S. Scarsella

Well into the 1960's, area residents eagerly saved trading stamps. These tokens were given out at gas stations, supermarkets, and other national retail outlets. Homemakers, businessmen, teenagers, and children all collected them, with hopes of exchanging full books of stamps for much wanted consumer items. Names such as S & H, Plaid, Top Value, and Gem stamps were well known and trusted. They were very much a part of our daily lives.

Corner grocery stores and garages were virtually doomed if they didn't award trading stamps at their neighborhood establishments. Out of town based chain stores and service stations dazzled local customers with modern conveniences, such as air conditioning, credit card acceptance, and most importantly, generous trading stamp giveaway policies. New suburban plazas and fuel stops lured in town trade to the fringes of the city with the help of trading stamps.

Throughout the Youngstown area, inhabitants could be seen during warm weather on spacious tree shaded porches dutifully sorting out various types of trading stamps. Children would lick and glue the penny single stamps in long rows on blank pages, under the watchful eyes of their elders. Fresh squeezed lemonade would accompany our stamp licking marathons, since it cut the taste of the stamp glue. Stamps valued at ten and fifty were the province of older adults. They did not want to take the chance that these stamps would be lost or disfigured. Teenagers would usually glue the stamps of five denomination.

Redemption stores were carnival-like experiences. Housewives that regularly frequented Loblaws, A & P, Kroger, and Century markets, all mainstays of trading stamp activity, always ran into friends at the redemption stores. Jokes were made, pictures exchanged, and stories were shared, all to the delight of onlookers. Everyone was in a good mood at these impromptu gatherings. After all, no money changed hands here. Despite attractive displays of the latest house wares, housewives usually redeemed their books for such staples as Cannon towels, Plakie toys, rolls of contact paper, hair dryers, strollers, Dutch ovens, mangles, deep fries, and steam irons. These books of stamps were integral parts of conservative household spending habits and used judiciously.

Engaged couples could be seen bashfully filling out bridal registry forms at redemption counters. Their wish lists included Melmac plates, metal venetian blinds, Toastmaster toasters, Art Deco blenders, Purcell bed linens, Japanese made silver plated flatware, and hen canister sets. Many newlyweds partially furnished their "honeymoon nests" by using the once ubiquitous trading stamps. Not surprisingly, many items from these stores still see service in frugal homes of the now aging baby boom generation.

Men liked trading stamps because they could obtain all types of hardware, tools, car, and home-improvement kits without spending tightly budgeted funds. Teen-agers loved redemption stores because they could test out and dream of getting dual speaker, stereophonic, hi-fidelity (hi-fi) stereo record players and radios at no charge. Children loved the toys. Lincoln logs, Monopoly games, Mr. Potato Head, and deluxe swing sets could all be had for just filling out books. How magical it seemed.

People all appeared congenial and full of camaraderie in the redemption lines. If someone was short a stamp or page of stamps, someone always helped out, knowing others would do the same for them. The ultimate embarrassment was to have glued the wrong stamps in a trading stamp book of another brand. This was a sure way to lose your place in line and be labeled a non-serious collector.

Many people looked down at others saving trading stamps. However, Youngstown's so-called "Greatest Department Store", McKelvey's, gave out much coveted Gem stamps, which could be converted into true luxury items. Tuesdays were double-Gem days. McKelvey's would be full of trading stamp aficionados on these days, proving that better-healed clientele also liked what they considered to be a bargain. Naturally, everyone heard of, but never met, consumers who supposedly collected trading stamps until they exchanged them for bone china, pearls, or a fur wrap. Such tales were legendary and were powerful prods for others who always redeemed books for less exotic goods.

Redemption centers provided scores of children with their first red wagons or Schwinn bikes. Many households obtained their first electrical convenience kitchen gadgets there as well. Electric can-openers seemed to epitomize America's fascination with gadgetry. The redemption stores had no shortage of these items or equally unnecessary furnishings. This was part of the trading stamp mystique. These stores were veritable dream factories, somewhat like the middle-class "Price Is Right" television show. They both fueled and whetted America's appetites for things that were consumable, contemporary, and status symbols. Best of all, we felt that we were owed these guilty delights, since we already had purchased items that rewarded us with "free" trading stamps.

Once thought of as novel, redemption stores became passé when discount stores and catalogue marts flooded the valley with huge selections of house wares at deep discounts. Impatient area residents no longer were willing to wait months or years to procure desired items in their quest for the good life. Easy installment plans, in-store credit cards, and two-income families now allowed most everyone to purchase anything one wanted, without saving trading stamps. Redemption centers could not meet such competition.

No-frills discount gas stations and warehouse food stores all offered low prices as their major marketing tools. Trading stamps were increasingly viewed in the 1970's as outmoded, costly sales gimmicks. Busy, dual income households had little time to seek out trading stamp vendors or redemption centers. The result? Trading stamps began a long, slow disappearing act in our metropolis. By the early 1980's, they ceased to exist locally.

Recently, when unpacking some old storage boxes, I came across some partially filled trading stamp books. I explained to my daughter how, at her age of eleven, I gladly sorted, licked, and glued S & H, Plaid, Top Value, and Gem stamps into their prospective books, in hopes that I could pick out something special at the redemption centers. She nodded her head knowingly and walked away speechless. This was a piece of Americana she would never know.

As I repackaged these vestiges of another time, a thought came to mind. History is not made of only great men and memorable deeds. Rather, it is also made of everyday experiences, both simple and sublime.

Transfiguration

by Richard S. Scarsella

Throughout our lives, the very familiar changes imperceptively. Seasons unfold. Flowers bloom. The gilded youth become decidedly middle-aged and ultimately the faded elderly. Time, after all, is relentless. No one escapes.

Civilizations are made and crumble upon the backs of noted personages. Augustus Caesar established the glittering Roman Empire. Emperor Napoleon left the French imprint upon the European continent. Germany's Hitler attempted to remake the world. Regardless of victory or defeat, larger than life individuals made history.

On the local scene, the Mahoning Valley emerged from rustic frontier land into a thriving industrial metropolis. Founding families of our rich heritage included Wick, Hillman, Powers, Tod, and Stambaugh. Many institutions and buildings still bear their influences.

Although few dwell on native historical figures, notable retailers still are oftentimes referred to in conversations about the not so distant past. Families still recall fondly being fitted for "adult shoes" at Lustig's shoe stores. This once popular chain of family owned shops outfitted generations before disappearing. Discount shoe stores became the vogue.

Strouss-Hirschberg's and McKelvey's were known region wide as purveyors of quality-made dry goods. These flagship downtown landmarks brought a touch of New York's 7th Avenue and Park Avenue into our area through the specialty departments they advertised. These grande dame department stores featured exotic furs, designer gowns, interior design, estate jewelry, and imported perfumes. Sadly, these once locally owned emporiums have past from our landscape. Large impersonal superstores have displaced them.

All fields of retail and wholesale have pioneers. The DeBartolo and Cafaro names are synonymous nationwide with strip plazas, malls, and suburban merchandising. The Handel name conjures images of homemade frozen confections. The Alberini's name is equated with gourmet food and fine wines. The Whitehouse name brings to mind apples, pies, and cider.

My father, Alfred "Al" Scarsella, Sr. was also a name known to area residents. As founder of the original Scarsella Furniture Company, established 1937, he touched the lives of many. Countless numbers of households bought whole housefuls of furnishings from his stores. Numerous homes count as heirlooms solid wood cedar chests, bedrooms, dining rooms, and desks obtained on lay-a-way and installment plans. Some families still retell how they found their first television, stereo, freezer, or dishwasher at my dad's original East Side store.

Unlike today's forgettable shopping experiences, visits to once celebrated stores of youth were memorable. Clerks were once dressed fashionably in black and spoke proper English. Displays educated consumers about the finer points of craftsmanship and bore the "Made in the U.S.A." logo. Generous free samples titillated our senses. The fragrances of Old World perfumes and the touch of pure Irish linen were representatives of lifestyles one could only dream of living.

Today's society seems hell-bent in pursuing modernity, efficiency, and pluralism at any costs. Seemingly, the individual is being homogenized into a mass culture, with stores offering a plethora of similar merchandise. Hand-made workmanship, personalized service, and knowledgeable salesmanship are all now practically nonexistent in the retail trades. Business has devolved from being customer driven to being profit driven. The shopping experience has become an alienating process, dreaded by many, and responsible for the detached on-line purchasing trend.

When my father recently passed away on 12/7/04 at age ninety, I recalled a phrase my Uncle Sam Scarsella once favored. He oftentimes said, "When an old man dies a library burns down." He was right. The wisdom of the ages is locked into graves. The forerunners of our environs are rapidly disappearing from our midst. My father lived to see it all unfold before he too passed into another dimension. He, like others, epitomized another age. What remains is a massive void.

Change is inevitable. It is not always for the better. It has been said that death is part of the life cycle. I now know what my dad meant when he remarked that "We are all in God's waiting room."

Traveling Son

by Richard S. Scarsella

Traditionally, summertime brings expectations of travel. Once June arrives, the "travel bug" emerges in us all. The result? We make plans to hit the road either domestically or abroad.

In my youth, it was not uncommon for local residents to head "up to the lake," which of course meant Lake Erie. Some traveled to the upper Great Lakes named Superior, Huron, and Michigan. Young couples and newlyweds headed towards romantic Niagara Falls and Lake Ontario.

Many families trekked to the Eastern Seaboard. The Atlantic Ocean beaches, especially in Atlantic City and Ocean City, were huge draws for valley residents. Beauty pageants, boardwalks, bingo parlors, and nightclubs all lured sedate Youngstowners to these legendary vacation communities.

However, not all were content to travel stateside. Some few of us embarked on grand tours of the continent. Our destination? Europe. Well into the 1970's, traveling to the land of our forefathers was considered a bit of a hardship. Our cousins across the seas did not dwell on such creature comforts as air-conditioned hotels, soft toilet paper, and readily accessible ice cubes. Going to Great Britain, France, Italy, or Germany was considered to be both exotic and foolhardy.

Nonetheless, many of us set out for the Old World girded with passports, visas, health cards, cash, Pepto Bismol, and toilet tissue. What we experienced both thrilled and confounded. Europe was not picture postcard perfect. It was more and less.

Big Ben, Windsor Castle, Parliament, and the Tower of London were regal, proper, and strangely familiar. These English landmarks evoked awe, curiosity, and closer inspection. Long tourist lines, kitsch souvenir stands stocked with Japanese made goods, and personal guided tours by Third World guides all made our travails here a bit surreal. Straining to understand the Queen's English was frustrating. Our British relations treated us with both respect and condescension.

In France, Paris oozed romance, elegance, and cold politeness. The Eiffel Tower, Notre Dame Cathedral, the Left Bank, and Champs Elysees all appeared to be Hollywood movie sets erected in an otherwise dirty, cramped, and inhospitable metropolis. Frenchmen, it could be said, like American dollars but not the tourists. Thankfully, the Italians were friendlier.

Rome lived up to its reputation as the eternal city. Vatican City, St. Peter's Basilica, the Pantheon, and the Coliseum, to name a few, made history come alive and stop still. Imperial Roman art, architecture, and culture engulfed untutored American sightseers. Here was a land that valued its heritage, we thought. When we viewed an occasional demolition or modernization of an aged building "for progress", we were disheartened. The beauty and treachery of the Roman Empire was enlightening and sobering. Was America the new Rome? Was our country destined for the same debilitating decline we wondered?

In Germany, World War II was still smoldering. The ugly scar across cosmopolitan Berlin named the Berlin Wall was a stark reminder that politics and warfare ruled the hearts of mighty nations. Visiting Checkpoint Charlie, the pass between democratic West Berlin and communist East Berlin, was bone chilling. Barbed wire, machine gun towers, and mine fields riveted our eyes. Here, East met in an epic standoff dubbed the Cold War. Bombed ruins of once sophisticated neighborhoods made Berlin, Hitler's once glittering capital city, appear melancholy and startling. Was this the "real" Europe? One could only ponder. After this dose of reality, we were ready to go stateside.

Flying home, I reflected that the dominant presence of America in our host countries was comforting and disconcerting. Coca-Cola machines, Hershey chocolate bars, Mickey Mouse toys, and Elvis Presley music seemed to be everywhere. Ironically, our polished European relatives relished symbols of American pop culture. We in turn cherished mementos of Old London's Trafalgar Square, French haute couture, Italian leather goods, and German pubs.

Today, travel around the world is commonplace. The Concorde supersonic jets now connect New York City with Europe in six hours. Cable television, fiber optics, and the new world economy all have made the world smaller, more interconnected, and less foreign.

I cannot help but remember when this was not always the case. There was a time when few Americans went overseas. Those that never left these shores kept intact their images of lands afar that most only read about in history books. In a strange twist, the United States has now become a favorite tourist destination for Europeans. My, how times have changed!

Tribulations

by Richard S. Scarsella

Americans have come to expect prosperity, peace, and security in their own land. When the ugliness of the world at large intrudes on this mindset, spirits sink and faint hearts fret. In true pioneer style, Americans always show true grit, enterprise, and perseverance, regardless of the threats at our doorstep.

When the British burned the president's residence in Washington, D.C. during the War of 1812, many felt despondent. However, the legendary Yankee resolve vanquished the former colonizer despite great hardships and odds. Demonstrating true courage and ingenuity, the Americans prevailed. After the conflict, the first family's burned home was repainted and dubbed the "white house".

In 1941, the Japanese attack on Hawaii's Pearl Harbor stunned the world. The United States was caught unawares by a militaristic kingdom lusting for land, natural resources, and geopolitical influence. Many wondered if the United States had the resolve and willpower to prepare for battle and see it through to victory. The unconditional surrender of the Japanese Empire, precipitated by atomic bombs leveling Hiroshima and Nagasaki, showed disbelievers that Americans would not tolerate violations to their freedom and safety.

When military warlord Hitler, along with Italy's Mussolini and Japan's Emperor Hirohito, planned world domination, Great Britain and France stood alone as defenders of democratic ideals and traditions. When the United States entered World War 11 as the "arsenal of democracy", critics voiced doubts that the Third Reich and its Axis alliance could be defeated. It was soundly vanquished in time. The resiliency, resourcefulness, and pride of Americans literally saved the world from autocratic servitude. Like it or not, the United States of America had to spearhead the drive to eradicate despots from the international scene.

The recent New York City World Trade Center bombings have begun a new page in the annals of American history. America's shock and revulsion have morphed into righteous anger and solid determination to rid the world of fanatical terrorists. If the past is any guide for the future, the United States will prevail over its present faceless foes. Americans never shirk from a challenge and do not like to lose.

As events unfold in front of our eyes, I am struck by the irony of it all. Our enemies know not the nation they have declared war on. The United States is not symbolized merely by oversized buildings and grand monuments. It is best defined as the embodiment of a love for liberty, equality, and self-determination. As an Imperial Japanese admiral once exclaimed during the aftermath of the Pearl Harbor attack, "We have awakened a sleeping giant." The era we have lived in will never be the same again.

Twilight of a Dynasty

by Richard S. Scarsella

The recent announcement that Plymouth automobiles will no longer be made after the year 2001 signals yet another milestone in American culture. This dependable, wholesome, no-nonsense symbol of our nation is the latest victim of the new worldwide economy. The recently created Chrysler-Mercedes Benz Corporation, based in Germany, has decided that this reliable Yankee brand is no longer competitive and is expendable. With its passing, another piece of living American history disappears.

Up into the 1960's, names such as Ford, Chevrolet, and Chrysler had definite lineages that were both protected and promoted as being special. Chrysler was known for innovation, Ford was built to last, and Chevrolet screamed style. Plymouth exuded reliability. The 1970's, besieged by imported sedans and gas rationing, homogenized the automobile industry. Both domestic and foreign cars became virtual clones, indistinguishable from each other, except for a nameplate. The 1980's push for economy and the 1990's international automobile conglomerates have minimized the once glorious car traditions that Plymouth personified.

In the 1950's, long, low, wide, powerful, chrome laden behemoths once glided down local streets. The President Dwight D. Eisenhower superhighways, built to speedily transport troops nationwide, fueled America's love affair with the "horseless carriages". In this Cold War era of escapism car design, vehicles sported exaggerated fins, whimsical taillights, and stately hood ornaments evocative of rocket ships, ocean liners, and skyscrapers. Prim, proud, practical and prodigious Plymouths shared the freeways with dignified DeSotos, hulking Hudsons, elegant Imperials, pachyderm-like Packards, and futuristic Edsels. Only Plymouth survived into the modern epoch.

Ironically, many cars to be unveiled for the millennium are boasting retrospective features. Chrysler, Plymouth's parent company, is in the lead. It is already advertising its "new" PT Cruiser, with an oversized 1940's front-end grille, encrusted with a honeycomb lattice work of chrome, any Plymouth owner would instantly recognize. Old is new again and chic. Unfortunately, Plymouth will not be part of this revival of the styling it once epitomized.

The imminent demise of the Plymouth is yet another casualty in the long fadeout of great, historic, distinctively American automobiles, we knew and loved in our youth. Its unfortunate exit marks the twilight of a dynasty of cars which once embodied the American spirit.

Unforgotten

by Richard S. Scarsella

When the spring season slips seamlessly into summertide, I am ever mindful of things retained in memory. Despite the inexorable passage of years, I somehow have managed to recall fleeting images of times past.

Local advertising once featured resorts at Lake Erie, the Poconos Mountains, and the Ohio River, long before it became fashionable and affordable to holiday in exotic places such as New York City, Las Vegas, and Florida. Of all the get-a-way destinations, Geneva-On-The-Lake was the most popular.

This Coney Island inspired beach town offered reasonable lodgings, food, and attractions for budgets of any size. Family owned cottages, rental cabins, campgrounds, trailer parks, boarding houses, and motor lodges all catered to those seeking soothing relief from the boiling hot Mahoning Valley environs. Lake Erie was considered a blue oasis, within driving distance from the industrial heartland.

Before Route 11 was built, vacationers "went for a drive" into the countryside as they headed north to the banks of the Great Lakes. Both Route 45 and Route 46 were traditional and familiar roads taken by Youngstowners heading for the sandy beaches. Verdant pastures, bustling farm villages, and old growth forests welcomed "cityslickers" on the move. Buying fresh laid eggs, sweet corn, and freshly picked strawberries from Amish roadside stands were standard practices during our summer treks. For those reared on store bought groceries, these homegrown fruits, vegetables, and dairy products were real treats to behold.

Geneva-On-The-Lake was a veritable bastion of Youngstown society. Professionals and laborers alike co-mingled. Some families summered there from Memorial Day until Labor Day. Others came up several weeks per month. Still others visited every weekend. Not to "go to the lake" at least once a year was considered quite odd.

Men particularly enjoyed fishing out on the lake or near the docks of the marinas. The blue perch—now extinct—were considered a delicacy. Fishing contests were held regularly and to win a prize was considered a great honor. Boys reveled in catching pollywogs, water snakes, and minnows. Bait and tackle shops were institutions and provided advice, camaraderie, and Coast Guard weather reports.

Women frequented the boutiques, antique shops, souvenir stands, and bingo parlors. Girls preferred the gold and silver vendors, the salt-water taffy and fudge stands, and miniature golf courses. Of course, getting one's fortune told by a gypsy was not considered unusual.

In the days when a dark tan was termed healthy, we literally encamped on the beach. Every family had a genuine Native American blanket they lounged upon, from morning until dusk. Oversized umbrellas, coolers, and board games were part of the beach culture. Come suppertime, the coast was aflame with bonfires. The aromas of roasted hot dogs, fried fish, melted marshmallows, and burnt driftwood filled the air. When the cool inland sea breezes moved ashore, we headed for the boardwalk.

During evening time, beach dwellers donned their "dress up' outfits in search of entertainment. Outside concerts catered to families. Nightclubs attracted a younger crowd. Children filled the Lakeview Amusement Park—a cousin to famed Idora Park. Parents danced to big band songs on the wooden floor of the waterfront ballroom. Grandparents sat on benches, in front of Eddie's Grille, and watched throngs of people march up and down the avenues eating fresh custard and hot doughnuts. From May until September, this lakeside community was a beehive of wholesome escapism.

When the long somnolent days were spent and it was time to retire, bedroom windows—usually without screens—were flung open to allow for air circulation. Inevitably, as our eyes grew heavy with sleep, we could hear the restless Lake Erie waves crash upon the shoreline. For those that cared to listen, the lake seemed to speak to us, just as Native American folklore said it did.

Uptown: Crossroads to Suburbia

by Richard S. Scarsella

Up until the early 1970's, Youngstown residents oftentimes shopped south of the crowded, bustling and car-choked downtown central shopping district. Where did they go to? To the Uptown!

This distinctive enclave started south of the Market Street viaduct and ended at Midlothian Boulevard, the boundary with Boardman. The Uptown featured expansive sidewalks, plenty of store-front and free store-owned parking, upscale shops, fine dining spots and chic lounges.

Unlike the gridlocked downtown, the Uptown welcomed both car and bus patrons. Numerous car dealerships—such as the old Donnell Ford and Stackhouse Oldsmobile—serviced cars, while you went shopping. Smartly dressed women would promenade up and down Market Street "window shopping". They made a day of it.

Fashionable shoppes, such as Esterlees and the Bride and Formal Shop, enticed fashion mavens by their haute couture collections. At night, cars would cruise on Market Street, pass the signature Amoco sign and slowly glide by colorful, multi-textured, eclectic display windows that catered to even more exotic tastes. Furniture stores lit their windows with a homemaker's dream furnishings.

A drive on Market Street was a veritable "Price Is Right" show on wheels.

Lunch at the Colonial House, Mansion, or Antone's was a dress-up occasion. Women still wore gloves and hats for "tea". Gentlemen, of course, dressed in an "Esquire" wardrobe, to "do lunch". The Oven Restaurant offered an elegantly casual ambiance, with its slanted, Colorado styled, wood hewn ceiling, and tinted windows.

After lunch, entertainment would be either a matinee at the sophisticated Uptown Theater or a stage production at the Playhouse, on nearby Glenwood Avenue. This was as close to Manhattan as one could get in Youngstown.

Cocktail hour could be celebrated with very dry martinis at the art-retro Cave Lounge. The more daring frequented the Club 54 styled Limelighter or Theatrical Lounge. Socialites shimmered here.

The ultra-modern Sears—with its drive-in automotive department and garden center—anchored stores such as W. T. Grant, G. C. Murphy, F. W. Woolworth, and Fanny Farmer Candies. The Uptown dazzled in the 1950's, as Americans rushed to spend their new post-war affluence. It lost its luster to new shopping centers sprouting up in the suburban fringes.

Ironically, just as the Uptown slowly sapped the energy of the downtown, it too was equally drained of life by the Mahoning, Boardman, Liberty and McGuffey plazas. The downtown malaise spread, like a cancer, and enveloped the Uptown.

Today, the Uptown is ghostly in appearance. Like the downtown, it is boarded up, forlorn, derelict, and barely occupied. Die-hards can still have lunch at the Colonial House. If they wish, they can pretend that time has not moved on so mercilessly. The Uptown area encompasses many shadows of other eras. Nearby, spectacular Mill Creek Park and the remains of Idora Park bear mute testimony to this incontrovertible fact.

Urban Legend

by Richard S. Scarsella

Any metropolis is rich in local folklore. Chicago is still known by the saga of Mrs. O'Leary's cow kicking over a candlestick and starting a catastrophic fire, which virtually leveled the city.

Many regions foster little known myths. In the Youngstown area, old fables still prevail upon the lips of a pre-World War II generation. The narrators are living fossils of and practitioners of oral history. Before television and computers dulled our collective cultural memories, the Mahoning Valley was a paradise of famous and infamous accounts.

I still vividly recall my grandmother breathlessly warning us to stay off the streets behind locked doors. Why? The dreaded and much maligned gypsies were passing through, like they were want to do. These vagabonds of East Europe, transplanted to the more hospitable American continent, periodically traveled westward from the eastern seaboard. The Midwest was considered a prime market for gypsy wares, medicines, "magic", and entertainment.

Oftentimes, following the carnival or circus, gypsy families, known as clans, silently slipped across the county lines and settled in on the outskirts of town. For upright conservative Christian adherents, these colorful transients added a welcomed change of routine. Male gypsies were renown for "getting up" torrid high stakes card games. Many heard undocumented stories of local citizens gambling away rent money, heirloom watches, and gold fillings of teeth in their quest to win the big pot. No one I ever knew "hit" the jackpot. However, I knew many that had wicked hangovers from gypsy spirits and elixirs.

Female gypsies were known for their earthy beauty, raucous senses of humor, and willingness to let their hair down—for a price. Although many adolescents supposedly were initiated into the ways of love by bewitching gypsies, their accounts were always a bit suspect. A visit to a gypsy woman meant having your fortune told. And many times predictions came true.

Child gypsies were characterized as compulsive liars, hardened thieves, and one step in front of the law. Whenever a bicycle was missing, a window broken, or a garden poached, gypsy youth were damned for their cleverness, stealth, and lack of conscience. To my recollection, no gypsy offspring were ever caught "red handed" by ever wary constables. However, we were always on our guard, lest these undesirables get the better of us.

Gypsies were much vilified for not having roots, for practicing white and black sorcery, for selling their wives and children into prostitution, and for fleecing unsuspecting patrons all too happy to part with their dollars. Many claimed they were cursed by a gypsy and had to buy their way out of a spell.

Preachers, politicians, and self-appointed guardians of morality all damned the gypsies for their alleged practices. Chilling yarns of gypsies stealing and selling sleeping youngsters, boiling and eating babies, and robbing graves of valuables made this subculture an outcast wherever they visited. Yet, they returned annually, like clockwork. Unbeknownst to us, many solicited their services.

Some elderly men and women found welcome relief from rheumatism and gout in the murky odoriferous vials of gypsy liniments and powders. Those that lacked "vigor" oftentimes found energy in love potions and concoctions brewed from ancient recipes. Children stricken with dropsy or a mysterious "wasting" ailment, were known to sometimes benefit from gypsy prescriptions for health.

The delicate fine laces, woven by blind Belgium nuns, amulets, good luck charms, and chants for sale all made industrious gypsy entrepreneurs important figures in the hidden economy of our valley. Old wives' tales always said to never cross a gypsy. Why? One could be afflicted by the dreaded "evil eye".

When I revisit these shadowy figures of my childhood, they still hold me in rapt curiosity. Did the gypsies really possess rare knowledge and exotic powers foreign to us, or did we just buy into their illusions? Were these celebrated anti-heroes frauds, or were they descendents of a civilization long forgotten? I still do not know.

Of this, I am sure. Living in a land minus the gypsies would have been bleak indeed. They gave our hometown a tenuous link to wonder, adventure, and mystery. In a true sense, they were ambassadors of another time and world.

I can now better understand why an aged relative once reverently whispered within earshot, "Thank God for the gypsies."

Vanished Tableaus Live on in Memories

by Richard S. Scarsella

In the greater Youngstown area, once familiar scenes have slowly dissolved into the landscape. Occasional artifacts act as reminders of what once existed in our midst.

Boardman, Austintown, Poland, and Canfield were until recently considered rustic inner suburbs to the bustling Youngstown central city. These bucolic townships were legendary agricultural producers. Corn, wheat, barley, and fruit were grown, picked, shipped, and sold nationwide by farmers in these now reborn bedroom communities.

For years, Idora Park and Midlothian Boulevard were the limits of Youngstown's south side. Going south to Route 224 was considered a "trip". Before the trend setting DeBartolo family developed virgin land into the pioneer Boardman Plaza and ultra-modern Southern Park Mall, Boardman was dotted with picture-perfect farmsteads owned by stolid and hardworking families. City folk were accustomed to buying fresh vegetables at stands, which could be found along the county roads. One such stand still exists on Shields Road, next to a fire station.

Route 62 was always a convenient highway for those destined to Canfield. This historic village was the county seat for years, until Youngstown business interests had the center of government moved to Youngstown. The old courthouse still remains astride the quaint Canfield Village commons, which was used as a place for grazing cattle. Canfield Fair, located south of the village green, has survived the test of time and has kept alive a rich Mahoning Valley agrarian tradition.

Austintown was once viewed as a way station for those heading towards Akron via Route 18. Horse farms were frequented here by urbanites seeking the great outdoors. Many area residents discovered the charm of Austintown's "wholesome living" when attending the old Meridian Road circus grounds. Others headed west to the Salt Springs Road in search of salt or mineral spring water. A huge truck stop on Route 46 gives testimony to the fact that this western enclave still is at the crossroads of transportation.

On Route 170, Poland touched our lives as we headed towards Pittsburgh. Stately homes, Connecticut Western Reserve architecture, and idyllic Yellow Creek watershed all created a sense of serenity. The Old Stone Tavern still exudes this characteristic. It is hard to imagine that only a few miles east lays a dirty loud crowded and blighted industrial corridor.

As suburban development homogenizes these venerable settlements of our forefathers, memories must work hard to recreate the backdrops of our youth. I can still recall seemingly endless acres of fragrant apple orchards in Canfield. The riding stables of Austintown still conjure clear images of jaunting horsemanship. Boardman's many weathered barns, with Mail Pouch Tobacco signs painted on their sides, are still unforgettable, long after they have disappeared from the landscape. Poland's old library bridge still is fondly revered by generations who threw rocks off of its' deck.

People, like trees and plants, need roots. Without them, a sense of impermanence sets in. We find comfort in landmarks that remain. These markers are guides to our lives. To this day, aged milestones survive around the countryside, signifying boundaries, water rights, and ownership.

Ancient Greeks and Romans cherished the past. Heritage was documented, preserved, and passed down to the youth. The Renaissance sought to recreate the best of the ages. A "Renaissance man" sought to acquire a universal knowledge by way of broad cultural and intellectual interests. Simply put, the future was based firmly in that which had preceded it.

Memories keep alive things, times, and places that still hold importance for us. As our former stomping grounds grow unfamiliar, we can still feel at home in our thoughts. Tomorrow can bring great sorrow for those not shielded from the harsh realities of modern life.

Remembrances are a lifeline, yet they are as tenuous as a wisp of smoke.

Vanishing Youngstown

by Richard S. Scarsella

When I returned to the Mahoning Valley, after living out of town several years, I felt like a visitor from another time. Why? The city I knew had vanished. The long fade-out continues mercilessly today.

Long-time residents know too well, of what I am speaking. A land-hungry state university is decimating Youngstown's historic North Side, which was once an architectural oasis. Beautiful, distinguished grand residences, echoes of a more gracious time, have been unceremoniously leveled, not recycled, only to be replaced by nondescript boxy structures or barren parking lots.

Visitors to Harvard University, in Cambridge, Mass., will tell you that both academia and residential areas can co-exist nicely, without one eradicating the other. If Harvard demolished Cambridge, Massachusetts, then one would not get the much vaunted Ivy League experience. Likewise, when Youngstown State University flattens its surroundings, it robs students of an organic learning environment. These flagrant actions also deny valley residents of their cultural legacy.

Downtown Youngstown is truly a ghost of itself. Millions of dollars, spent on urban renewal, mall construction, and traffic reconfiguring, have produced a shell of a central district. Surprisingly, much money is found for the razing of priceless structures and the construction of yet more parking spaces. Little funds are readily available for the gentrification of once thriving edifices. Is the pulling down of the legendary McKelvey/Higbee building really progress? Surely, this building could have been better secured—and mothballed—until a viable revitalization project could be implemented.

Generations of shoppers still wistfully recall the eye-catching McKelvey show windows, eclectic displays, diet-busting restaurant, and Santa's Toyland. This definitive, ornate, neo-classical mercantile monster of a building screams "Youngstown"! The death of this landmark—for a parking lot—will leave yet another hole in the wounded psyche of the downtown.

The Palace and Newport Theaters, Idora Park, Tod House Hotel, Elms Ballroom, St. Joseph's Church, and the Jeanette Blast Furnace are all victims of wanton neglect, greed, and a callous disregard for our heritage. These familiar places only exist in our memories now. Yet, they all once played major roles in our daily lives. Collectively, these buildings defined the essence of the Mahoning Valley. Can we afford to let more symbols slip through our fingers?

Concerned residents and leaders of vision should advocate for the preservation of the State, Paramount and Uptown theaters, Wick Building, B & O Railroad Station, Smokey Hollow, Isaly's, and Idora Park Ballroom, to name a few. They are all in great danger.

Should these trademarks of our valley evaporate into thin air, our community will no longer be readily discernible from other post-industrial settlements. With the loss of identity, comes the loss of spirit and heart. Then, we will have a decidedly defeated metropolis.

Victuals

by Richard S. Scarsella

Memories are made rich by our senses. Older generations still swell with pride and patriotism when they hear matronly Kate Smith's version of "God Bless America". Images of W.W. II ration lines, p.c. coupons, U.S.O. dances, and Americans in uniform still seem fresh for those who lived during this epoch.

Baby-boomers can vividly recall the feel of wool carpet prevalent in 1950's décor. Elvis Presley's crushed velvet sweaters, sweaty polyester materials used in "leisure suits", and genuine leather covered, down filled bus seats all were once familiar sensations in the 1960's.

Kodak's brownie camera black and white snapshots, President John F. Kennedy's post-assassination "martyr" portraits, and downtown mill-produced smog were once commonly in sight. Look Magazine's inferno-like Viet Nam photographs, Walter Cronkite's moon landing television panoramic news broadcasts, and counter culture record album covers, complete with hippie colors and symbols, all are embedded in our collective consciousness.

Fragrances such as Evening in Paris and Lilies of the Valley still remain in my mind, along with the scents of witch hazel, glycerin and rosewater, and Princess soap. Cod liver oil, linseed oil, vanilla, and turpentine are all aromas no longer commonly found in most homes of today.

Everyone has cherished recollections concerning food. Idora Park's vinegar drenched French fries, creamy egg white Parker's custard, and Strouss' malts still linger on the palette. Why? These tastes were integral parts of our past lives in previous times. In turn, they have become part of our local urban lore and legend.

A skillet-made pepper and egg sandwich enjoyed at the downtown Brass Rail is unequaled to this day. Drinking a phosphate at a Gray's Drug soda fountain, licking a Whitehouse skyscraper cone at an Isaly's Dairy Store, or eating peach chiffon cake in a booth at Woolworth's are all rituals that have passed imperceptibly from the modern scene.

Consuming a grilled wiener at the Dog House corner coffee shop, mixing Golden Age, NeHi, and Holly orange and cherry pops to create a "pink lady" cocktail, and buying bridge mix by the pound at Fanny Farmer's confection shoppe are all customs in which we no longer indulge. Times have changed, but our tastebuds still remember.

The Palace Grille, in the Palace Theater building, once served a buttery fried cheese sandwich, which had no rival in town. In Boardman, the Golden Drumstick's "secret recipe" seasoned breadcrumbs had throngs coming back for more fried chicken suppers, week after week. On Youngstown's North Side, the art deco Twentieth Century Restaurant featured homemade macaroni and cheese and indescribably rich German chocolate cake. When these landmark establishments reluctantly closed, their culinary talents were sealed in time and frozen in our remembrances.

Today, families enjoy fast-food hamburgers, frozen yogurt, franchised pizza, and microwave dinners. Still, I can not help but reminiscence about the singular qualities of long gone victuals. Never again will I ever know the aftertaste of Howard Johnson's HoJo cola, the texture of Fifth Avenue Pizza crust, or the sumptuous dark chocolate Forever Yours candy bar.

These things and many more are precious little luxuries the current generation will neither experience nor miss. Unbelievably, after all these years, I still sometimes yearn for these once common items of a bygone era.

Virtual Family

by Richard S. Scarsella

Well into the 1940's, local residents usually lived near their paternal or maternal families. It was typical for children of the Mahoning Valley to marry, settle down, and raise their children near grandparents, aunts, uncles, and cousins, oftentimes in the neighborhoods they were born and raised in. If one moved across town, an efficient transit system or affordable fleets of cabs made visiting economical and convenient.

The post-World War II economic expansion fueled the growth of a dramatic change in lifestyles. A tight housing market confronted ex-GI's and their wives. The remedy? Moving to and building homes in the suburbs ringing Youngstown. Boardman, Canfield, Austintown, Poland, Liberty, and Lincoln Knolls rapidly became the homesteads of young families by choice, necessity, or default. Nuclear families began a long, slow, irreversible transformation into contemporary households. Extended families were split up across the valley. Many families were transferred to or lured to out-of-town jobs, as the Mahoning Valley shifted from a wartime economy into a peacetime economy.

The 1950's made the kinescope, later called the television, popular. Growing families adopted this new medium as one of the household. The friendly broadcasts of Romper Room, Art Linkletter, Dorothy Fuldheim, and Margie Mariner helped fill the vacuum of loosening family ties. Captain Penny, Barney Bean, the Disney Musketeers Club, Kookla, Fran and Ollie, and Howdy Doody became baby-sitters, surrogate family, and confidants to a legion of youth. Family dynamics would never be the same again. Telefilm took hold of one's life.

As the downtown Youngstown movie palaces began to dim in popularity, television enthralled modern families with free, live entertainment. Television antennae sprouted up all around town and became status symbols. A "night at the movies" meant watching network rebroadcasts of Hollywood films in the comfort of one's own home. Special made for television teleplays and movies sapped the monopoly Hollywood once enjoyed. Television aggressively targeted and marketed various genres to different members of the family. Soap operas, sports spectacles, educational programs, and variety shows captivated Americans, wary of the 1950's conformity, nuclear threat, and bleakness. News broadcasts enlightened parents. Cartoons like "Mighty Mouse" and "Bullwinkle" amused their offspring.

Film giants such as Gloria Swanson, John Garfield, Joan Crawford, Gary Cooper, Bette Davis, and Clark Gable were replaced in the 1950's and 1960's by more approachable idols. Viewers felt they "knew" Chet Huntley, David Brinkley, Walter Cronkite, Fulton Sheen, Lucille Ball, Ernie Kovacs, Milton Berle, Jack Paar, Dinah Shore, Rod Sterling, and Alfred Hitchcock intimately. These larger than life figures visited one's homes weekly, months on end. One felt comfortable with them. Families saw more of their television "family" than they did of their blood related clan. Subsequently, one's attitudes, styles, tastes, and behavior began to closely mimic one's new, readily accessible role models. Absentee parents, siblings, and other kin no longer were sole influences in one's lives. Families began to drift, splinter, and disengage, as one found comfort, solace, understanding, and acceptance in make-believe virtual families.

The pictorial images of television soon became the standard of how and what Americans believed family life should and could be. Women strove to be "Leave It To Beaver" June Cleaver clones, replete with heels, pearls, and a spotless kitchen. Men tried to emulate the solid, no-nonsense, cool detachment of Raymond Burr's "Perry Mason". Meanwhile, children dreamed of inhabiting the worlds of "Lassie", "Sky King", and "Sea Hunt". The excitement, adventure, glamour, and accomplishment of our celluloid heroes made one's life seem drab in comparison. The "American dream" was co-opted by network magnates and was no longer rooted in the heartland values of decency, hard work, patriotism, and common sense.

Ironically, as television tightened its grip on our psyches, it was the agent of its own debunking. The quiz show scandals, McCarthy era trials, Kennedy assassinations, and Viet Nam horror made previously naive Americans critically question the illusion of truth that television purveyed. Americans grudgingly acknowledged that television could and did manipulate news, war, tragedy, fads, and conjecture all for the sake of selling advertisements and gaining market share.

In the year 2000, the broadcasting industry has fragmented. Cable and satellite has pierced the stranglehold the big three networks once had on America. The World Wide Web has siphoned off both viewers and advertisers. Television, like Hollywood of old, no longer reigns supreme. Yet, one still clings to classical 1950's tableaus of family life that still flicker across one's screens as reruns. These vintage shows are a type of recorded living history. They are time capsules of another era in American life.

Those who have seen the full scope and breadth of media unfold, from the crystal set days of radio, Hollywood's golden era, and television's bright promise, realize the computer age is here to stay. However, the warm, fuzzy familiarity of "Father Knows Best", "The Donna Reed Show", "Ozzie and Harriet", "My Three Sons", and "I Love Lucy" can still bring a tear to one's eyes. These stereotypes of American families became integral parts of our own families. These shows hauntingly represented an American era that was as real as it was transparent.

War Fervor

by Richard S. Scarsella

I remember well uncles and great-uncles retelling glorious stories from the past. The most vivid were tales of World War II conflicts, escapes, and maneuvers. For a young boy, going to war seemed adventurous, glamorous, and manly. It was not until later that I discovered the unseen realities of war.

Many do not know or fail to recall that the United States was slow to enter the conflagration Germany ignited. The thought of being in London, Paris, Rome, Berlin, and Warsaw was thrilling to those of us unfamiliar with the carnage of mortal combat. Armchair soldiers are quick to sentimentalize the gruesome tasks war entails.

Unlike modern wars of today, which depend upon computer guided missiles and sophisticated technology, World War II was a blood and guts campaign dependent upon such World War I standards as guns, tanks, and trenches. The fact that vintage World War I armed services issue was used in the early World War II years seems both ironic and foreboding. My elders, some of whom served in both great epic confrontations, always ominously intoned "Blood flows freely and red in any war."

Looking back, it is hard to believe that such titans as Churchill, DeGaulle, Hitler, Mussolini, Stalin, Hirohito, and Roosevelt all shared the international scene at the same time with such tragic results. It would seem that such astute students of history could have avoided the bloodbath that ensued. Did Hitler really think he could wage a two-front war and win? Did Mussolini feel he could reclaim former Roman Empire splendor with an unstable ally renamed The Third Reich? Did Hirohito believe that the Empire of the Rising Sun was destined to rule all of Asia and the Pacific basin? Did Stalin presume his non-aggression pact with the "mad dog of Europe" would buy Russia enough time to arm itself for an inevitable attack? Did Churchill surmise that America would eventually come to England's aide? Did Roosevelt secretly prepare for battle while mouthing neutrality and claiming, "No American boys would fight in a foreign war", to a believing war-wary nation? The answer to all of the above is unbelievably yes.

History is full of such incongruousness and oddities. My relatives were always quick to point out that war knew no boundaries and no one was spared its ghastly grip. The veterans of these calls to arms were both philosophical and realistic about the causes of bloodshed. Apparently, nations could be as temperamental, narrow-minded, and deceitful as their citizenries.

When visiting my maternal grandmother, it was always fascinating and somber to view the wartime effects of an uncle missing in action during World War II. Lost over the Atlantic Ocean in route to the German front during a tour of duty as an Air Force navigator, his body was never recovered. All that endured was a purple heart, part of a uniform, and a black and white eight by ten photo of him in full uniform. His tragic death at a young age made the toll of war both personal and heartfelt. Warfare was not just made up of John Wayne movie victories and propaganda. No, battlegrounds were full of the remains of broken bodies, shattered lives, and decimated cultures.

The call to arms is a seducing invitation that oftentimes prevails over common sense and diplomacy. Toy soldiers, such as G.I. Joe action figures, continue to be best sellers, during peacetime and war years. History is a rich chronicle of titanic struggles between proud peoples intent upon victory at all costs. I oftentimes wonder if the cost of war ever truly registers upon those that so zealously wage it? One can only hope. As my grandmother always said, "May the saints and angels preserve and protect us all."

Water Delights

by Richard S. Scarsella

Youngstown and the surrounding communities evolved around water. Connecticut bred John Young encamped upon the banks of the once pristine Mahoning River Valley, since this watercourse provided a drinking supply, a means of transportation, and plenty of fish to eat.

The development of the iron and steel industry depended upon and far surpassed the capacity of the Mahoning River in due time. Subsequently, dams were erected to insure water for industrial purposes. Further population growth required reservoirs to be built to quench the thirst of a burgeoning populace.

Undoubtedly, water was always perceived as a necessity of life and prosperity. However, most now consider water in lighter terms. Indeed, water now conjures images of vacations and recreation. Water diversions are very much a part of our lives, despite our distance from the nearest ocean.

Lake Milton always featured boating, skiing, swimming, and cottages. City dwellers found inexpensive and convenient escape at this man-made resort. Craig Beach, located upon the shores of the lake, was once a popular destination spot for vacationers. The amusement park, replete with concessions and carnival rides, offered affordable attractions for children and teenagers. Nightclubs and cocktail lounges provided adult entertainment. Taking a stroll along the beach at night was a favorite pastime.

Nearby Lake Erie was the choice for the more daring. The Great Lakes' "deep sea fishing" appealed to avid fishermen. Charter boats catered to these fans. Maritime races of fiberglass motor craft brought out a competitive spirit landlubbers loved. Aquacade-styled exhibitions, in the vein of Atlantic City and Hollywood, thrilled audiences safely ensconced on the piers. Geneva-On-The-Lake and Mentor-On-The-Lake featured boardwalks with saltwater taffy and homemade fudge stands, games of skill, handcrafted souvenirs, and bingo parlors. Refuge in a lake enclave was a time-honored practice in the Mahoning Valley for many years, before cheap airfares and super highways lured patrons to other venues. Indeed, many generations still fondly recall being "brought up" in a lakefront cabin during summertide.

Many valley residents did not have the luxury of time or a surplus of funds to go to an out-of-town vacation spot. Mill Creek Park became a popular choice due to its proximity and many offerings. Lanterman's Falls, originally called Idora Falls, was a favorite natural wonder. Its cool mist and multi-colored hues were idyllic and soothing. Lethargic Lake Glacier and Lake Newport were literally aquatic jewels in the heart of an industrial corridor. Having a canoe ride, catching frogs, fishing for catfish, swimming, and skating all were pastimes once enjoyed at these waterholes. Taking home a jug or bottle of mineral water from park springs was once an area tradition for those heading home after a day spent in Youngstown's "green cathedral".

Most will agree that of all the water delights available in the area, the Dutch windmill-styled waterfall amusement ride at Idora Park was clearly in a class by itself. Known as the Old Mill, Tunnel of Love, The Rapids, and Lost River Ride, it was a blend of gentle gondola-like boat ride and a jarring roller coaster descent. The refreshing cascade of water, illuminated by rainbow lights, made this midway landmark legendary, until a 1984 fire reduced it to ashes.

Sadly, in our modern world we no longer take pleasure in simple water activities as we once did. Yet, even now, the youngest of children and the young of heart still find great joy in a fountain. Neptune and Poseidon would be proud.

Whatever Happened to...

by Richard S. Scarsella

Things, places, and people we once took for granted no longer are part of our lives. Regrettably, one scarcely has the time, energy, or presence of mind to contemplate these contemporary losses. If one thinks back, the deprivations are both great and small.

Whatever happened to Isaly's recipes for banana, Whitehouse, and rainbow ice creams? The thought of nickel skyscraper cones we once bought at neighborhood Isaly's dairy stores still brings a smile to my face.

Whatever happened to the summer outside concerts held in Wick Park? These free north side musical programs drew crowds from throughout the valley. A hot summer evening of serenades amidst the shadows of elegant Stambaugh Auditorium and stately mansions was an unmatched experience for young and old alike. Youngstown's version of the Boston Pop's was a summertide tradition for many years.

Whatever happened to an Esther Hamilton type column in local newspapers? Her inimitable chatty style of local society news, human-interest stories, and wry political comments gave one a bird's eye view of local happenings.

Whatever happened to the Community Chest trademark? Once these charities were folded under a new umbrella organization, old-timers still lamented the absence of this once formidable fundraising organization.

Whatever happened to the Camp Fire and Bluebird scouts? At one time, they were as near ubiquitous as the Girl Scouts and Brownie troops. It seems not long ago hordes of girls would canvass the streets, dressed in prim uniforms and merit badges, selling candy, cookies, and hand-made crafts.

Whatever happened to Forever Yours candy bars? This dark chocolate cousin of the Milky Bar candy bars was once an American favorite.

Whatever happened to NeHi, Golden Age, and Holly soda pops? These soft drink refreshments were once standards at any church, school, or birthday party. Cherry and orange flavors were the most popular. Many a white dress shirt never recovered from their stains.

Whatever happened to double matinee movies? These two-for-one specials were a real treat. Attending the picture shows at the Schenley, Belmont, Home, or Uptown theaters for a twin bill was once a local past time. Many a boy and girl received their first kiss during these lengthened attractions. Uniformed ushers armed with flashlights kept a watchful eye on the audience.

Whatever happened to going to a corner drugstore or variety store luncheon counter for a malt, phosphate, or grilled cheese special luncheon?

Whatever happened to the carnival freak show performers who once came to town? Did local uneasiness with natural deformities deny victims of birth defects a livelihood?

Whatever happened to the burlesque queens who once graced the stage of the local Park Theater? Did Busty Russell and Chesty Morgan retire gracefully or are they still appearing live somewhere as geriatric showgirls?

Whatever happened to the shoe repairmen, knife sharpeners, and lace salesmen who once frequented our environs? These traveling artisans were once important contributors to our households. Their expert skills, kind words, and worldly wisdom left indelible marks on our lives.

Whatever happened to the tramps, hoboes, and gypsies who once regularly traveled through town? These colorful street people were both mysterious and enthralling. They seemed pathetically romantic and free.

Whatever happened to passenger rail travel? I recall vividly awaiting family to arrive at area depots. Watching long, sleek, chrome-plated Pullman cars discharge well-dressed world travelers at local stations was like being in a novel. The railroads were once considered our lifeline to the outside world.

Whatever happened to ballroom dancing, the likes of which once dominated the Idora Grand Ballroom? Guy Lombardo, Lawrence Welk, and Glenn Miller once created magic in our midst. Soulful timeless harmonies, mixed with the midway odors of fresh popcorn, vinegar drenched French fries, and sweet cotton candy, made Idora an oasis in a gritty steel valley. Nothing has ever replaced this legendary cultural landmark in our lives or memories.

When I hear folks state how lucky, prosperous, and modern we are today, I cannot help but look longingly back to former days. Like shadows, they follow us everywhere. It's true. Time is nothing but personal history.

When I Go Shopping

by Richard S. Scarsella

After all these years, old buying habits still linger. Although the retail climate has changed vastly, I still catch myself making references to things that have long ago passed into local history.

When I go shopping I still expect to find shelves stocked with Ivory soap flakes, Sealtest cream and ice milk, Barth farm eggs, and Amish country handmade soap.

When I go shopping I still look for Golden Age ginger ale, Holly cherry and orange soda pop, and NeHi root beer.

When I go shopping I still hope to find Forever Yours dark chocolate bars, Chuckles jellied candies, and Beeman's and Black Jack chewing gums.

When I go shopping I can't help to compare the friendly intimacy of now closed Loblaw's, Kroger's, Century, and A&P grocery stores to the gigantic antiseptic supermarkets we now patronize.

When I go shopping I no longer see butchers wrapping soup bones for children to give to the family dogs. I also don't see chicken skin being wrapped for free to be fed to the family cats.

When I go shopping I never observe elegantly dressed matriarchs dispersing wise advice to young brides about how to make a house a home.

When I go shopping it is rare to come across displays of canning jars, beeswax, and preserve labels.

When I go shopping magazines with titles such as Look, Life, and McCall's no longer dominate the checkout lanes.

When I go shopping I have noticed women no longer wear Chanel No. 5 perfume, men no longer reek of sweet cherry pipe tobacco smoke, and children no longer smell of Fels Nappa soap.

When I go shopping I cannot help but recall when there was only one kind of Cheerios and the Wheaties box champion changed only every several years.

When I go shopping I still seek out fruits and vegetables grown in Ohio or in the United States. Somehow, buying "fresh" produce shipped in from Mexico or Latin America strikes me as being contradictory.

When I go shopping I have to ask the baggers for old-fashioned paper bags for my items. The now commonly used plastic bags just do not seem sturdy enough for a week's supply of foodstuffs.

When I go shopping I have to concentrate in front of the milk cooler. I carefully read all the carton labels, for milk now is available as fat free, 1%, 2%, whole, flavored, or lactose-free. Such was not always the case. Indeed, milk in a redeemable glass bottle was the only selection offered at one time.

When I go shopping checkout clerks no longer ask me if I save S&H, Plaid, Top Value, or Gem trading stamps. Those once esteemed tokens were diligently collected, glued into trading stamp books, and cashed in at redemption centers for much sought after consumer goods.

When I go shopping I can no longer find stacks of cardboard boxes in front of the plate glass windows free for the asking. Now, these cartons are collapsed, bundles, and recycled.

When I go shopping I still miss the brown paper signs hand-lettered in red ink proclaiming the daily specials. A sale on sunflower seeds, boric acid, or Vick's Vaporub once created a stir of activity amongst shoppers in another era.

Even now, I have to remind myself that grocery stores are opened for business after six o'clock and on Sundays. No longer can I take for granted that I will know someone when I go out to purchase a weekly order in the sleek cavernous aisles of our modern supermarkets.

However, when familiar aromas of vanilla, cinnamon, or Milsek furniture polish fill my senses as I shop, I have a flood of comfortable memories to accompany me when I go shopping.

When Youngstown Turned Irish

by Richard S. Scarsella

Well into the 1970's, the Youngstown area heartily celebrated the Irish holiday of St. Patrick's Day. Every March 17, Mahoning Valley residents became Irish for the day as they shook off the winter blues and prepared for spring. This Roman Catholic saint's day united all classes of people, regardless of religious affiliation or national origin, by the food, spirits, and frolic that accompanied it.

Like the Fourth of July and Thanksgiving parades, the grand St. Patrick's Day parades were held in once bustling downtown Youngstown. Thousands of revelers and their families lined East and West Federal Streets. Many children would wave both Irish and American flags. Irish step dancers, units of the Royal Order of Hibernia, high school marching bands, cheerleaders and flag crews, Boy Scout and Girl Scout troops, and veteran groups all were on display in their finery. Whether it was a sunny day or a snowy day, parade watchers dutifully turned out for this yearly ritual. This parade was very much a part of our lives.

Men wearing colorful, plaid kilts and playing booming bagpipes was a special attraction in an otherwise conservative, gritty steel town. Politicians all vied for the honor to be on the review stand. Speeches flowed fast and furious before the spectacle. Floats, with all matter of green adornment, were striking contrasts to soot covered buildings and the remains of Christmas decorations. It was an oddity to see anyone in the crowd not wearing a green hat, shirt, button or costume. St. Patrick's Day had much of the whimsy of Valentine's Day, the emotional release of Mardi Gras, and the escapism of Halloween. Everyone hoped the luck of the Irish would befall them.

Downtown merchants capitalized on this unofficial holiday. Final winter merchandise markdowns lured people into such mercantile landmarks as Strouss', McKelvey's, and Livingston's. Their show windows were a riot of green decorations, mystical Irish symbols, and early spring attire. Lustig's and Baker's shoe stores unveiled their Easter display windows on this day. Hordes of buyers would flood the stores and make purchases or put items on lay-a-way.

Variety stores did a brisk business in related St. Patrick's Day novelties. Leprechaun cut-outs, blarney stones, shamrock sweatshirts and jewelry, green hats and scarves, noisemakers, invitations, trimmings, and cards all could be purchased cheaply at Woolworth's, Murphy's, Grant's, McCrory's or Kressege's. These all-American stores were turned into a bit of Ireland for a weekend, in tribute to a man who Christianized Ireland and drove its snakes into the seas. The fact that St. Patrick was probably not of Irish descent mattered little to anyone. St. Patrick's Day was a reprieve from the everyday routines and responsibilities during a month that seemed to never end. A visit to Irish Bob's Bar was a surefire way to bring a little warmth into our lives. For here, one could find the congeniality, humor, and family that was inherent in Irish culture.

Many area residents attended church services on this day. St. Patrick's Parish, on Youngstown's South Side, would have standing room only available for late worshippers. This Gothic edifice would be brimming with prominent Irish families, politicians, professionals, and clerics. Roman Catholics throughout the valley would commemorate this famous patron saint with glittering high masses. St. Patrick's Day was one of the few holidays where priests, nuns, brothers, and monks could be seen in public witnessing secular events. Non-Catholics were big participants in this day of jubilation, as well. Unbeknownst to most of us, St. Patrick's Day was a powerful tonic for those who believed in the power of a historical figure to bring joy into their lives.

St. Patrick's three-leaf shamrock, which he reputedly used to explain the nature of the trinity, also symbolized the cross. The color green represented not only the shamrock, but also Ireland and the season of spring. One's search for a "lucky" four-leaf clover offered hope to anyone. Finding one was considered a good omen. Children would search high and low, in their earnest searches for this talisman. The old wives' tales of Ireland became part of our modern American culture. St. Patrick made Irish folklore engaging to all who would listen.

Although schools and government offices were open on St. Patrick's Day, many folks took all or part of the day off. The Twentieth Century Restaurant on the North Side served up heaping portions of corned beef and potatoes to hungry patrons. Across town in the Fosterville area, Courtney's Grille filled pitchers with green beer for thirsty merrymakers. Neighborhood drug store soda fountains blended green milkshakes and phosphates for the younger crowds. At society functions, green punch with greens sherbet would be featured, alongside finger sandwiches. Even parochial school kitchens would whip up something special, such as green mash potatoes, green ribbon Jell-O, or St. Patrick's Day cookies. Florists would have brisk sales on green carnations and green corsages, many of which were given to non-Irish and non-Catholic celebrants. On this day, most everyone pretended to be Irish. Adding an O to your name, such as the famous O'Hara's or O'Dea's, made everyone feel Celtic.

St. Patrick's Day began a long weekend of song, dance, and party making. Ursuline High School, home of the "Fighting Irish", always premiered its annual Irish Show on March 17. The school choir and band, along with local, national, and international "stars", performed classic Irish tunes, choreography, and comedy sketches. Oftentimes corny and maudlin, these productions grew in popularity. Eventually they had to be moved from the Ursuline Theater on Bryson Street to Stambaugh Auditorium, where they continue today.

City high schools had a large Irish connected student body. Lavish dances were held in most of the high school gyms and cafeterias during St. Patrick's Day weekend. In the 1930's and 1940's, big band music, performed by Sammy Kaye or Kay Kaiser, once entertained the W. W. II generation. Later, in the 1950's, the Mills Brothers and the Ink Spots gave St. Patrick's Day a more urban flavor. In the 1960's, Natalie Wood, Sandra Dee, Troy Donahue and Tab Hunter all encompassed sophisticated innocence. St. Patrick's Day was a rerun of Valentine's Day for many. It was a chance to be seen in public formally with that "special" someone, before graduation day in June. Many precious memories and broken hearts were made over St. Patrick's Day weekend. It's no accident that beer is associated with this day, since some drank to give thanks for good fortune and others drank to forget.

Throughout the valley, house parties, Greek fraternity societies, Hibernian lodges, church socials, high school dances, patriotic gatherings, and reverent church services all continued a centuries old tradition of honoring a former slave turned liberator on a once pagan land. Old-timers oftentimes stayed home on St. Patrick's Day weekend. They were content to read the newspaper accounts of all the festivities. They also listened to Arthur Godfrey on radio and watched Lawrence Welk on television. As a child, I can still remember the famous tenor, Joe Feeney, crooning "Oh Danny Boy" and "When Irish Eyes are Smiling". This music could melt the most hardened heart. It tugged mercilessly on our emotions. Our elders shook their heads knowingly.

From the Club Merry-go-round, to the Elks lodges, on the Elms' dance floor or in the Idora Ballroom, Youngstowners yearly recreated a little bit of the Irish heritage in our midst. We all wished each other health, happiness and longevity on St. Patrick's Day. As we went about our merriment, we paid scant attention to the ever present power of history in our contemporary lives.

Whispers of Time

by Richard S. Scarsella

The greater Youngstown area has changed much over the years. Farmland and forests slowly were consumed by ever expanding neighborhoods. The once mighty iron and steel industries fueled both urban growth and suburban development. As the area became a post-industrial metropolis, our lives no longer were centered on the strip of mills, which clung to the banks of the muddy Mahoning River. A way of life changed. However, remnants of another age still exist in our midst. They are whispers of times past.

Throughout the city, an occasional red brick street can still be viewed. These latter-day cobblestone avenues were built to last generations. And they did, only to be paved over by inferior quality asphalt, which has given birth to the dreaded potholes. South Avenue is the lone widely traveled example of these once common thoroughfares. This road is symbol of a time when both horses and motorcars needed to be accommodated.

Trolleys once linked the four sides of towns. A transfer from the downtown terminal could connect one to the nearby towns of Campbell or Struthers, to the farm villages of Lisbon or Washingtonville, or to Western Pennsylvania's New Castle. Most of the rails were melted down for the World War II salvage drives. Almost all of these lines were ripped up or paved over by the late 1940's with the ascendancy of the diesel-fueled bus coaches. The Southern Boulevard tracks still survive and connect downtown Youngstown and Boardman to Columbiana County.

Downtown Youngstown, Uptown, the corridors of Oak and Market Streets, and Belmont and Mahoning Avenues all once were beehives of business, professional, and social institutions. Boxing clubs, billiard parlors, and dance studios once dotted the cityscape. These colorful establishments were anchors for neighborhoods. Outsiders were held suspect and had to "prove" themselves to be accepted. Your affiliation with one of these locales could easily open doors elsewhere in town, due to a deep sense of fraternity, which once existed in them.

Sadly, these trademarks of urban life have perished along with the environs they once so typified. Only hollow shells of facades remain to remind us.

Corner dairy stores, such as Lawson's and Isaly's, have long faded from the scene. Family-owned and operated fruit stands and vegetable stalls are rarely found in the city or suburbia. Pyatt Street open-air market is a ghost of itself. There are no drive-in theaters left in Mahoning County. Neighborhood cinemas have also vanished. Mass transit benches, bus stop poles, and taxi stands are also near extinction. The sight of a traveling Bible, encyclopedia, globe, or cemetery lot salesmen would startle the eye. All of these once-common places and things bespeak a not too long ago era when life was simpler and less hurried.

Sometimes, as I travel through once prosperous urban enclaves, my memory drifts back. I can still vividly recollect metal milk boxes on porches, back-yard grape arbors, front-yard American beauty rose trellises, old world herbal gardens, and spectacular fireworks displays over beloved Idora Park.

These landmarks of time still dwell deep within us. In a very real sense, we are our memories.

Wonderland Lost

by Richard S. Scarsella

Springtime brings memories of years past in the Mahoning Valley. Mill Creek Park, since 1891, has been a haven for area residents seeking to throw off the wintertime blahs. Newport, Glacier, and Cohassett Lakes all continue to attract nature lovers, despite the soulless parade of progress, which surrounds them. These nautical jewels, filled with lily pads, pollywogs, and waterfowl, are still very much part of our contemporary lives. The same cannot be said for their unlucky neighbor, venerable Idora Park.

Bucolic Mill Creek Park borders these vast twenty-seven acres of National Historical Registry property on three sides. Idora's fate was sealed by this green boundary, for it had nowhere to expand. As Kennywood, Cedar Point, and Geaugua Lake amusement parks grew and prospered, Idora was frozen in time. This timeless quality gave Idora unique appeal. Unfortunately, time marches on and takes no prisoners. Idora became a fatality.

Youngstown's "Million Dollar Playground" became an extension of Mill Creek Park. Midway smells of vinegar drenched French fries, deep fried corn dogs, buttered popcorn, and fresh roasted peanuts all enticed Mill Creek denizens to glittering Idora Park. The mist from the Rapids/Tunnel of Love waterside drenched Mill Creek's trees, much to the delight of park dwellers. Idora's once fabled botanical gardens and lagoons, full of exotic flora and fauna, flowed seamlessly into the Mill Creek watershed. These facilities were truly interconnected in fact and in our minds. They were both safe havens from cement urbanity.

Idora's Grand Ballroom, once a fortress of Coney Island Moorish art deco architecture, reigned regally on a hill overlooking Mill Creek's gorge and Old Mill complex. This bastion of big band music, style, and culture was once the heartbeat of the area's summer season. Dancing under the stucco suspended cloud ceiling, which seemed alive with hues of the rainbow, reflected in a revolving mirrored sphere, was hopelessly romantic. Cooling off on the wide, pillared verandas, with panoramic views of Mill Creek Park, was sublime.

Mill Creek Park was best seen when riding the chrome-plated jets. These gliders, suspended on cables from a concession stand tower, provided unimpeded vistas of not only primordial Mill Creek Park, but of bustling downtown Youngstown and the smoke belching steel mill corridor. Idora made all of the environs seem dreamlike, with height, speed, fantasy, and carrousel calliope music creating magic in our midst.

From the roar of the Jack Rabbit, Wild Cat, and Baby Wildcat coasters, to the throaty whistles of the Idora Limited train, these were all once springtime sounds found in Mill Creek Park. Mill Creek remains. Idora stands smoldering. Spring will never be the same again.

978-0-595-37269-0
0-595-37269-4